D1497239

CONFESSION OF A REFUGEE

A Journey to the Unknown: August 21, 1968

by

Z. George Mesko, M.D.

For Irne Rosenthal:
"our Good Samaritan of
June 1969 and to loving memory of
Ami, her husband & dear friend.
With compliments, fondly

Z. G. Mesko — "Zoltan".

DORRANCE
PUBLISHING CO
EST. 1920
PITTSBURGH, PENNSYLVANIA 15238

Washington, Spring 2020.

Dorrance Publishing Co
585 Alpha Drive
Suite 103
Pittsburgh, PA 15238
Visit our website at *www. dorrancebookstore. com*

ISBN: 978-1-6461-0851-0
eISBN: 978-1-6461-0051-4

Motto:

"Give me your tired, your poor,
Your huddled masses yearning to be free,
The wretched refuse of your teeming shore.
Send these, the homeless, tempest-tossed to me
I lift my lamp besides the golden door."
Emma Lazarus — Statue of Liberty.

For Judith, who shared this unforgettable struggle with me

CONTENTS

Z. George Mesko, M.D., FAAP, FACC.
Emeritus, Assoc. Professor of Medicine, SUNY

PROLOGUE

U nforeseen events can come in surprise or as a brutal assault in our life, along
our very personal path. Their crucial importance — at that very moment —
we can't or are not able to appreciate, let alone understand. They appear unexpectedly out of the blue, and their pivotal consequence and central importance in
our very life will show up only many years later, as these "accidents" turn to our
evanescent history.

It was on a crystal clear summer day in June 1960, when the golden rays of
the sun were penetrating sharply across the beautiful summer scene of the manicured gardens in the park of the Spa Sliač — in the heart of Slovakia — with
patches of sprightly yellow and crimson red colored snapdragons with their lovely
bilabial flowers, as the morning air in this haze soothingly shimmered on this
sleepy break of the day.

At this early time, an elegant, middle-aged lady arrived at the reception desk
of the Heart Institute for Children. She was a rather short, petite, but striking lady
in an unusual attire, which testified that she was from a different country or perhaps
another world. She had a smart, "boyish," salt and pepper coif of well-matching
undulating waves of hair, wore an elegant dress of colorful silk with spring flowers
and matching white summer shoes. She presented herself with a self-assured physique and attitude, with an inquisitive expression on her face, underlined by subtle
makeup for a lady of some age.

At the reception of this attractive-looking interior of the institution, at the front
desk a small, local women sat with her attentive, bright eyes, dressed in her garb
from the local provinces with her inviting but curious expression. It was Mrs. Maria

Čiampor with a laced scarf covering her head, as she was ready to kindly welcome this "foreign," elegant lady.

It remained a mystery how these two women communicated coming from different worlds and tongues, but somehow it transpired that this foreign lady would like to see the physician in charge.

Aunty Čiampor — as everybody called her — briskly ran up the few stairs to the elevated mezzanine and reported to the managing lady in charge that a lady — most probably from abroad — wished to see their physician in charge. My office was right behind the lobby at the same level, thus I could hear the conversation of the two women. I descended then to the reception hall to welcome and face this foreign visitor.

It was in the middle of the summer, and "my bronze" was pleasingly contrasting my white attire in my slim frame as I was curiously descending to the lobby to face this unexpected visitor. As I glanced and eyed up this middle-aged lady, it was highly probable, from her whole appearance, that this lady was from the USA. This could pose a problem for me, since my colloquial English was not up to the par at that time. But a year before, I was on a trip in Cairo, Egypt, where for twenty dollars, peddled on the black market, I was lucky to purchase the most modern textbook of Pediatric Cardiology of Canadian authors, which I industriously studied. I hoped that this professional course of the English language would suffice in my communication at that moment.

I welcomed this elegant lady from abroad as a welcomed guest with my kind expression and asked her, "How can I help you?"

The lady introduced herself with an inviting smile as Dr Frederica P., a doctor who worked at the Beth Israel Hospital in Boston as an external pediatrician. At the same time, it soon transpired that the roots of her ancestors went back to the times of Emperor Franz Joseph and the Austro-Hungarian monarchy to the town of Eperjes (today Presov) in northern Slovakia. Consequently she was still fluent in Hungarian, as I was. Hence "presto," the problem of our smooth communication was suddenly resolved.

Right away I invited this lady — quasi a countryman — into my office, which was the most elegant office I ever in my life had. The office was quite spacious with a smooth, pastel beige tapestry. I had a large working table from Swedish teak wood that faced every guest of mine. Behind my table chair, there was a cabinet from the same pale wood with some bookshelves as well. In the middle of the office as a centerpiece was an oval coffee table surrounded by two comfortable easy chairs with beige tapestry with a pattern of intertwined light green leaves of Canadian maple. Behind them was a comfortable sofa of the same color and fabric.

I decorated the office with original oil paintings of the well-known Czech painter Václav Špála and the Slovak Janko Alexy, which had been in 1948 removed from the lobby of the directorate of the spa by the Communist coup in Czechoslovakia. I saved them from this ignominy when I found them abandoned and dirty in the cellar of the building. Now these exquisite originals, on this sunny day of summer, were showing off their colorful beauty and charm.

I offered an easy chair to this elegant foreigner, and she accepted it in gracious delight. She was visibly surprised by this enticing and picturesque interior in a country behind the Iron Curtain. I asked now my manager to provide us with coffee in Carlsbad china, laced with its typical blue onion-shaped ornaments and some ginger cookies.

Now the curtain of my personal "prologue" to my future fate started to quietly unfold!

My guest, the lady from Boston, had a vivacious personality, pleasant demeanor, and an observant expression in her hazelnut-tinted eyes. During our initial conversation and exchange, she explained to me that she, as a pediatrician, was curious to learn about our protocol of care of these children after the acute attack of rheumatic fever or even in convalescence after heart surgery.

In a very friendly conversation in my narrative, I informed her that our institution with her logo "Slovakia" had a history as a treatment facility since 1878 as a part of European balneal culture in waters rich of carbon dioxide for ailment of heart and high blood pressure in adults.

In 1950 this former hotel was converted to an institution for children with heart disease with rheumatic fever, which was then — in the pre-penicillin era — rampant in Slovakia.

The institution accommodated 120 children who were hospitalized for two month on average, but children with severe heart disease remained there for longer periods. These were the children with severely afflicted hearts after repeated bouts of rheumatic fever (Figure 1).

As I learned, Dr. P. had come with her dear friend, an older gentleman who came to "take the waters" of the renown spa. The two families had been friends for many years, even if separated by the Iron Curtain, and her friend was her guest in this spa, and his daughter was sponsored to study abroad by his doctor friend.

After a pleasant chat, I escorted Dr. P. to the elevator, and we ended up on the top third floor, where the new patients were admitted every month for initial triage and assessment of the severity of their heart problems. Here we established a treatment plan for the child, as it was many times transferred directly from the hospital after the acute phase of the rheumatic fever.

The doctor was surprised that the children were accommodated in a room for two with a small anteroom equipped with a wash basin and a cabinet for wardrobe. As a former renovated hotel, the institution was quite a modern facility even in a socialist country behind the Iron Curtain.

On every floor — in the middle of it — there was a sunny dining room with set-up tables covered by clean, checkered tablecloths, and in the middle of them a small vase of fresh flowers gave a bucolic impression. At one end of each floor, there was a small serving kitchen, while at the front end of it there was an office for the nursing staff. The floors were shining clean — even for an unexpected visitor — thanks to our punctilious manager.

Dr. P. seemed to be pleased and impressed while walking along with me, as she did not expect in this socialist country to see such a professional setup. We visited the other floor amidst friendly conversation of medical give-and-take, and I showed her some of our really sick patients and presented her with our protocol.

On the first floor, I introduced her to our laboratory for microbiologic testing of the invading "strep," as the patients were screened on a monthly basis. Then I took her to our "sanctuary," the electrocardiographic laboratory with its special electrical shielding, where a technician was performing the required tests. I showed her that we were also performing sound tracings and graphic tracings from the jugular vein in the sick patients, and she was really taken by surprise. When at the end of my review I presented to her our Masters two-step staircase (Arthur M. Masters, 1953), she was really astonished in disbelief that in the early sixties we were using this stress test for testing the endurance of our patients.

The doctor was visibly taken by surprise, if not disbelief, by the modern, up-to-date diagnostic and medical protocol, which was up to the international standards of its times. She congratulated me for my leadership of the institution, which I took with grain of salt, or as a gesture of her courtesy, but it made me happy. She left the institution with best impressions.

In the following days, we met on the "colonnade" of the spa with her friend, holding a cane, who was probably in his eighties, a gentleman of some better times in the past. Incidentally I could now introduce to her my new wife, and on first sight she took her into her heart and labelled her "the belle Judith."

Through my professional responsibilities in the district, the state assigned to me a car that I could purchase, a small, French Renault CV4. With the help of it, I could show the two guests the charming countryside of hills and forests in the surrounding mining towns (Zvolen, Banská Bystrica). We visited another neighboring spa — Dudince — with its sulfuric waters used since Roman times in basins hollowed out in stone, which were still there. But in this small spa, the facilities were much more modest, only a small basin for patients with eczema and psoriasis even though the healing power of waters were remarkable. There were no formal hotels, only some rather primitive wooden shacks.

But the surrounding countryside was beautifully lush green with undulating hills and fresh, green fir trees and bushes, with daisies and country flowers on the surrounding meadows. The guests liked these short outings, where we always could find a small restaurant for a drink or refreshments.

After three weeks of "cure" while taking the waters, Dr. P. was preparing for her return to Boston. At the time of her departure, she addressed me with a question: "So if I come next year with my friend, what can I bring you as a small token of your hospitality?" Her visible willingness to be of help or assistance to a colleague behind the Iron Curtain was unexpected. After my surprise, I raised my courage, and after a short cogitation, I answered, "If you want really to help, purchase for me an American stethoscope of Rappaport brand, and I will reimburse you for it." She gave me her petite hand with a smile, and we departed with an "au revoir."

Indeed next year Dr. P. showed up again with her older friend "to take the waters," and at our first meeting, she almost victoriously presented me with a brand-new stethoscope of my desire. On the elegant box, there was a bill attached for twenty U.S. dollars. I reimbursed her in a realistic "black-market" exchange rate with an amount of Czechoslovak crowns that probably covered the majority of her expenses in our spa.

Again after the month of relaxation and pleasures taking "the waters," Dr. P. came to see me at our institution, and I welcomed her to my stylish office, where she admired my pictures. At the end of our exchange and the coffee, she looked in my eyes and said, "Zoltan, would you be interested to come to Boston for a fellowship to the famous Children's Hospital of John Harvard Medical School, where I know the professor and head of the Department of Pediatric Cardiology?"

In my astonishment and surprise to this offer, my eyes almost popped out of their sockets, and after some hesitation, I answered, "As you know, it would be a dream for me to study in Boston, but you know well I am living in a country behind the Iron Curtain, and I really don't know if that would be politically possible."

She looked at me and said, "Look, I will do what I can do in Boston, and you do your job according to the political possibilities." We departed with a soft hand-shake, and I was really moved.

In the spring of 1962, I was dismissed as the physician in charge from this be-loved and upgraded institution into which in five years I had invested a lot of energy and intellect. But I was a politically unreliable person, not a member of the Com-munist Party. I was supposed to be transferred and put in charge of a Department of Pediatrics in a rather small district mining town (Banská Štiavnica). I was very un-happy that my career as a pediatric cardiologist was finished. I totally forgot my pos-sible chances in Boston; now my professional neck was under political guillotine.

Fortunately our institution was under professional patronage of the Children's Hospital in Bratislava and its chairwoman who had founded the institution. She visited us periodically to assess and assure my professional prowess, as she had chosen me to lead the institution at the time when the quality of care had slipped down. She had chosen me as a top young specialist and was very proud of her choice, as I upgraded the dilapidated institution from bottom up and gave to it a direction of modern medicine. Between the professor and me, a professional re-spect readily flourished, as well as a personal friendship, as she considered me her professional disciple from the previous year when I had attended her course in pe-diatric cardiology in Bratislava.

The professor regarded my removal and degradation as an unfounded political act and as a loss of a young talent in pediatric cardiology into a small "backwater" town. She summoned now her professional and political clout, and in the summer of 1962, she offered me a place as an assistant professor at her Children's Hospital, making me extremely happy. My political fall thus turned to be a professional "up-ward kick," and as such, it significantly advanced my professional career.

In summer of that year, I started in my new position at the Children's Hospital, and the only thing that I took with me was the "Canadian bible" of pediatric car-diology, purchased in Cairo, as my professional scaffolding, probably the only textbook of this kind in the whole country.

My dear wife, Judith — as a technician in physical therapy — had to remain in in the spa and endure all of the ignominy for her kicked-out husband. She had to leave our apartment of the physician in charge and joined me many months later in Bratislava.

At the Children's Hospital, in a bout of my audacious initiative, I wrote to Mayo Clinic in Rochester, Minnesota, and asked the editor in chief of the *Mayo Clinic Proceedings* if he could send me their monthly *Mayo Clinic Proceedings*.

The Mayo Clinic was, at the time, in the front of and a pioneer of a new diagnostic method called "dye dilution curves method," which measured or followed the dilution and streaming of an injected dye into the circulation in children with congenital heart problems, to discern the abnormal circulation or connections in the heart, that is "holes" in their hearts.

By the great generosity of the *Mayo Clinic Proceedings* for a colleague behind the Iron Curtain, I received their journal for many years gratis! Within two years, our institution acquired — by stroke of luck — a Cambridge LTD apparatus from the United Kingdom for starting research and measurements with the dye dilution method. We started quite an active research with this technique, and in 1964 we presented with the professor the results of our research in children with abnormal connections in their hearts at the International Congress in Split, Yugoslavia. While my professor presented the paper in English, I pointed to the figures concomitant to the narrative with the important points of the research. Our paper was very well-received, especially from countries behind the Iron Curtain, as this technique was new and was not yet utilized and applied in these countries or in their diagnostic workup.

Split was a beautiful city on the bank of the Adriatic; it was the summer residence of the Roman emperor Hadrian (AD 117-138) with a huge, well-preserved palace. We trotted through its corridors, alleys, and gardens, and walking on the beautiful, seaside promenade at the sea, it was the first time seeing it in our lives. We were anxious to visit a neighboring island of Brač, where, at the beginning of the twentieth century, our prominent Slovak writer Dr Matthew Bencúr, alias Martin Kukučín, was active as a general practitioner and a writer of fine prose. We visited his small house with great reverence, seeing the exhibition of some of his works. We left Split with a well-accomplished job and pleasant memories.

A year later in 1965, I received a fancy envelope that, at its heading, in beautiful, crimson letters, stated, "University of John Harvard, Boston," and presented its elegant crest, which almost shouted for me: "Veritas-Truth" (Figure 2). I was taken totally by surprise by this unexpected letter, and at that point, I could not fathom who could write to me from that prominent university. Very carefully, almost with reverence, I opened up the envelope, spread out the elegant letter of fine paper, and could not believe my eyes.

The Chairman of the Department of Pediatric Cardiology at the Children's Hospital Medical Center (CHMC) sent me an invitation and offered me the possibility for a "fellowship" and specialized training at his department at the University of J. Harvard. I almost lost my composure or breath and had to sit down for a moment.

At home I showed this letter of invitation to my wife, just when she was offering a spoon full of cream of wheat to our son, Robert. At that moment, she had to stop and was totally beside herself — till Robert demanded the next portion.

Of course, the letter stipulated some preconditions and requirements, which were totally unknown for me as prerequisites to receive this prestigious position for a foreign graduate. I would be able to work under the supervision of an attending physician with the patients while not having an American license. It jolted me to a certain degree, but it was obvious that the professional and legal standards and requirements in the USA were quite different as in European countries, especially countries behind the Iron Curtain.

The letter gave me the instructions that I would have to pass an American examination over the entire medicine as a foreign physician, to test my professional knowledge and prowess, and also to pass an examination in active English, to show that I was able to communicate in English. The examination acronym was Educational Counsel for Foreign Medical Graduates (ECFMG), and it was arranged to be done on one particular date in the whole world at the Cultural Center of the U.S. Embassy, in my case in Prague, Czechoslovakia.

I said to myself, "Good Lord, this will not be a fun!" It was thirteen years after my graduation, and I would have to cram again the body parts in anatomy and all the formulas in general chemistry, physics, and, lo and behold, gynecology?

The letter had also an application form — how to apply to the ECFMG with the requirements of all additional documents translated into English and notarized, such as a copy of my "index book" with the list of all courses and their passing grades and my medical diploma in English. It was not a small investment for me in my present position and income. I sent all the documents in a registered letter to Boston, USA, to the admission office of the University of J. Harvard, Cambridge, Mass., from where the verified documents were advanced to CHMC. The fact that I sent all my documents to Boston in 1965 will have pivotal importance in my near future. I did not fathom then how lucky I was going to be!

It was most helpful that the instructions in the letter from Boston listed the appropriate references from the medical literature and what each candidate should study from for the particular exam.

At that time in a somehow politically "softened" situation in Czechoslovakia, probably after the consequence of the Hungarian Revolution of 1956, I was able "somehow" to purchase the "bible" for the review of the whole medicine in English by J. Rypins: *Medical Licensure Examinations*. To boost my English, I purchased a guidebook for the English language by C.E. Eckersley, *Essential English*, (Fig. 3) by Oxford Press, which, in four colored booklets, introduced the student not only to the basics of English, but also to some grammar and idioms as well in this richest language of the world.

During my studies, I used, of course, Slovak medical textbooks as well. In the second half of the year, I studied and "crammed" as much information as I could from these resources and books, and I studied hard every day after my return from my work. With the help of strong coffee, I studied daily at least till midnight. I also upgraded my English by listening to the BBC on the radio, but I decreased the volume of the wireless, putting my ear on the speaker — thus my neighbor could not hear that I was listening to the imperialist enemy.

My determination and stamina were boosted by the knowledge that perhaps I will have a small chance and will get to the hospital in Boston, to get away from that ossified and mechanical intellectual atmosphere, even though I appreciated the Department where I worked.

Those times were difficult for my family as well. Sometimes exhausted, my nerves gave up, and more than once I wanted to quit. But my wife and my reason just gave me more strength and determination to clench my teeth and hold on with the help of the dictum "sursum corda," lift up your heart!

In spring 1967, I went by the morning train to Prague, where in the Cultural Center of the U.S. Embassy I had a chance to take the ECFMG exam in hope that I will cross that hurdle successfully to get to the U.S. Before my departure, with a sinking heart, ruffled emotions, and being exhausted, I gave farewell to my beautiful wife, a small, three-year-old son, and a few-month-old baby girl. Then I took the trolleybus and rode to the train station. I secured a hotel not far from the central Saint Wenceslas Square, where I arrived in the evening. In the morning, I took a taxi, which took me that spring morning to the picturesque hills of "Mála Strana" (the Little Side), where at the marketplace called "Tržiště," I noticed the beautiful, classical building of Schönborn Palace (1656) where the U.S. Embassy was located. On the side of it, a similar smaller building stood by, the Cultural Center of the Embassy, in a colorful spring garden. In my haste, I did not have the time to admire the beautiful petals of the spring trees in the manicured garden, and I quickly entered the building. At the entrance, I faced an officer in an American uniform, a guard with a gun. I presented him with my papers and identified myself and was allowed to enter.

I entered the spacious lobby of the Center, which, in early fresh springtime, was pleasantly warm. The interior was inviting, with soft-colored, wall-to wall rugs, elegant, mahogany easy chairs, a long sofa, a large picture of George Washington with his majestic demeanor, and pictures of other founding fathers, whom I did not recognize.

I was obviously in a different world, in the world of a "decadent" West, with no coarse socialism but an inviting smell of Arabian coffee was emanating from a silver-coated coffee machine. And look! As a miracle, on the side of it, a classical Russian "samovar" stood by for an afternoon tea. These two machines, representing the aromatic culinary pleasures, stood side by side without any ideological stride or struggle. A few of us, with some hesitation, approached those two — for us — new "contraptions of pleasure," either the aromatic coffee or the perfumed Darjeeling tea, with or without milk, offered in a small, china decanter. On the side on a delicate plate, a line of gingerbread cookies were served, lined up like the U.S. Marines, and beside them on a silver plate, a discretely placed line of napkins in different colors were offered with a logo: "Be sociable"! I could not resist, and I pilfered a solitary napkin, that is, a "capitalistic napkin," into my pocket as a souvenir from the "free world" and kept it for many years as a secret talisman till I unexpectedly left my native country.

We were twelve physicians — like the apostles — from the Czech and Slovak lands and one colleague from Budapest, Hungary. To my surprise, I met there a friend, a surgical resident from the Department of Surgery. Obviously nobody advertised his desire or secret dream to study in the USA. As we were waiting and sitting without a word in the inviting lobby, suddenly the door opened, and a gentleman in an English tweed jacket stood before us with his welcome to the U.S. Embassy. "I will be your 'proctor,'" he announced, "and together with my assistants, we will supervise the proceedings of the ECFMG test."

Then he invited us into a larger room where, like in a classroom, there were twelve tables and chairs prepared for us. On each table were two No. 2 pencils, already sharpened for our use and answers. On the proctor's suggestion, we took our seats. Between the tables was a space of about three feet, dividing one from another like an invisible wall. In his remark, we were reminded that any communications between us during the test was forbidden and would mean disqualification of the person. The time was 9 A.M.

The proctor standing before us explained to us that on his command, we could break the seal of the exercise book and start to work. He repeatedly underscored that no communication was permissive. Well, I reminded myself that it would not be an examination like in the socialist system!

The proctor then reviewed our team with a sharp eye and gave the command: "You can break the seal and start to work. This session will end at 12 noon." The other assistants started to swirl around our tables with an encouraging smile, but no words were uttered.

We were quite well-prepared to answer the rather new and unusual multiple-choice questions from the J. Rypins textbook, even though these "real questions" had many unusual and unexpected variations.

In this first round — lasting three hours — we concentrated on the right answers for many tricky questions, but we were allowed a break for the bathroom or, in this cultured milieu, for a cup of coffee or tea to sharpen up our attention or intellect. That is, we could be "sociable" during our unaccustomed struggle, as the napkin was suggesting. This was not in line with the known "cultura bolshaja," that is, the Russian culture.

At noon the proctor promptly arrived with his command: "Please stop the work. Close the notebook." These were taken away by his assistants. A huge sigh of relief and relaxation followed in this "camp of retched refuse" (Emma Lazarus). Everybody stretched his stiffened back, and most of us ran for a "healing" coffee.

We had an hour for recess. The group as a whole went to the closest diner and gobbled up a hot dog and a roll or two and splashed it down with a glass of small "Pilsen bier" and was running back to the embassy and to the coffee machine, and tanking up a cup or two of his choice of "ecrasite " for another fight.

At 1 P.M. the proceedings were repeated, and we had to work till 3 P.M. In this section, I faced a question about a midget two feet, three inches tall, and I tried to convert the inches into the metric scale, familiar for me, to reach a reasonable conclusion regarding the etiology of this affliction. Even though I had drilled the formula to translate the English measures to metrics before the test, in this stressful situation, my brain somehow failed in his faculties, and I was not successful in getting to a plausible answer. Fortunately a young proctor with an encouraging smile just passed by, and I raised my courage and, with some indecision, asked him, "How much is two feet, three inches, in metrics. He replied with a smile and quipped, "Sorry," and passed by. Probably I did mess up the answer.

In the last part of the test at 4 P.M., we had to solve diagnostic questions from a series of pictures of body parts of a patient, the color of his skin, X-rays, electrocardiograms, or a sample of urine in a test tube. All the pictures were in natural colors. As I opened the first page of my test book, I got my first cultural shock, and I almost lost my breath and bearing. The picture portrayed the genitals of a black male, that is, his penis, with an ulcerated lesion with gray demarcation on his borders of the glans of the penis, with a yellow, purulent center. It was the first black patient in my professional practice, and I did not have a clue about the correct diagnosis or its etiology. Thus I mechanically marked the column C. What the result of my haphazard answer was, I never learned.

At 6 P.M. the third part of our test or struggle ended. On the command of the proctor, we put down our pencils, closed the exercise book with our answers, and returned it to the assistants of the proctor.

A huge sigh of relief followed in the whole group. Again we stretched our stiffened neck and back, and one of us exclaimed, "Christ, this was not a joke!"

It was already sundown in Prague, and the first lights were on over the town when we took our suitcases and overcoats, said short goodbyes to the proctors with frozen smiles, and got out into the fresh air of the spring and took deep breaths to raise our spirits and moods. The whole group took a streetcar, as a group of prisoners whom bad luck or fate had forged together at that time of our lives. As the streetcar pushed ahead, I was so exhausted that I really did not know if the streetcar was moving forward or backward. I was groggy indeed! But the other chums were no less wretched, and we all looked for some relaxation to unwind or have some fun, to raise our spirits in our numbed souls, after we had crossed this Rubicon.

Four or five of us, with my surgeon friend Ludenko, decided that we really deserved some "fun extraordinaire," and we sauntered into a high-priced nightclub, Alhambra, named after the exotic Spanish fortress Qualat Al Hambra in Granada, Spain. To heck with the cost!

This nightclub, or "cabaret," had been entertaining patrons of the higher class since 1915 as part of the hotel Ambassador on the Wenceslas Square. In the spring of 1967 — in a country of socialism — this was the main attraction for foreign tourists, with its show of cabaret dance and dancers in skimpy bikinis and high prices in this country behind the Iron Curtain. We expected that its boisterous and rowdy program would, at least for a while, erase our concerns about the results of our exam and entertain us amidst light and lively music (Fig. 4).

With the decision made by five of us, we purchased our high-priced tickets into a rather spacious box, where in its intimacy we could have our dinner and drink. It was probably the best idea from one of us — not me — for a two-hour entertainment and relaxation.

The main hall of the theater was elegant and ornamental. At the entrance were two gilded, half-clad caryatides, and inside were rows of easy chairs with their Bordeaux-colored upholstery and gilded armrests. We got a box on the left side of the parterre in the main hall, facing the stage, and from the opulent dinner menu we ordered a fancy dinner and a bottle of Riesling. At the beginning of our dinner, we clicked our glasses with the golden Riesling, and our tense moods started to slowly mellow.

Below the parterre and under the stage, the orchestra suddenly started the program with a loud and brisk swing of jazz. The lights went dim, and suddenly on the stage under the strobe light, a young gentleman in an impeccable tuxedo and spritely bow tie introduced the particulars of the evening program.

It was a great surprise that in this city, a center of socialism, the first person who started the show was a famous German actor, Kurt Jürgens, with his charming and warm smile. While already in middle age with silvery whiskers, he sang in his sonorous baritone a well-known chanson while around him some beautiful girls swirled and danced, exposing their voluptuous lines. The crooner received tremendous applause and cheers, which went for the girls as well (Fig. 5).

Then on the scene the members of the famous Prague "black theater" showed up, where, on a black background, actors clad in black — thus invisible — were portraying and showing different figures or clowns lit in phosphorescent lights and colors, telling a story or singing a ditty. The audience was thrilled with these picturesque and glittering stories in their witty presentation. At the end of this presentation, the lights came on, and we could see the actors themselves, all in black, moving the different figurines and pictures in the stories. A great applause followed to this ingenious and witty presentation.

The last part of the program was the performance of the world-renown "Laterna Magica (Magic Lantern)" where in three-dimensional projections and views, the presentation of the barcarole from the opera *The Tales of Hoffman*" by Jaques Offenbach were displayed on a large screen. Everybody was thrilled by this magnificent show, famous since the World Fair in Brussels at Expo 1958.

It was a memorable, if not unforgettable, evening of a spectacular show with delectable dinner and wine, a best medicine for our exhausted minds. After a good night's sleep and a sumptuous breakfast topped by an Italian espresso, our trip came to a memorable end.

In the morning, a fast train took us back to Bratislava. At home I had to narrate to my wife in great detail our adventurous experience of the ECFG test, followed by the boisterous celebration in the Alhambra cabaret, amid her joyous astonishment, giggles, and chuckles as well.

In the hospital, I concealed my experience and the trip, with its potential interpretation of a "conspiracy" undermining the socialist state! My professor knew about my adventure, and she approved and stimulated me to get a fellowship abroad. In this awkward, subtle subterfuge and plot, nevertheless, I was happy that I had dared to struggle and perhaps had jumped over a bar, whatever the result of the test would be. Consequently I increased my stride to study and advance in my specialty in hope, eventually, to study abroad.

In May, the same year of 1967, my professor was, for the first time in history, "mysteriously" invited to participate in the World Congress of Pediatric Cardiology in Rome, Italy. Her expenses of the trip were, of course, covered by the Medical School. A slight chance to attend this Congress showed up as well for myself, and I could have the opportunity to see the research and clinical results from the USA in that specialty. It gave me an impetus to try having a fighting chance at the possibility to attend the meeting, even if I would have to absorb the expenses by myself. I was always willing to sacrifice my means in the interest of my advancement in my professional career and know-how. Lo and behold, I was successful with the authorities to get permission to go abroad, provided my family stayed behind as a hostage. Unexpectedly I was thus turned as an "altar boy" and escort to the professor during the trip. As such, it was socially advantageous to her as well, as I helped her with her luggage and my English was in better shape and could be of assistance to her for communication.

The congress was organized on a weekend in early May. At least two hundred specialists and experts were invited for the event. Most important, of course, were the scientists from the USA, where pediatric cardiology and surgery was well advanced vis-à-vis the other countries.

We took the train — both of us coming from behind the Iron Curtain — from Vienna, Austria. There on the train, suddenly a gentleman joined us in our compartment with a measured "good morning." It was a handsome, middle-aged man in an elegant, blue business suit with salt-and-pepper hair and sideburns. It turned out to be a lawyer from Wellington, New Zealand. His heavy Hungarian accent gave away that he was an émigré from Hungary after the Hungarian Revolution of 1956. He spoke in fluent English, and I tried with him my English in a colloquial conversation just to get some experience. The compartment was a very pleasant, first-class coupe with a nice Bordeaux upholstery, and amidst the mutual give-and-take in discourse, the trip was very pleasant. At his departure in Rome, he wished us a "bon voyage."

Our lodging was in a hotel or a transformed Roman palace with large rooms and beds with baldachins, like in a fairytale. Friday morning on the first day of the conference, we had a quick breakfast with authentic Italian espresso, giving us an appropriate wake-up call. In addition there were scrumptious brioches available with real butter and marmalade from different fruits, which boosted the sugar level in our blood and sharpened our curious intellects.

Bolstered by this exquisite breakfast, we entered the beautiful, baroque conference room, and lo and behold, we unexpectedly noticed other colleagues from countries behind the Iron Curtain, such as Dr. János Kamarás from Budapest, Hungary, and Dr. Jerzy Swidersky from Warsaw, Poland. We welcomed each other warmly (Fig. 6).

The presentations and the chosen topic were excellent, mainly the results of the research of the American pediatric cardiologists. Their lectures covered a wide range of problems with instructive, statistical data and graphic presentations with slides. We convincingly realized, as physicians behind the Iron Curtain, that we are significantly limping behind these "pioneers" of science from the free Western world. But the physicians from continental Europe — except perhaps those from the United Kingdom — were rather behind as well in experience, knowledge, and technology from their American friends.

Dr. Abe Rudolph and Dr. William Rashkind presented to the audience their new approaches and advances in the technique of cardiac catheterization (passing a plastic tube into the heart). Dr. Rashkind presented his new "balloon catheter," which he used to create a new communication (opening) between the two atria (upper chamber of the heart) for certain types of heart lesion, thus avoiding surgical intervention. A new world of different, innovative approaches in the treatment of congenital heart problems were presented in this discipline, to the astonishment of many. During the intermission, all the participants were mixing together in a cordial exchange, as the pediatric cardiologists in the world were still a rather small club. We surrounded the athletic and jovial Bill Rashkind, whose ancestors originated from Poland. He was exceptionally cordial to colleagues from behind the Iron Curtain. At the end of this informal "tête-à-tête," he offered some samples of his "miraculous" catheter to some of the surrounding colleagues. I boosted my courage and asked for a catheter, and he generously offered me one of his samples. That catheter gave me a problem on our trip home: how to smuggle this "contraband" through customs. Eventually, in the critical moment, my professor had an ingenious idea, and she hid it in her bra, and we passed! Eventually two months later, I used this catheter in a critically ill baby.

The congress was, for us, a God-sent revelation that opened our eyes and fundamentally shook us up from our professional lameness and marasmic condition!

Saturday, after the professional program, there was a farewell dinner where the Chairman of the Congress, the dapper Dr. James Du Shane from the Mayo Clinic, expressed his great satisfaction with the professional presentations of the Congress and underscored his pleasure that for the first time in the history of the Association, he could welcome colleagues from the Eastern Bloc of Europe. It was a welcomed and heartwarming sign that we from the Eastern Bloc were not forgotten and perhaps that somebody even cared.

A social program followed where waiters in Roman livery were offering heir tasty hors d'oeuvres, attached by a toothpick on a special green cabbage, which had the shape of a papal miter. It was the first time we had seen that witty, appetizing presentation of the tasty hors d'oeuvres at this lavish Lucullan banquet. A lavish dinner followed, boosted by a red ruby Chianti with its tarty aftertaste, which was a nice complement to the juicy rack of lamb. During the dinner, a string orchestra was entertaining the guests with mellow European songs.

Suddenly, out of the blue sky, Dr. Sam Kaplan from Cincinnati came to our table and asked my professor for a dance. She was quite surprised, but her eyes reflected a great joy at this honor, and she probably felt that she was indeed in heaven. Here she was, a daughter of humble origins from the small village of Liptovský Peter, in the heart of Slovakia, and she was now dancing with an "American imperialist," who, with grace, swirled her to the tune of "Blue Danube" by Johann Strauss. I was really very happy for her at that moment. Many times the happiness of our friends makes our happiness more pronounced or joyous at such a moment. I was really delighted to see my "boss" elated in her bliss like in a fairy tale.

The next day, the day of our departure, while still quite sleepy after the evening of festivities, we rushed for a strong espresso and a quick bite and said a hasty farewell to our friends and took a cab to the train station. We were concerned, as "ignoble foreigners" from behind the Iron Curtain, how we were going to smuggle our "contraband catheter" through customs, but the Italian customs officer just let us go through his post nonchalantly: "Avanti!"

At the Italian border to Austria at Tarvisio, we missed the connecting train, and we had to wait for the next one.

On the train in the department, I left the three-padded seat for my professor to stretch out, and I, the "manly man," climbed up into the net for the luggage compartment to catch some sleep and settle down, as in an hammock. It was quite an experience! Before I stretched out, I pulled out from a small bag my hairnet for the night — thus in the morning I would look well-groomed. As the professor noticed this never-seen contraption on my head, she burst out in an explosive bout of laughter, with tears bursting out from her eyes. I giggled as well, from my height in the hammock, but eventually we tried to catch some sleep on the noisy train. When we returned home, we showed up on the morning "journal" in the hospital. We presented to the members of the department our professional and social experience, but at the end of the report, my hairnet turned up to be the main social event, with a lot of laugh and bantering. Eventually we underscored, in a rather somber presentation, our professional backwardness being behind the Iron Curtain, especially in technology and diagnostic tools.

Suddenly the sunny summer was upon us, and everybody looked for some weekend escape and relaxation to the neighboring woods or to the waters of the Danube. For a summer vacation, we had very limited means and only the well-to-do went to the sea in Bulgaria, and only the well "chosen" could afford the Adriatic Sea. A trip to the west was out of the question unless you were a political bigwig.

Our two children were small — our baby girl was only one year old and our son was four. Our outlook for vacation was financially quite bleak, even though as an assistant professor, theoretically I could have had a vacation of two months, since the teaching started in September. It was an unbelievable academic and socialist luxury.

Yet unexpectedly my sister, who worked in the eastern metropolis of Kosice as a secretary in the local college, found an inviting solution. The college had a "socialist friendship," or a contract, with a college in Debrecen, Hungary, located ideally in a "Great Forest" of the town. Here my sister could rent two apartments in the student dorm for us and my dear mom and her so she could be with her grandchildren.

The summer was sunny and lazy with luscious, green gardens all around. The leafy trees offered a gentle screen over the playgrounds for the children in that ideal setting. The main attraction of the campus was a group of large swimming pools, where in the largest, hidden hydraulic pumps created huge waves for the swimmers every hour. These artificial waves were so powerful that we had to keep our kids tightly on our side, since the waves could smash them against the wall of the pool. My dear mom had the experience of such a jolt of splash, and I had to rescue her at that moment from being thrown to the wall of the pool. But it was great fun for all of the children and adults, amidst a lot of laughter and cries in that swirling, champagne atmosphere of the pool.

On and off, when the children were under the watchful eyes of their "Ó ma" (as they called my mom), my wife and I escaped to a local inn (csárda) for a spicy fish soup followed by a fried "fogas" (tooth perch) from Lake Balaton, splashed down by a glass of golden Riesling.

On the last Saturday of our vacation, the students in the dorm could invite and have some visitors. There were Russian students there as well who were visited by Russian soldiers stationed in the town, who after the Hungarian Revolution of 1956 still remained as part of the Red army's occupying force, keeping in check the restless Hungarians. Those young soldiers, of course, brought some vintage "vodka stolichnaja" to their compatriots.

After dinner around 8 P.M., the students with the visiting solders started to sing Russian songs on full throttle in the apartment above ours. The singing soon turned to boisterous shouting, and the whole floor started to tremble, especially when they started to dance or tramp on the floor the Russian stomp called "kozak."

Around 9 P.M. we tried to put our children to sleep, but the noise and tramping was unnerving everybody on our floor. At 10 P.M., when the dorm had a compulsory silence on order, still the singing and stomping continued aloud. My mom, a resolute and energetic woman, started to be annoyed. She dressed up in her nightgown and went down to the ground floor to see the doorman and asked him to calm down those boisterous students. But the doorman was at visible unease, saying, "My dear lady, who can order something to these Russian soldiers? I don't have the power to order them anything!" My mom was not happy with this development and was quite exasperated. In our room, she pulled out a broom, and with its stick, she pounded on the ceiling, to no avail. The students and their guests did not pay any attention to that knocking, and with their yelling, they probably did not even hear it. Then from the other apartments, some other guests were coming out and lamenting as well, but everybody was afraid of those Russian soldiers. But when it turned 11 P.M. and the "bacchanal" continued, my mom got really mad. She picked up again her fancy nightgown, bobbed up her snow white hair to look like a fairytale sorcerer, climbed up the stairs to the next floor, and forcefully banged on the door of the rambunctious students. The door was opened by a Russian soldier, who in his surprise almost froze like the biblical Lot when he faced this angry white "witch."

My mom gave him an angry dress down in her native Slovak tongue, which had some similarities with the Russian language, so the Russian got the gist of her anger. She reprimanded him for the ruckus they were causing at that time of night and threatened him that she would file a complaint with his local commander of the Russian forces!

The soldier was totally shaken by this attack of an exasperated, old, "white lady." In his embarrassment, he did not know what to say, but he understood the word "silence" from this Slavic tongue, and he tried to mutter something like, "sorry," but my mom did not understand that either. From that moment, the howling stopped, and heavenly silence spread over the whole building. My mom then made a victorious retreat and returned to our rooms, exhilarated as a champion of the day.

The next day, as we toured with our children in a stroller into the park, my mom marched as a victorious peacock in the gardens, and the doorman pointed to her: That is the woman who gave a dress down to the rambunctious Russian last night. Our neighboring guests greeted her with a smile of appreciation as to Joan of Arc, who had defeated an aggressive dragon.

Yet the balmy summer had to come to its end and, thus, our vacation as well. Soon we had to return home to Bratislava and start to work and go back to our routine.

In the fall, I received an official letter from the Council of ECFMG with a note congratulating me that I successfully passed the examination with the resulting eighty points, which was quite high and fully satisfactory. It made me really very happy, and we had a small celebration at home with my wife. Yet with those political times and in that atmosphere — as I inquired — the possibility to study in U.S. was quite bleak, and so I tried to search for some other possibilities.

A few weeks later, I received a letter from a Swiss peer review journal, *Annales Pediatrici*, where they informed me that they had accepted for publication my case report about a very rare heart condition in a three-year-old patient. As was customary, with the congratulations from the editor, I received twenty separate copies of the article to be available for other interested professionals. To my surprise, I soon received a letter of interest from an associate professor, Dr. Jürgen A., from the Children's Hospital in Tübingen, West Germany, and I was happy to supply him a copy of the article. In my cover letter to him, I probingly asked the professor if there would be a chance to work at his division of pediatric cardiology as a fellow. He was kind enough to suggest that I should apply for the West German scholarship at the Alexander van Humboldt Foundation. I complied immediately and was happy to have another chance or possibility to apply to an institution interested in my work in West Germany.

Alexander van Humboldt (1769-1859) was an acknowledged scientist and researcher in natural sciences. In 1799 he sailed and traveled in South America around the Orinoco River and Amazon and climbed the volcanic mountain of Chimborasso (5,200 meters high), where he collected over two thousand samples of plants and different species of animals as a kind of forerunner of Charles Darwin. He also studied the local climatic conditions and the different ecology in the changing geology of the land. He summed up the results of his research in a monumental treatise, *Cosmos* (Fig. 7). In 1953 the federal government of West Germany, under the premiership of Conrad Adenauer, established the Foundation of Alexander van Humboldt to advance postdoctoral research for young researchers from all over the world. The Foundation had its headquarters in Bad Godesberg, close to Bonn, the capital of the Federal Republic of West Germany.

As my chances for study in the U.S. looked bleak — from political perspective, as I was not a member of the Communist Party — I submitted my application to the prestigious Foundation for a scholarship, with all my professional documents translated to German and notarized as well. In addition I presented to the Foundation also the list of my professional publications. My goal was to get a position at the children's hospital in Tübingen, West Germany, where Dr. Jürgen A. was the Physician in Chief of the Division of Pediatric Cardiology.

Simultaneously in June 1968, two pediatric cardiologists came to visit our Children's Hospital in Bratislava, one from Budapest, Hungary, the other from Subotica, Yugoslavia, who was also an ethnic Hungarian. These two professionals, learned by word of mouth that in our institution in Bratislava, we, the pediatric cardiologists, took over the technique of the cardiac catheterization of the heart from our surgical colleagues. I previously had learned this technique of the so-called "percutaneous" insertion of a catheter (tube) in a vein without a surgical cut down — originally developed by Swedish radiologist Sven Seldinger — from adult cardiologist Dr. Jiří Endrys of Hradec Králové in Northern Bohemia.

I demonstrated the technique to our guests during a diagnostic workup and showed them the technique, inserting via a special needle a small tube into a vein of a child in his groin. These friends were impressed to learn this ingenious, rather simple-looking technique that avoided surgical intervention.

In reciprocity these friends were eager to show us their research in noninvasive techniques of diagnostic tools in workup of children with heart disease, mainly by selective sound tracings or phonocardiography. Our professor was very happy about this exchange of different experiences and techniques in cardiology, and a nice friendship developed, not only between us, doctors, but also between the two institutions in Bratislava and Budapest.

I also invited these friends to our house for a dinner, where my wife hosted the guests with some of her choice culinary home cooking, complemented by a fine wine from the region of the Small Carpathians.

The two of them were trained in Budapest by Prof. Dr. Gegesi-Kiss Paul, native of southern Slovakia. In 1953 he published the first textbook of pediatric cardiology in the Eastern Bloc, where the part about congenital heart diseases in children was not up to par to American textbooks. Still that was the best available textbook at that time in the countries behind the Iron Curtain. It was my first textbook of pediatric cardiology, from which I learned a lot.

We spent professionally quite a productive week, with the two guests and my professor very happy with our teaching and demonstrations for these colleagues from Hungary. At the departure of these two friends, as a small souvenir I gave to each of them a small coil of original Swedish catheters, which came very handy to Steve from Subotica. He left me with his business card with his telephone number. Never did I fathom that this telephone number will come to me very handy in few months.

After their departure, we in my family made a bold, if not audacious, plan to spend our vacation on the Adriatic Sea. This was our dream, as we had heard about the pristine and turquoise blue waters of this southern paradise of Croatia, surrounded or walled in by the rugged Karst mountains.

We had no idea or any premonition and never fathomed that the vacation would have fatal consequences for us in the political maelstrom of the Cold War that would forever change the fate and trajectories of our lives.

THE FATAL VACATION

Since the last fall, 1967, I almost had forgotten that I had a possibility or chance to study abroad in the West. We were now looking forward with great expectation and joy for our planned vacation in the turquoise waters of the Adriatic.

Unexpectedly in the last days of June 1968, I received a letter, and in the first moment of that surprise, I did not fathom who could write from West Germany to me. But the crest of the Alexander van Humboldt Foundation raised my attention, and I quickly learned that the Foundation was informing me that I was being awarded with a prestigious stipend for the academic year 1968-69 to study in West Germany. I was, of course, elated by that privilege, yet I did not fathom that it was again my "blue fairy" offering her magic hand, and in the near future, I will desperately need that fellowship at the dramatic turn of political events. It looked again that our future fate was indeed unforeseeable or unpredictable.

In the very last days of the month, we said farewell to our friends at my hospital and on June 30, 1968, the whole family was riding in my small car to see my in-laws, the parents of my wife, to bid farewell to them with the two grandchildren. On the last day of our visit, we went for a dip and our first suntan on the nearby Hron River, to have some mischievous fun with our two small children (Fig. 8).

Early the next day, amidst many hugs and tears, we said goodbye to the grandparents without a premonition that we were not going to see them for many years to come.

Our small car was really "small," in conformity with the "socialist realism" of our days and in that country behind the Iron Curtain. It looked like a box out of tin with a small, frontal trunk that could accommodate only a medium-sized bag.

Under the back trunk, a small, four-cylinder motor was hidden that could master only three speeds while driving and switching speeds by a stick. But we liked this small "bugger," and we nicknamed it Bobby. He served us very loyally and well and was an immense advantage in our dramatic turn of events and unexpected emigration (Fig. 9).

With our two small children, Robert, five, and Patsy, two, we needed to carry some supplies for them like diapers, dried milk, and some amount of canned food — just in case — since our foreign-currency supply was rather meager. In that tight arrangement, one bag went to the front trunk while the rest of the luggage was piled up on the seat beside me, the driver.

My wife, with the children, took the two back seats. Behind my front seat, our grandfather had made up a small shelf out of wood for the children so they could stretch out for a nap or sleep. We were crammed in the car like sardines, but it was important that we were all together in this small, but for us beautiful, car.

The foreign currencies — the dinars in Yugoslavia — were our most important concern. We could not just go to our bank and buy dinars since the leader of Yugoslavia, Josip Broz Tito, in 1948 defied Joseph Stalin and detached his country from the Soviet Bloc countries. Consequently the dinars were then like Western denominations, tightly regulated by our state.

A friend of my wife, Ann P., who had her roots in northern Yugoslavia, gave us "contemporary" advice of the times. If we could bring or smuggle through the border of Hungary some "cigarette papers" (to roll a cigarette with tobacco in them), her relatives would reimburse us in dinars.

Since spring we had started to buy and hoard rather large boxes of cigarette papers. Those were like a fine paper membrane from which the peasants or blue-collar workers could, with great skill, roll their cigarettes. It was, for them, cheaper that way — a half century ago — than buying cigarettes. We were able to accumulate twenty-five boxes of that merchandise (a box was 8 inches by six inches by two inches in size). We divided them into two heavy-duty plastic bags that we hung on two hooks on the side of the engine in the back of the trunk. In other words, those could have been like two explosive devices. Fortunately the plastic bags did their job!

In the last moment, we still returned to Bratislava, just to finish up our packing, and the next day we set off south to Hungary for our vacation. Never did we fathom that we would never see our home again, nor our new condo with brand-new furnishings, an art collection, and all the amenities!

We crossed the border to Hungary at the small village of Rajka, and we drove toward the border town of Mosonmagyaróvár. As I was driving on a two-lane asphalt road, suddenly I noticed, to my misbelief, in the adjacent fields about half a dozen heavy Hungarian tanks turning their turrets and guns toward the north, that is Slovakia. "Look," I exclaimed to my wife, Judy. "Do you see what I see? These tanks are aiming their guns toward our country! What does it mean?" I got into a nervous panic attack of anxiety and had a bad premonition. I got so agitated that I had to stop the car on the side of that narrow road. I reached for my medical supplies and quickly swallowed a tablet of Valium to regain my calm and composure. My wife tried to calm me down. "Well, these are probably just some exercises or a small maneuver." But in few weeks, we learned that it was anything but a small exercise!

Yet there was no time for sentimental tribulations, and we pressed forward, bypassing Budapest, and at dusk we reached the second-largest city in the Hungarian south: Szeged. We quickly found a friendly inn, and there we had no problem with the Hungarian currency of the Eastern Bloc. We took some rest and then looked for a classical Hungarian restaurant with local folklore in that part of the picturesque town.

We were eager to try that cozy restaurant, on the banks of the Tlsa River, the famous spicy fish soup. It was indeed very tasty but a little bit "hot" from the famous red paprika of Szeged, so for our children, we asked for the familial chicken soup with angel-hair noodles.

Following the soup, we wanted to try the famous "tooth fish" (fogas) from the river, which was tasty and very tender. Our children had mashed potatoes with meatloaf to avoid the bones from the fish. The fish, of course, wanted to swim, and we splashed it down with a golden local white wine, which had a very appealing bouquet. The following dessert were the local "crepes suzette" with cottage cheese and raisins, which were indeed scrumptious. For children an ice-cold spring water from the courtyard well was very refreshing.

At this time, we were all tired, and we quickly fell asleep in the fresh air coming through the open windows from the garden.

It was our first time in this beautiful and historic city. We visited the famous shrine of the Holy Mother, built in a gothic stile. The interior was magnificent with its mosaic windows of different colors and biblical themes. Interestingly, leaning on the back of the cathedral was an open-air theater built in 1931. The summer performances in that arena were a feast of operas, concerts, and dramas for the whole country (Fig. 10). We also visited and strolled through the rich and picturesque local farmers market with beautiful and fresh vegetables and all kinds of fruits, like juicy peaches, which my wife eagerly purchased for our trip. Of course, here was the land of the famous "Hungarian paprika" in piles, sweet and hot, in beautiful, ruby red colors. I knew as a physician that in the thirties, at the University of Szeged, Dr. Albert Szentgyörgyi isolated from this paprika vitamin C, for which he was awarded the Nobel Prize. (Eventually he ended up doing research in Woods Holes in Massachusetts.) My wife could not resist buying some sweet variety of this famous vegetable. But the time was pressing, and we had to continue in our trip. After a short bite for lunch, we hurried southward toward the Yugoslav border.

In a short while, we crossed the border without a problem with our "contraband," and in about two hours of rocky drive on dirt roads, we arrived in the small town of Bácky Petrovác, where in 1745 the Slovak Southern Slavs settled. After a short search for the house, we quickly noticed it, where Ann was already anxiously expecting us with her family. This was a family of Slovak settlers, who welcomed us warmly and offered us their heartfelt hospitality. The two "girls," Ann and my wife, greeted each other emotionally, with lot of hugs and kisses, and our children and myself were not spared of them either by Ann or her kind parents. The family offered us a spacious bedroom where we felt quickly at home.

Soon we were invited to a large table in their living room, where a large bowl of steaming chicken soup was on the table, with its inviting smell and fragrance of fresh vegetables right from their garden, such as orange-colored carrots and snow white parsley. They were floating with angel hair and large golden circles from the chicken lard. Before dinner we clicked our tumblers with local plum brandy: "To your health — cheers!" It lifted our fatigue and mood as well.

Next a big serving plate showed up, brought in by Ann, with chunks of fried chicken, new spring potatoes sprinkled with fresh green parsley, and homegrown cucumber salad, dashed with red paprika and black pepper. It was quite a culinary show for us, the hungry wanderers. In the crystals for wine, a golden local Furmint wine was served as an appropriate compliment for the main course. The children enjoyed the crystal clear water from the well in the court. Around the table, a lively conversation developed about our trip to the Adriatic and about our lovely children, but the comment about the Hungarian tanks evoked worrisome glances from the parents.

In the morning after a good night of balmy sleep, a sumptuous breakfast of scrambled eggs with bacon and a fresh, crusty, home-baked bread was served.

Then I went to my car and pulled out from the back trunk the dirty but intact two plastic bags. From them I presented, in the kitchen, to the father of the family twenty-five untouched and sealed new boxes of cigarette papers. Anne's father was surprised by such a generous supply of cigarette papers, but he was very happy with the high quality of the merchandise. Right away he presented me with the amount of dinars as the price on which we had agreed upon in advance. Both happy, we shook hands as two men, and the business was closed.

Later on Ann took us for a tour to see and view the small but historic town, where over 70 percent of the local inhabitants were Slovaks or had Slovak ancestors. We were surprised how far our ancestors had spread out their wings in the past. We visited the Slovak Lutheran church in baroque style, quite ornamental, and the historic and famous Slovak high school of Jan Kollár, where the well-known Communist journalist and writer Ján Siracký (1925-1988) studied and was later a member of the left-wing literary group "Dav" (Crowd) in Slovakia. Nearby stood the theater of Vladimir Hurban, another prominent clergyman, and the town was the center of the southern branch of the Slovak Cultural Society-Matica in Serbia. We were rather surprised by the rich, cultural environment in a relatively small settlement. While well-aware we were proud to see that our forefathers remained always true to their native language, cultural heritage, and religion, as we later experienced in the USA.

The next morning, with great tenderness and many hugs, we said good-bye to Ann and her parents, full of emotions. Never did we fathom that we would never see again our beloved Ann.

We were facing a shorter drive to the capital of the country of Yugoslavia, Belgrade (white castle), where we were expected by our old friends from Bratislava. They invited us to take a rest before our trip to the Adriatic. Paul was a typical southern Slav-Serb with his dark mustache and vivid black eyes. He was an engineer in a local factory. His wife, Chyrianna, was a blond beauty with brown eyes, a fetching young woman indeed. They welcomed us with great affection and warmth, especially our two lovely children since they were childless. We stayed and enjoyed the hospitality of that lively pair, who were just delighted by our two children, especially Chyrianna. They had been a year ago our guests in Bratislava for a week.

The next day, they showed us the historic center of Belgrade, which was built at the confluence of two rivers, the Danube and Sava, as a formidable fortress, well-known from the turbulent history of the Balkans, where in the fifteenth century, the

Hungarian general Jan Hunyady fought a great battle with the Ottoman Turks, and Europe was saved for years to come from their invasion.

We were surprised by the elegant, rather modern city center, where historical manor houses and luxurious and chic boutiques were built in with plenty of Western merchandise, such as Italian clothing, shoes, shirts, and colorful, silk neckties. We could not even dream about such an assortment in Bratislava.

It was obvious that the Yugoslav leader Joseph Broz Tito made a wise political move to say farewell to Joseph Stalin.

In the afternoon after a light lunch, Chyrianna took Judy and the two children into a beautiful, green park, Kalimegdan (Fig. 11), where the kids could roam around and have some fun while Paul and myself followed them from a small distance in a slow stroll. The park was surrounded by the crumbling walls of the old fortress, and from its banks, we could see the picturesque confluence of the two majestic rivers, which were of different colors. I sat down with Paul on a bench, and as the men in July 1968, we tried to untangle or foresee the menacing political situation in Eastern Europe under the control of the Soviet Union, where the winds of political freedom were piercing through the surface of the oppressed public as a raging epidemic. The times were obviously very ominous and menacing.

The next day after a most pleasant meeting and relaxation with our dear friends, who cherished our lovely children, we said an emotional goodbye, or "auf wiedersehen" (see you again) in a month, and we dashed with our car south, well-supplied with the "grab" from our generous friends. We took the direction to the southern district town of Čačak and farther south, crossing the town of Biele Pole (white field), and in late afternoon, we could already see the turquoise waters of the Adriatic as we descended from the mountainous region of Karts to the deep valley of the sea. There, squeezed between the crevices of the mountains, lay the small town of Budva in the southern tip of Croatia (Fig. 12).

Budva is an ancient, picturesque town, the oldest settlement on that embankment of the southern Adriatic. It was inhabited first by the Greeks 2,500 years ago when their leader, Cadmus, was expelled from the historic Thebes, and he came to settle there with his wife, Harmonia. After the Greeks came the Romans and the Byzantines, in the sixth century, followed by the Avar tribes and their king, Duklis, and finally the Slav tribes with their Vlastinovič dynasty. In the seventeenth century, the area was governed by the Venetians, and at the beginning of the twentieth century, the government was taken over by the Habsburgs.

The old town was still surrounded by its formidable bastions, with the main entrance Porta di Ferma, which led to the main thoroughfare, Avenue Njegoševa. Nearby stood the Citadella and the church of Saint Ivan from the seventeenth century, the Santa Maria di Punta from the nineteenth century, and the Temple of the Holy Trinity. For history buffs and lovers — as we were — Budva was a place with tremendous historic heritage.

As we reached the center of the town, our first task was to look for the tourist office, where they eagerly offered us to rent a room, or "soba," for our whole family. We could not look there for a Hilton — fortunately they did not have any! But our spacious room was in a house in the green part of the town, looking more like a cottage in a big garden, full of plum and mainly fig trees with their large, leafy foliage. Already the figs had started to ripen, as their fruits were greeting us with their sweet aroma from the sugary syrup that was already oozing from their plump bodies.

From the small house, a young woman showed up, in her twenties, with a baby in her arms. As we entered the small ante garden, we noticed the lush, red geraniums and the snow white daisies. We showed her our papers from the tourist bureau, and she nodded and welcomed us with a gentle smile. She was a fetching, blue-eyed women, with her braided hair the color of flax and a slender figure. It was obvious that she was coming from the northern provinces, as all the other people were all dark-haired and black-eyed, with the Creole complexion of people from the surrounding province of Monte Negro (Black Mountain).

In the kitchen — as we entered — the young woman put her baby in a cradle that she could rock with her feet.

She showed us our spacious room, quite ready for a family with two big beds and an additional smaller bed. We hinted that we knew how to manage. Through the open window into the garden, we could feel the pleasant, dulcineous breeze and hear the chirping of the birds. Behind the house, a proud rooster, with his red crest, was tending his harem of hens. As we made our way into the kitchen, the young woman was rocking her baby with her left feet while on the kitchen table kneading a piece of dough and spreading it out with a beer bottle. We looked at each other, and I quipped, "I guess it can be done this way as well."

Already dusk was descending on the town, and we were famished indeed. We had to hurry into the center. Not having a folding baby carriage or stroller (none were available in those countries in those years), Patsy was mostly in my arms or on my shoulders, but she was a muscular little toddler, so she jumped around like a young filly most of the time. We soon arrived in the commercial center of the town on the main street and saw different food vendors and shops welcoming us, as we wanted to stock up our bags with some provisions after we finished our dinner.

On a small side street, we stumbled on a quite small but lovely garden restaurant to appease our hunger and rumbling stomachs.

The restaurant was surrounded by a patch of lovely flowers that reveled in their lively colors, such as the Croatian blue iris, the ruby red begonias, the golden yellow dahlias, and the rusty resedas. This colorful symphony lifted our spirits, especially when we sat down around a nice, red, checkered-cloth-covered table with a small vase of white daisies, a salt shaker as well as a pepper mill, and toothpicks between the two. A Montenegrin waiter, with his pitch black hair and fiery eyes, welcomed us at the table and offered us the menu of the restaurant, written only in Serb. We tried to figure out the intricacies of another Slavic tongue with some difficulty.

The menu was quite inviting, such as the local čevabčiči or ražniči — cubes of meat with onion and pepper on a skewer — or barbecued kebab, as well as different kinds of fish from the early morning catch. Also spicy goulash and pork "vesalica"-grilled meat with tomato sauce was available.

We ordered a local spicy stuffed pepper, complemented with a black rye bread, quite a tasty, rustic combination. The children chose the kebab with mashed potatoes and tomato salad with onions. To splash down the spicy hot pepper, we chose to drink a fruity, local white wine, and the children had their refreshing lemonade. For the last course, we had a fresh cheese strudel with raisins, and our son, Robert, liked the Greek baclava.

We were most pleased at that balmy evening of the seaside, especially when we noticed, in the corner of the garden, a proud, red ruby hibiscus shining in the sunset. We enjoyed the beauty of that intimate restaurant, and we thought we had found our culinary headquarters.

On our way "home," my wife purchased all the gastronomic provisions that the family needed for a week. Here, for the first time, we noticed that milk was sold in plastic tripods as an import from Italy. My wife also bought a brick of butter, only in our home we noticed that the butter was salty. She was surprised because she never had seen salty butter for the kitchen in our country. The next time she asked for sweet butter, and the family was happy to have bread and butter glazed with a sweet, golden honey. Yum, yum for the children!

The first night after our long trip, we slept like logs, with our dreams in the land of fairy tales, but the rooster woke us up with his ill-started, high-pitched crowing in the early morning. Defiantly we turned on the other side after this un-expected and unwelcome wake-up call, trying to steal some more dreams in our sleep.

After a sumptuous breakfast, we were eager to see the beaches where the sand had a pinkish tint from the flint of the nearby mountains of Karst and where the tiny crystals were reflecting the beams of sun in the sleepy morning. Subsequently my wife produced the ubiquitous "Nivea cream" at that time, when the need for protection against ultraviolet rays was still unknown. First we started with the children to apply this white goo on their face, shoulders, hands and back while my wife unpacked the linen hats for protection against the sharp sun. After this sticky maneuver, we entered the refreshing turquoise waters of the Adriatic, hand in hand, with the children with their floating rubber rings around their waists. And now the bantering started in the cool waters, with lot of screaming and laughter amid squirting water on each other. That was the first time that our children had enjoyed the salty water of the sea.

After a while, we started to build some castles on the beach with sturdy sand walls, tunnels, and channels till a playful wave came and smashed away our newly built "kingdom." There was a lot of laughter and disappointment, but resolve as well to build the castle again. The sandy beach was warm and cuddly as we spread our simple blankets to have enough comfort in this lazy and beautiful environment.

We made our times livelier and more joyous with light music coming from my transistor Phillips radio, which I had purchased in a store that sold merchandise from the West only in Western currencies. Only this way, by means of the so-called "gray market," could we have technology of higher quality from the "rotten" West.

From the beaches, we could see the silhouettes of Italy afar and enjoy their romantic chansons from some of their movies directed by the famous Italian Vittorio de Sica with the voluptuous leading lady Gina Lollobrigida in the movie, *No Peace under the Olive Tree*. All the youth were singing the beautiful chanson from this movie, even behind the Iron Curtain, with his "cant":

> "Voláre, oh, oh,
> O cantáre, oh, oh, oh,….
> Nel blue, dipinto di blue.
> Felice, di stáre rassu!

"While gliding, oh, oh, And singing, oh, oh, oh….Through the blue painted sky oh, oh, oh, In the bliss of this happy blueness indeed!"

We were still young and happy with our lovely children and did not fathom that the "sword of Damocles" was hanging over us.

At noon we usually came back to our little cottage, where my wife in the kitchen could accomplish her culinary miracles to the full satisfaction of our appetites. A short siesta followed, and then the children could play in the luscious garden. They also cherished rocking the baby in her wooden cradle, made by her dad and painted over by some local, colorful flowers. We had a great time and relaxation in this bucolic paradise of sweet aromas of the impinging figs. Really we had not had any such blissful vacation in the short past of our marriage and our family!

If the weather got cloudy, it was a good time to explore the old town. Our son wanted to see the citadel with its heavy guns and cannonballs. We also visited the shrines in the old town, with their cool and sweet atmosphere of frankincense within the peaceful piety in the dusk of the church, where only the eternal red light led us to the altar.

In other times, with our small car we could make some explorations into the rugged countryside, where the limestone of the Karst mountains came down to and under the sea and submerged in it.

We visited the known tourist attraction, the picturesque Saint Steven Island, connected to the mainland only by a narrow, man-made path (Fig. 13). There we enjoyed the sandy beaches as well and its exquisite restaurant with its choice, local specialties.

Not far on a higher promontory was a small settlement of Cavtad, right above the sea, where in a tiny cemetery, a mausoleum was erected from the white limestone of the island of Brač (Figure 14). It was a resting place for the family of Račič, a well-known and rich family of shipbuilders, whose lives were wiped out by an epidemic of typhoid. The mausoleum was built by the famous Croatian sculptor Ivan Meštrovič (1882-1962). This world-famous artist was eventually in his last years sculpting in the USA.

The majestic chapel was built in veneration of "our Lady of the Angels" on the promontory of the mound of Saint Roche. The entrance of the chapel was guarded by two angelic caryatides, with their arms resting in the shape of the cross on their chest, projecting an impression of solemn piety. Through a heavy gate of bronze decorated by biblical motives, we entered into the twilight of the sanctuary, where on the marble floor we faced the picture of the four evangelists in mosaic presentation.

In front the altar of Saint Roche revealed the symbols of birth, life, and death as a cycle in our life. On the walls of the chapel were the oil paintings of the members of the Račič family. The ethereal beauty of that shrine and her spirituality was deeply moving. Our children stood beside us in an amazed awe, and somehow they snugged up closely to our side at that moment.

During our other outing, we went to see the famous Boca Kotorska (The Gulf of Kotor), a town wedged between formidable rocks that were assaulted in perpetuity by the ruffled turquoise waters of the sea (Fig. 15). These menacing rocks of the embankment served as a protective shield of the town in the Roman times, from the time of Emperor Justinian in year AD 535. After the Romans came the Dalmatian and Serbian monarchs, and in the eighteenth century came the monks of the Bogomil order (loving God), with their prayers and chants invoking the ever-present Almighty.

The architecture of the town was greatly influenced by the Venetian culture from the eighteenth century on when those knights were battling for that strategic town and its advantageous harbor. After them came the Habsburg generals and their ships, and they built a formidable military bastion there.

The town was proud of its many and beautiful churches and the monumental cathedral of Saint Trypolit (A.D. 1116) and two Orthodox shrines for the majority (80 percent) Eastern Orthodox worshipers. The Catholic bishop was present as well with his bishopric and palace.

The roads to Kotor were full of narrow and dangerous paths, right above the sea, where the waves were forcefully abating the embankments. Driving through that tortuous dirt road was dangerous since we were just above the sea.

We visited some of these ancient shrines while I carried my daughter on my shoulders, and we reviewed the embankment of the bastion with its formidable guns, part of the past defense and glory of the town.

We had our lunch on a promontory above the sea, with its nice breeze that was refreshing during our culinary feast.

In the afternoon, we headed back to our small cottage, where Svetlana was waiting for us at the entrance with the small baby in her arms.

Yet our vacation was slowly coming to its end. As a farewell, before our departure in the first week of August 1968, we wanted, for the last time — and so it was — to see the Island of Saint Steven and take a short dip on the beautiful and well-kept beaches. To have some fun and entertainment with our children seemed to be a good idea before our departure. After some bantering altogether in the water,

I went for a last swim, not far from the edge of the beach where the depth of the water was about ten feet deep. On my ring finger of my left hand, I had my wedding ring from my dear father, which was unusual because it was about a quarter of an inch wide. As I was swimming with my breaststrokes, suddenly I noticed, to my disbelief, that the precious ring was starting to unwind from my finger like a bolt from the nut to the tip of it and to the very end of my finger. Eventually it separated or wound off from my finger, and to my dread and astonishment, it started to sink to the bottom of the sea, where its golden color blended with the sand, and I lost the ring from my sight. I dove into the sea in a frenetic attack to look for my precious jewel with all of my physical strength. As I searched frantically in the depth of the turquoise water, as well as its sandy bottom, its beige color obfuscating my sight, to discern and find my ring. I tried repeatedly, with all my efforts, to recover my precious gem, but, eventually and tragically, I had failed.

Totally exhausted and out of breath, I came out from the water like an angry Poseidon, running to my wife and revealing to her my loss and shocking experience. She turned pale, as she regarded it as some kind of bad omen or augury for our future. Good God, what did it mean for us? Was it some kind of fatal warning or sign? Even my left hand was somehow different or foreign without that "shackle" of our love.

Some kind of dark cloud lurked into our subconscious, and the feeling was intrusively invading our soul, afflicting and disturbing our peace of mind. We did not say anything to our children, but our lovely vacation was now mortally wounded. Did we perhaps inherit some habits of premonitions from our parents or from our native culture? My dear mom used to have some foreboding, which fortunately never came through. But this genetic inheritance or propensity to it was not easy to erase, even with academic reasoning or rationality.

Following that unfortunate event, on the next week in August, with great regret we said our farewell to our "gingerbread house" and to that island of bliss as well, in the weaning summer days. We had a teary farewell with Svetlana and her lovely baby, especially our children.

The next day, we departed Budva along the rugged coastlines of the Adriatic, and as a solace, we wanted to spend few days in the "pearl" of the Adriatic: Dubrovnik (Figure 16).

This historic town, once the seat of the Republic of Ragusa, rose out from the stony embankments of the island of Laus. The town had a turbulent history through the times of Romans, Ostrogoths, Byzantines, and the Republic of Venice, which took over the town in the thirteenth century. From the fourteenth century on, the town of Ragusa was more or less under its own jurisdiction but soon turned to be a vassal of the Austro-Hungarian Empire. In 1805 it was conquered by the army of Napoleon and incorporated into the Italian Kingdom. In 1815 it returned to the protection of the Habsburgs till the end of the World War I, when it turned to be part of the new State of Yugoslavia.

From the fifteenth century on, this town had its own "lazaret" (hospital) pharmacy and arboretum, "Trsteno." The Venetian times gave the town its classical architecture, with many ornamental palaces of the Rector and Sponza along the main artery of the town, "Stradum," with the known shrine of Saint Blasius, the Jesus the Redeemer, and the Cloister of the Dominicans all surrounded by formidable walls of this fortress town.

We stayed in a small hotel outside the walls of the town, which was virtually wedged into the rugged stone of the embankments. Only by built-in iron steps could we descend into a small bay of the sea where the children could play or swim under our watchful eyes.

The next day after the sunset, we entered the centrum of the town through the gate of its drawbridge with its heavy chains. We entered the main street "Stradum," hemmed from both sides with a chain of elegant boutiques and small shops, wedged into the rocks of these mini-palaces, where they were showing off their elegant Western merchandise, mainly from Italy, and jewelry of local artisans, mostly from silver. The richness of the town was surprising. Nevertheless, we had to be frugal with our resources since we had only a limited amount of dinars for our trip home, as our homesickness started to show up with our longing for our "home sweet home."

After a pleasant and sunny week, finally on August 18, 1968, we started our trip home, and we left the beauty of Dubrovnik and drove to the western town of Metković and then turned sharply north toward the historic town of Sarajevo. Here in the summer on June 28, 1914, the regent of Austria-Hungary, Prince Franz Ferdinand, and his wife, Sophie né Chotek, were assassinated, which triggered the beginning of World War I. Who could avoid the opportunity to see this historic jewel-town?

After our arrival, we visited the tourist office and rented a room in the home of a retired gentleman, right in the center of town. Almost at dusk we entered the centrum of this unusually interesting and architecturally exciting town, with historic mansions, cathedrals, and places of worship for the different denominations of the faithful, including Eastern Orthodox, Roman Catholics, Jews, and Moslems as well. No wonder that the city was called the European Jerusalem.

Suddenly we noticed for our first time a Moslem mosque with an onion-shaped dome and nearby a slender and tall minaret flanking the main building. Unexpectedly at the sunset, the muezzin, with his rasping voice, was inviting his faithful for a prayer.

On my initiative, we looked for the so-called "Latin bridge" over the ever-so beautiful green Neretva River — reflecting the local algae — and nearby we indeed found the cafe of Martin Schiller, where just in front of it on June 28, 1914, Gavrilo Princip assassinated the regent for the Austrian throne and his wife. A commemorative plaque was the only reminder to this murder, which led to the tragedy of World War I. Obviously I took a snapshot of this historic plaque.

We were then tired but content after that historic search, and on the banks of this picturesque river, we found a small restaurant and had a quick dinner from the local specialties. After the dinner, we were darting home to our apartment and, quite tired, went for a sound sleep.

The next early morning, on August 19, 1968, we drove northward through the towns of Ložnica and Šabac, and at dusk we reached the city of Belgrade, where we found our friends already waiting for us with some concern.

We were received with a warm and joyous welcome from Chyrianna and Paul, who was somehow shyly sniggering in the background of the "crowd," as sometimes men do. We were right away invited to the prepared rich dinner table.

After we refreshed ourselves, at the dinner a piquant stuffed pepper was served with local golden, boiled potatoes. It was quite spicy, but the crispy local wine softened the hot pepper, and soda was also offered as well. The children were rather tired; thus my wife put them quickly to sleep. Then we had to narrate the story of our marvelous six-weeks-lasting vacation in the turquoise waters and sandy beaches of the Adriatic in that romantic and beautiful countryside, where the blue waters were soaking the rocks of white limestone.

Through the whole time, we had not followed the news on radio (in Serbian) or read any newspaper, and we did not have any idea what was happening in the world or around our country. We had totally forgotten our "meeting" with the Hungarian tanks at the start of our vacation. Yet Paul, with a worrisome expression on his face, informed us and shared the news of the sharply worsening political situation between Moscow and Prague at the Conference between the leaders of the two countries, which supposedly was to alleviate the ideological differences between them. But the meeting on the border of the two countries in a small town in Eastern Slovakia and the USSR could find no agreement. The political tensions between Leonid Brezhnev of the USSR and Alexander Dubček of Czechoslovakia — his former accolade — got even worse.

The next day, we tried to get rid of our fatigue after our long drive from the southern coast and went with our friends for a stroll to the park of Kalemegdan, where some of the leaves already had started to change to the color of ochre or rust, foretelling the coming of the fall.

After a short dinner and the last clicking of our glasses, just before our departure on the next morning, we retired for sleep, quite tired but hopeful that everything would be in order and were happily looking forward to seeing our "home sweet home" in Bratislava.

The next day, the fatal August 21, 1968, Paul woke up early and at 6 A.M. went to the nearby farmers market to buy some pears for the children for our trip home. He returned around 8 A.M., and at this time, we were slowly waking up and somehow — perhaps in our dreams? — were hearing some howling, like air-raid sirens. But we were in a foreign country, and we did not fathom what that meant. Suddenly Paul entered the apartment, visibly upset and anxious. His whole face was red from excitement or discomposure while we were just sipping our morning coffee with Chyrianna.

We all looked up at his excitement and anxiously asked, "What is going on?" He started, with some hesitation, while he was facing us, and then he blurted out, "You are not going anywhere because the Red Army invaded your country, Czechoslovakia, and its tanks occupied the whole country!" It was, for us, an unexpected consternation and shock. Suddenly a menacing fear started to creep into our minds as a consequence of this menacing news of the unforeseen invasion of our homeland by the brute Soviet Bolshevik Army. We had no idea what we were going to do at that moment, in that tragic and menacing situation. What to do now was the key question because we acutely realized that we were in big trouble. In my desperation and outrage, in a tragicomic way, I invoked the dictum of Russian revolutionary scientist Nikolay G. Chernychevskyj: "Što zdelat'" or "What to do now?"

BELGRADE

In the summertime of August 1968, there were about fifty thousand tourists from Czechoslovakia in Belgrade who were on their way to return home from their vacation, just as were we. Likewise they were caught in an unforeseen shock and, likewise, were bewildered in that situation: What to do?

At that time, the citizens of Belgrade demonstrated an astonishing magnanimity and generosity of heart, as all these "lost souls" were invited into the homes of the local people, who offered them their lodging and food to "love thy neighbors" and alleviate their unexpected misery and misfortune. All the tourists were accommodated and taken care by the local authorities as well. Those who had cars got gasoline free of charge by coupons because in socialist times, on return from a vacation, everybody had almost empty pockets, us included.

In the whole city following the invasion, the emotions flared up, and the tempers of people were boiling with anger and defiance. Marshal J.B. Tito was praised, who had extricated the nation from the brotherly love of Joseph Stalin. The next day, after the invasion of the Warsaw Pact Armies under the leadership of the Red Army into Czechoslovakia, huge demonstrations erupted in the city, and hundreds of thousands of local citizens, boiling with anger and indignation, demonstrated against the brutality of Moscow and in support of the Czechs and Slovaks.

While my wife stayed at home with our children, who were frightened as well, not knowing what was going on, Paul and I joined the crowd of demonstrating citizens. Those were thousands marching hand in hand toward the Parliament, a huge, white building and a seat of the government. To our surprise, on the long balcony, the Czechoslovak banner was hoisted, together with the Yugoslavian flag. To my bewilderment, among the governmental officials, I recognized Mr. Jiří Hájek, the secretary of state of Czechoslovakia, as well as Otta Šik, the secretary for economy and some others officials, who likewise were on their vacations at the sea. These officials, while smiling and beaming toward the crowd, were waving their hands, appreciating their passionate support. The crowd of people was chanting, "Hands off our Republic! Russians get out!" They were saying Brezhnev was a traitor and cheering for Alexander Dubček as well. We were likewise yelling and chanting, with Paul on full throttle, as we took active part of that demonstrations against the Russians. The passion, indignation, and hatred against the Russians was in full display, and the demonstration lasted the whole morning.

In the evening, Yugoslav TV started the news with a welcome and introduction by a fetching young lady: "Dragi slušavci, dragi gledavci" (dear listeners and viewers), and we listened to the frightening news and pictures from Prague, where the Red Army tanks, with their red stars on their turrets, occupied the whole Saint Wenceslas Square around the equestrian statue of the saint. The people were yelling and red, shaking their fists at the Russian paratroopers in their raw hatred. "Get out of our country!" Some of the people were trying to argue with those soldiers, but everything was in wain. Everything was useless, as we learned how some resistors were shot, not only in Prague but also in our hometown in Bratislava, where a university student was shot dead before the main building of the University and another man before the main post office. We had seen the occupied eastern metropolis of Slovakia, Košice — my birthplace — where other people were shot as well.

After that heart-rendering news, we were shocked and depressed, indeed facing the question: What to do? Go home to our brand-new condo with the new, elegant, pear wood living room and matching hand-woven rugs of Slovak folk art? As a young physician, I had decorated my pale ash wood study with original oil paintings of Slovak artists like Marka Medvecká and the graphics of Orest Dubay. These were precious acquisitions of mine as a young art lover and physician. Fifteen years after my graduation, we had finally had our home, and we were comfortably enjoying our family life together. That was a major economic and emotional investment, especially in a socialist country behind the Iron Curtain! And now should we lose all those gains of our years' long hard work?

For the time being, we decided to stay with our friends. But it very soon dawned on me: How long can we be a burden to our precious friends? How can we make a living? And where?

In my nightly tribulations, out of the blue sky it occurred to me that I had a friend in the town of Subotica, about one hundred miles from Belgrade, Dr. Steve C., who had been a guest and visitor in our hospital in Bratislava in May 1968 with his friends from Budapest. I looked up his telephone number, and Steve was indeed surprised by my call, but he was happy to hear my voice. I explained to him my unexpected and dire situation, being with my family in a foreign land as the invasion of the Red Army into Czechoslovakia caught us on our way home in Belgrade. He was, of course, well-informed and indignant about the Russian invasion and was well-aware that I was in a calamitous situation.

But he tried to be help full and gave me the telephone number of his good friend in Belgrade, Dr. Mirko M., who was the head of the department of infectious diseases and a member of the Children's Hospital board of directors. In between, Steve called him up and introduced me to him as his friend and a professional in pediatric cardiology who had hosted him as a visitor in our hospital in Bratislava. Steve asked him to be at my help and assistance.

The next day, I went to the Hospital for Mother and Child, a gift of the U.S. Government to Belgrade, a tall, white, eight-story building. On the third floor, I found Dr. Mirko M. in his office, a shorter, blue-eyed, blond-haired man with a curious gaze. He welcomed me with a kind smile and a warm handshake and offered me a seat before his large, mahogany table. I explained to him and portrayed our misfortune and difficult situation at these turbulent times, being in a foreign country without any means. Mirko was well-informed by Steve that I was an Assistant Professor in Pediatric Cardiology from the children's hospital in Bratislava. Mirko promised me that he would present my case and my precarious situation to the board of directors and their political branch, the Unions.

In the following days, my anxiety was exponentially growing, and I was almost getting desperate and had no idea how these new friends of mine could be really helpful. It was a stressful situation full of concern and insecurity for the future.

But after two days, Mirko invited me to the hospital by a phone call, and he introduced me to the chairman of the hospital, a surgeon, with whom I had a short but friendly interchange. He realized my precarious predicament, and his goodwill to help was obvious.

Mirko took me then to the chairman of the Physicians Unions, Dr. Lenka Nedelkovič, a very pleasant, middle-aged lady, a slender blond with blue eyes and welcoming disposition, originally from Poland. She unexpectedly surprised me when she informed me that yesterday the Board of Union had an extraordinary session, and it was decided that the hospital would employ me as a pediatric cardiologist, and they would advance me a one-month salary: 1,500 dinars!

I got speechless in my surprise, seeing this generosity of mind and the magnanimity of these physicians who never had seen me before and never had worked with me. I was deeply moved, and my eyes welled up with tears seeing that embodiment of real humanity. I uttered some incoherent words of deep appreciation and thanks to the chairman and shook her hands with great affection. Surely I never had expected such a solution! Following that meeting, Mirko took me to the Department of Pediatrics and introduced me to the physician in charge. He was very friendly and kind, and right away he took me to the electrocardiographic laboratory, where I was supposed to evaluate the daily tracings for the department. I was pleased to get to my elements. Other physicians joined in and were very happy to hear that I was joining their team.

As I was leaving the institution, I hugged Mirko with affection for his immense engagement in my case and thanked him from the bottom of my heart for his more-than-friendly help. At that moment, as we warmly shook hands, he told me that he and his wife, Irma, would be honored if we could except their invitation for a dinner, as we were heading for the weekend.

When I returned "home," that is, to our friends' home, I had to share with my wife and our friends my exceptional encounter and experience with my new colleagues and friends. When I showed them a cheque for 1,500 dinars, the disbelief was complete! We were not expecting such exceptional support from friends whom we had only known a few days. It was like help from a brother not seen for long time. Never had we experienced anything similar in our lives like such generous help in Belgrade! Suddenly, for a crazy moment, I pointed to the cheque and exclaimed to my wife, "Look, we are now indeed rich!"

In the evening, our whole family was heading to Mirko's house in our best tourist attire since we had nothing else. Our friends lived in a new socialist panel house, about ten-stories high. We were welcomed by the lady of the house. Irma was a young, fetching women with black hair and light blue eyes. She welcomed us cordially with Mirko in their evening attire. The sartorial difference between us was appalling, and we felt like hillbillies in our sparse tourist outfit.

Right from the beginning, they expressed their sincere compassion for our distress and unenviable situation.

The couple had a nice, blond son the same age as our Robert, and so a new friendship was quickly in making. But our Patsy did not let herself get pushed to the sideline, and she actively joined in to a "menage a trois!"

After taking our seats in a spacious living room of beige furniture and making ourselves comfortable in plush easy chairs, we were welcomed by a small tumbler of local Serbian plumb brandy. It was a strong drink, and I just took a small sip while my wife boldly gulped down the whole tumbler. I just looked at her, but she ignored me. She probably needed an "oomph."

Our arrival at Mirko's house was just in time for the evening TV news. The whole half an hour was portraying pictures of how the occupation by the Red Army was spreading and overtaking the whole country. They had taken over all the military posts, barracks, and airfields of the army and key structures of the political and governmental structures, and in a week, they had the country under their thumb. The Russians took over all the information services, such as the radio, telegraph, and TV stations and the whole media with newspapers. We just looked at each other in fear and bewilderment. Fortunately the tasty dinner lifted our spirits to some degree, starting with a piquant, green, fresh bean soup. It was followed by a plate of so-called "vešalica," that is, sliced pork with fresh tomatoes. The next course was a local "gibanica," that is, kajmuk cheese pie supplemented by sliced, fried veal. A fine, local red wine "Procupac," from east Serbia along the Timok River, was served, with its mild, tarty taste and appealing bouquet, which somehow lifted our dark mood.

At the dining table, our children participated on our side as well, well-trained in their table manners, even though Patricia occasionally needed some help from her mom.

Our conversation was somehow subdued, but friendly and cordial. Unfortunately the topic was invasion all around while myself and Mirko were trying to figure out or solve the unsolvable and desperate situation. We were very thankful to that lovely couple for their friendship and hospitality whom, just a week ago, we did not even know. Perhaps there was some tribal Slavic sap that brought us closer together in that trying time.

Just before our departure, lady Irma called upon my wife, Judy, and took her to their bedroom and presented her with a small package. My wife did not know what it was all about or what was in the package, but we were between a rock and a hard place, and she accepted that friendly gesture, whatever was in the package. Our departure and farewell were quite emotional, especially between the two "girls," and we never saw Irma, that gracious lady, again.

As we returned to Paul's house, my wife opened the delicate package, where to her surprise she found a set of new lingerie. My wife was quite surprised by this ingenious and practical gift. The fact was that we were now two months on the road, during which my meticulous wife regularly washed our linen with the West German detergent Persil; thus our laundry was always snow white. Obviously Irma was very intelligent and practical in the feminine world of two young moms.

All the next week, I labored and evaluated the ECG tracings and presented the results in abbreviated medical English. I was also called for consultation to evaluate children with heart murmur and to evaluate chest X-rays for assessment of the size or shape of the heart and to come to the diagnostic conclusion of the case, as I was now the cardiologist of the hospital team.

The next Saturday, for the weekend we were invited by Steve to his house in the town of Subotica, a distance of about a hundred miles from Belgrade. It was a blessing that, in our misfortune and predicament, we had a small car at our disposition. This invitation was most welcomed to give a break to our generous and dear friends in Belgrade.

We departed in the early morning, and in two hours, passing the district capital of Novy Sad, we soon arrived to the outskirts of Subotica, where Steve and his family lived. The welcome was really more than cordial, with a real Hungarian bear hug and a warm embrace between the two ladies, Irene and my wife. They had two handsome, somehow older boys, Earnest and Dennis, who welcomed our son and daughter. Steve and his family were part of the Hungarian minority in Northern Yugoslavia. They lived in a large country house, like a hacienda, with the parents of his wife. The home was surrounded by a spacious garden with manicured patches of colorful, summer flowers. In the nearby garage, Steven's English, snow white Philip Morris car was on display.

Irene was a local Hungarian beauty with her large, chestnut brown eyes and rich coif of hair, indeed a fetching young lady of attractive proportions with a kind and warm disposition. She was the daughter of a well-to-do local joiner. Since Steven and Irene had no daughter, our Patricia turned out to be the star of the day. The boys took our kids into the large courtyard, communicating mostly by gestures even though our Robert had some rudimentary knowledge of the Hungarian language. But the outbursts of cheerful guffaws indicated that they understood each other quite well in their interplay.

Steven and Irene invited us into to their spacious house and gave their bedroom to our disposition. They were indeed very generous and hospitable. The house was full of flowers since Irene owned a flower shop, supplied by flowers from her own garden.

In the spacious and pleasant living room, we were seated in comfortable chairs and offered a glass of well-chilled white wine of Furmint from the famous Tokay region. The wine had a delectable, fruity bouquet, golden color, and a pleasant, refreshing taste. It gave us a well-deserved lift into our weekend mood. On the side of the table on a small plate, fresh, golf-ball-sized cakes of pork crackling were offered with their piquant and inviting aroma. We hadn't seen those for a long time. At that moment, the grandparents joined in and were introduced to us. They were the local patricians of the town, and they were warmly welcoming of us as well. All of them shared with us our concerns in our uncertain predicament and future after the barbarian invasion of our native country.

Even though my Judy did not know a word of Hungarian, somehow she communicated with Irene and Steven through her native Slovak, which had at least some common roots with the Slavic local Serb. The two girls, of course, got along very well.

After a while of lively conversation, we were invited to their spacious dining room, where the children were seated on the side of the large dining table. Robert occasionally gave his help or assistance to his little sister in a moment of her need.

The lunch had all the supplies and ingredients from their own farm and started with a tasty chicken soup with giblets and angel-hair noodles with slices of fresh greens, such as carrots, white turnip, and even kohlrabi. Large circles of golden fat were floating effortlessly on the surface of the soup, offered in a large, ornamental tureen. The soup looked like a symphony of colors in the impressionist painting of August Renoir. And it tasted heavenly indeed!

The next course was an extension of the chicken menu, and a large plate of fried chicken breasts and thighs was presented by Irene, with golden potatoes with a dash of fresh, green chopped parsley. On a separate plate, a summer cucumber salad was presented with red paprika and black pepper sprinkled over. In the crystals by the plates, the golden wine already glittered, being filled and refilled generously by Steven. On the side of the table, a classical blue soda syphon stood by for the youngsters or for a well-liked "spritzer" for others.

My wife occasionally glanced with love toward our children, mainly Patsy, and was ready to cut her meat into small portions, but our son, Robert, handled it skillfully, to our satisfaction. Thus the children dined merrily without a problem.

After the main course, we slowly relocated all of us into the sunny living room for coffee and warm and tasty apple "pité," or tart. The kids chose a rich, chocolate ice with a dollop of whipped cream.

Despite the warm and friendly atmosphere amidst our generous hosts, still our conversation swirled about the solution: What shall we do? Go back home? Stay in Belgrade? Go to the West and try our luck there? But the picture of the Russian tanks dwelled very deeply on the mind of my wife and gave her some nightmares regarding the future of our children.

At the same time, the children were in full swing of their afternoon fun, where Ernest and Dennis were cruising our children on their bicycles, as the highlight of their trip.

In the afternoon, Steven took all of us by his Phillip Morris to see the old town with the magnificent cathedral, where we fell on our knees and asked for the help and blessing of the Almighty in our precarious predicament. Afterward Steven took us to a small but idyllic lake of Palič, where he built for his family a cottage in a circular shape, like a watchtower on an airfield. It was great fun for our children, especially when they had seen the bunk beds lined up around the cottage like in a merry-go-round. We were not ready to take a dip, but we had a great pleasure to see the golden-tinted reed that was gently swooning in the breeze like a young odalisque. The yellow reed almost surrounded the whole picturesque lake, and in a gentle breeze, it gave a mysterious, rustling hum. It was a beautiful, almost intimate moment at that golden sunset, which brushed aside our dark dreams. I don't remember the menu of the sumptuous dinner because we were anxiously waiting to watch the evening TV news. A young, handsome anchor started with its obligatory, "Dragy slušavci, dragy gledavci" (dear listeners and viewers). Unfortunately the news was still menacing and dark; the Russian tanks were spreading their wings and cannons all over the country.

The demonstrations, protests, or discussions with the soldiers were fruitless, as were the turning around and changing of the road signs from west to east or the opposite to confuse the transports of the Red Army. The Red Army was now in full command in the country, and new reinforcements were arriving from Moscow to finish the job.

With heavy hearts, we retired to our quarters. At this time, we wanted to give our children a bath in this Western-style bathroom with an electrical grid to warm up the "frotteé" towels. What a luxury. No such sophistication was available in our country behind the Iron Curtain! The children had great fun in the bath, where they could play with newly discovered plastic, yellow ducklings. That eventually ended up in a cheerful ruckus, eventually fishing out our kids from that happy frolic in the bubble bath. We just took a quick shower to get rid of the dust of the day and went quickly to sleep, as our host retired as well after a day full of events.

Sunday morning was a lovely sunny day. We had strong cup of coffee for breakfast with scrambled eggs, provided by their own hens, and fresh rolls or "kaiser semmels" (emperors rolls) with the butter churned from milk of their own cows and pear marmalade. Then all of us went to the local cathedral for the Sunday mass with our heavy hearts and evanescent hopes.

During the mass, we called on the Almighty to show us the right decision and direction in which we were supposed to go, with his blessings in our unforeseen, treacherous, if not hopeless, pilgrimage. We were indeed totally lost and disoriented and in a quandary. What path should we take at that moment? We asked for His counsel and blessing.

We returned to Steven's house for a sumptuous lunch, but we were already restless and wanted to return to Belgrade. An emotional goodbye was full of hugs, tears, and sobbing, where not only the tender women but also the "hard, indubitable" men wept as well. As the parents were sobbing, the bewildered children joined in, as they felt that something sinister indeed was happening in our destiny.

With Steven we stayed in touch for years to come till his death in 2000, and with Irene we are still communicating via internet. They both visited us in New York in the nighties in a joyous reunion indeed.

Monday morning I continued to work in the Children's Hospital, making consultations and examinations of children with heart problems and evaluating ECG tracings for the whole institution. In the following week, it started down on me that in that position and type of work, I didn't have any future there.

In the first days of September, I was able to make contact with Professor Dr. Jürgen A. in Tübingen-West Germany through the international telephone directory. He was quite surprised by my call. When I informed him that I was calling him from Belgrade and in what kind of political and economic predicament I was in, he understood the reason of my call. My information, that just before our vacation in June 1968, I had been awarded the stipend of the Alexander van Humboldt Foundation, he very much welcomed. The stipend was able to cover my salary as a resident physician at his department at the Children's Hospital, and he would have the advantage to gain an assistant for his division.

We agreed that I would visit the embassy of the West German Republic in Belgrade and apply for an entrance visa to that country. Consequently I would be able join him and work at his hospital.

In those times in Europe in the fall of 1968, many institutions and citizens tried to be of help and assistance to about 150,000 citizens — Czechs and Slovaks who were stuck out of their country following the invasion of the Russians into Czechoslovakia. The professor, consequently, tried to help one of the unfortunate refugees and offered a temporary solution for me and my family.

I, of course, shared this option or intention of mine right away to our friends, Paul and Chyrianna, regarded this option the best one at that time.

The next day, I asked permission to have a short leave from my job, and I visited the West German Embassy, going there in my car. The building of the Embassy was settled in a well-manicured and picturesque green garden in that part of the city, surrounded by hedges and thick bushes. In front of it was a sizable square as well. I parked my car in a small, neighboring street. As I approached the square before the embassy, I froze like the biblical Lot. I could not believe my eyes as I suddenly saw the scene before me.

The whole square was full and packed by the so-called "gastarbeiters" (seasonal workers), who wanted to have entrance visas and work permits to be able to work in West Germany. But why so many? Around five hundred blue-collar workers were standing in tight lines on the square to get into the embassy for their visas.

In 1955 the diplomatic ties between West Germany and Yugoslavia were frozen between the two states when Yugoslavia — against the so-called Hallstein Doctrine of the German Parliament — diplomatically recognized the East German Republic. The West German Republic did not except this decision and broke off its diplomatic relationship with Yugoslavia.

As it was rumored, another reason was that the Serb terrorists wanted to settle their accounts with the German Nazis from WW II and initiated terrorist attacks in West Germany after the war, giving another reason to break off the diplomatic relationship with Yugoslavia.

Fortunately few months before in the spring of 1968, the diplomatic relationship was reinstated, and now a huge number of blue-collar workers lined up seeking visas and jobs in West Germany. Now I was one of them.

What was I going to do? I racked my brain. I had no time to stand at the end of the line at least for a week to get to the embassy. Somehow I raised my courage and elbowed myself through the restless crowd up to the front, just before the door of the embassy. Suddenly the door opened, and a middle-aged man in Western attire of a beige, checkered jacket with golden-rimmed glasses showed up, suggesting that he was from the staff of the Embassy. I raised my courage, stopped the man, and addressed him in German. "Excuse me, sir, that I dare to impose on you, but I am a physician from the Russian-invaded Czechoslovakia." I showed him my passport. "I am trying to apply for an entrance visa to West Germany. Trudging through this huge crowd of blue-collar workers is almost impossible, even though I am almost in an emergency." The gentleman looked at me attentively and cautiously — I was now dressed more appropriately than in my tourist garb, and eventually he handed me his business card with his remark: "Come to see me in an hour. I am going to have my breakfast in the nearby restaurant." It looked that my courage paid off, and I kept holding that business card as my last straw.

After an hour, I rang at the door of the embassy and presented to the concierge my card, who took me to an office. Soon the councilor of the embassy showed up and offered me a seat before his large, mahogany desk.

The councilor started his interrogation by identifying my personal passport and my family data and then asked me what my problem was. I succinctly presented my situation related to the invasion of my country by Russian armies, that I was caught with my family in Belgrade, and we were concerned to return to our country in such turmoil.

I explained to him that, coincidently, I was at the end of June 1968 awarded the Alexander van Humboldt stipend, which was giving me a chance with its financial support to accept now the invitation to work at the Children's Hospital in Tübingen at the Division of Pediatric Cardiology. As I mentioned the name of Tübingen, his eyes lit up, and a smile appeared on his face. He remarked that the University of Tübingen was his alma mater, where years ago he studied for his graduate degree in political science. The magic word of Tübingen softened up the atmosphere, and that coincidence made our professional relationship more human.

The councilor then took some copies of my passport and my wife's as well and remarked that he had to verify that I was indeed awarded with the Alexander van Humboldt stipend at the center of the Foundation in Bad Godesberg, near the capital of Bonn. He also asked me for the telephone number of Professor Dr. Jürgen A. to verify my invitation to work at the Children's Hospital in Tübingen, as this part of the equation should be in order as well. Our conversation was ended with his friendly remark that if all information was verified, he did not see any problem to issue the entrance visa to West Germany for me and my family.

He discharged me with his remark, "Come back in a week," and shook my hand with a smile. I returned home with the good news, to the satisfaction of us all. Still I continued to work in the hospital for another week.

In the first days of September, the autumn and its colder weather surprised us all. Before our departure, we purchased from my salary two warm overalls, a red for Patricia and a blue for Robert, with hoods for the winter. For my wife, we bought a three-quarter-sized winter jacket of imitation leather but with a good, wool lining. For me I could only afford an Italian, paper-thin raincoat, as the expected rain was just around the corner.

The week in the hospital went by quickly, and on Friday I returned to the German embassy with my precious business card of the councilor, and the receptionist took me right away to the councilor's office. He showed up from the adjacent office in a good mood with a smile and revealed the good news, that he could issue the entrance visa for me and my family, and he processed them right away into our passports. The councilor shook my hands with a smile and advised me that I should go to the Austrian Embassy and apply for transit visa since I would have to cross Austria to get to West Germany. At the end of our deliberation, he wished me "gute Reise," that is, happy journey, to Germany.

Right away I drove to Austrian Embassy, not far away. I expected that with visas to Germany, my transit visa would not pose a problem. To my unpleasant surprise, I faced a stubborn officer who was not interested that I already had entrance visas to Germany and insisted that, as citizens of Czechoslovakia we must first return to our native land — crossing Austria — and then again via Austria, we could turn back and travel to West Germany. It did not make sense to argue with this stickler even though I was boiling mad that this "pünctlich" (punctual) paper pusher did not consider our predicament at that time. At the end of our tit for tat, the officer gave me the transit visas without specifications of where I could and could not go. I was quite upset by this Austrian administrative pettiness.

At last I drove to the embassy of Czechoslovakia, where I asked the officer for help, as I would like to legally transfer our condo apartment in Bratislava from my ownership to the ownership of my sister, Catherine. All the officers were exceedingly helpful to all the new refugees. They presented me with all the appropriate papers, which I filled out on the spot. The officer then verified it with a stamp of a notary public. He also added to that document the frontispiece of my passport and notarized that as well.

I put all those documents into a heavy-duty envelope, and with my short note to my sister, I sent the letter to her. I had great doubts that those documents of the change of the ownership of our condo would be honored legally by the local authorities. Despite all the legal formalities confirmed by a notary public, the Communist authorities did not accept the validity of the document, and its value was annulled. A few months later, my sister was forced to leave the apartment, as it was seized by the authorities with all its content. The chairman of the board of the condominium, a prominent Communist, had a personal stake and interest in our apartment for himself, and eventually he was able to take into possession our new condo with all its artwork and oil paintings and embezzled it for himself. We learned about these events years later.

In Belgrade after a week at the hospital, I informed Dr. Lenka Nedelkovič, the chairwoman of the board of the Unions, who had appointed me to my position in the hospital, that I had decided that I would accept a position in West Germany, as I was awarded the Alexander van Humboldt stipend. She was sorry that I was leaving her professional team, but she understood that, for the long run, I had limited options in Belgrade.

I said a goodbye to the chairman of the Children's Hospital, with my many thanks and my special gratitude to Dr. Mirko M. and his family. At that time, I did not fathom that in 1985, seventeen years later, I would welcome Lenka in New York at the World Congress of Pediatric Cardiology, to our mutual joy. Then we informed our friends, who had offered their gracious hospitality, virtually being part of their family, that we had found a more realistic solution in our present predicament as refugees and that I had accepted a position as a physician in West Germany.

At our last dinner before our departure, we shed many tears, crying and laughing and at the same time expressing our everlasting gratitude that they had adopted us — our family — at the time of our dire needs, amidst our unexpected tragedy. At the same time, we were well-aware that we were going to face a totally new and unknown world with new and difficult struggles and responsibilities for our whole family.

In the early morning on September 13, 1968, we woke up early and quickly finished our packing. Our children were already huddled up in their overalls on this cold, autumn morning, as our little car offered only warm air from the engine, the only source of heating inside the car. Then we transferred all our belongings to our small Bobby car, which was packed up "to his neck."

Then we had to begin our last and very difficult goodbye to our dear friends, which was very emotional. We were so in debt to those good people! We, the "tough men," Paul and myself, tried to keep our emotions under control, but our eyes welled up with tears at our last manly embrace. My wife, Judy, and Chyrianna, as two sisters, cried and sobbed profusely while our two small children stood insecure and bewildered and did not understand the human drama. They got a lot of hugs and kisses, as they were indeed their own children. But it was inevitable to break off the emotional crisis because a new reality was really pressing on us.

As I entered the car, I looked at Paul and his frozen smile and slipped the key to the engine, and suddenly I collapsed with all my weight on the steering wheel and started to uncontrollably sob, my shoulders shaking as I was helplessly crying. My wife understood the drama in my soul and tried to calm me down by caressing my nape. Suddenly I felt that somebody was pulling on my left earlobe, and I heard the cry of my daughter. "Daddy, Daddy, don't cry." Our son, Robert, looked bewildered and in awe — he'd never seen his father cry. Our friends followed in astonishment the drama of mine through the window. But at that moment in the depth of my soul, I realized that then, for good, I was leaving my beloved country and my home, and I was turning into a refugee, or an émigré, for my whole life! At the peak of that emotional crisis, something hit me: "Hey man, rise up and be a master of your fate. Follow your dream and freedom and take your destiny in your own hands!"

In a minute or so, still teary and red-faced, I straightened up, and my wife offered me a clean handkerchief. I blew my nose while she offered me her loving smile. I entered the first speed with my shift, pressed on the gas pedal, and, as a rocket, launched forward, toward the free West. There was a deadly silence in the car, except the humming of the engine. I had to take couple of deep breaths to regain my composure. In a moment, I looked into the back mirror to see my wife, son, Robert, and the baby, Patricia, and through my still-misty eyes, I gave them a warm smile of my great love and devotion.

The weather in mid-September was sunny but cooler. The sun lifted our spirits as we drove through the city toward the highway to Zagreb. We were expecting a distance of about 400 km (250 miles). Fortunately it was already after the peak of the tourist season, with fewer cars, and the highway was straight and smooth with three lanes of solid concrete. With my "precious cargo," I kept my small car in the slowest right lane even though our little Bobby was able to master about 70 miles per hour, just in case. After two hours of an uneventful ride, we stopped at the first Yugoslav "autorest." This was a modern establishment of Western style of a bridge over the two-way highway. There was a big shopping mall with fancy stores, nothing to be seen in our country. We did not have even a highway, let alone a fancy autorest. We walked around along the stores to stretch our back and bones, but we did not have the means for a fancy restaurant. We returned to our car, and my wife produced our sandwiches, prepared with love by lovely Chyrianna. Water from a water fountain — cool and fresh — quenched our thirst. On the side of the parking lot, there was a small but tidy playground with swings and slides. We spent an hour there, frolicking and playing with the children.

Around 2 P.M. we passed by Zagreb, the Croatian capital, and we took a break again. Nevertheless, in this autorest, we had a small, warm lunch with some soft drinks and a strong espresso for me "de rigeur" (a must).

As we departed in a southwest direction toward Ljubljana (capital of Slovenia), my wife put the children to sleep with the help of a wooden shelf that served as an extension of the back seat where they could stretch out. We wanted to reach the Austrian-German border before dusk; we faced another hundred miles. Eventually we arrived at the small border town of Jessenice before the evening was upon us. We found a small guesthouse, as we looked for the advertisement of a "soba" (room) for a night, and we were the only "tourists" at that time in September.

The guesthouse was virtually empty; the room was cold with poor lightning, and the curtains were depressingly gray. We were not pleased with the conditions, but there was not too much to choose from. The guesthouse had no restaurant either, but there was a small one nearby, where we had our modest dinner. We quickly retired to the uninviting beddings, dead tired. In the morning, the breakfast was an improvement with a strong espresso coffee and warm croissants.

We were now heading to the Austrian border and customs, with some anxiety with our transit visas, but the Austrian border guard just nonchalantly "banged" his stamp into our passport and yelled, "Weiter"(continue). Thus we quickly passed the ramp and entered Austrian soil with a sigh of relief.

From the border town of Villach, I called Professor Dr. Jürgen A. and informed him that we were already in the West, that is, in Austria, and we were heading toward Salzburg and would cross to West Germany toward München (Münich), and I expected that in the evening we would be in Tübingen. He reassured me that an official at the entrance of the Children's Hospital would be informed and waiting for us and that we would be taken care of. The professor also advised me that as I entered the town, I should drive toward the center and the municipal park, as the Children's Hospital was right nearby.

At that break, my wife took the children to the toilets and washroom. She was startled by the meticulous, German cleanliness, where all the pleasing white and blue tiles were shining brightly and the sidewalls as well. The washbasins and toilets were working automatically, of course. She met here the first "Gastarbeiter" (seasonal worker) from Yugoslavia, who fiercely guarded her "kingdom" and industriously rubbed and cleaned the walls with a fragrant detergent and the toilets as well. Obviously we were in a different world of a cultured West in contrast with gray socialism behind the Iron Curtain.

As we were in a hurry, we drove across Austria toward Salzburg, another 150 miles, but here the Western highways were wider, and powerful Mercedes and Porsche cars swished away in a crazy speed while we stayed always in the slowest right lane. Here in the Austrian hillside, as the road started to climb toward the hill of Salzburg Alps, I noticed with uneasy surprise that the engine of my car was laboring, and I had to switch to the second gear while my car was angrily growling. I started to worry about that unusual, rumbling sound from my car, and of course, I had no idea what was wrong with my engine. After Salzburg the highway fortunately was going downhill, what somehow — to my relief — eased up the rumbling noise. We crossed the border without a problem with our entrance visas into West Germany and were speeding toward Münnich, another one hundred miles.

Before Münnich we stopped at a German auto stop, which was indeed as luxurious as a grand hotel. We risked there a sumptuous lunch and a dessert, reinforced by an espresso coffee, which boosted our adrenaline.

Still we could not resist but quickly perused this super-rich shopping mall with all its delicacies in food, chocolate, wine, cheese, and other specialties and allowed some fun for our children in an exclusive children's playground nearby, with all its fancy amenities, while we stretched and exercised for a short while.

In the afternoon, we took the highway toward Stuttgart, another one hundred miles, and then turned sharply southward toward our destination Tübingen for another thirty miles. I was very worried about the condition of my car, as we had to drive in second gear all the time, and when the highway turned uphill, I had to use first gear, and that never had happened before with my car. I knew something was very wrong with the car and was afraid. What was I going to do if the car gave up on me in a country totally unfamiliar to me. But in the early evening, we crawled south toward our goal to the periphery of the town. Eventually the car dragged us forward slowly, but fortunately the town was well-lit, and I easily found the center of the town, and in the nearby park stood the majestic building of the Children's Hospital. "Hallelujah" was in my thoughts. I drove the car to the entrance ramp and shortly honked for the officer in a small booth. He knew about our arrival, opened up the ramp with a "good evening," and showed us to the side entrance of the hospital and to an adjacent parking space.

I took a great sigh, and as my dear mom used to say, "thanks to God," and we all thanked the Almighty that indeed we had made it.

Suddenly the side door of the hospital opened up, and a middle-aged, chubby, blue-eyed blond in nursing attire greeted me. "I am Schwester (sister = nurse) Hilde. Welcome, Herr Doctor (mister)!" Suddenly the tired children woke up, and seeing a pleasant, smiling, welcoming nurse, they were happy to reciprocate with a cheerful smile of their own.

Schwester Hilde helped us with our luggage, directing and chaperoning us toward the elevator. We were all guided to the fourth floor of the hospital and entered into a so-called "gallery" under the roof, where other nurses were lodging as well.

The sister opened up the door to a spacious room with two beds, and my wife immediately noticed the beautiful and shining parquets, as they just recently had been varnished with a golden beeswax. It was obvious that we had entered a realm of German impeccable cleanliness in the "schwabian"(southwestern rural) part of Germany, where "putzen," cleaning, was a national sport. Schwester Hilde opened another room as well of similar interior with two beds, and we, as refugees, were indeed not prepared for such a luxury.

In the first larger room, fresh sandwiches with ham and cheese were prepared for us on a coffee table with a pitcher of hot tea. We were dead tired, and we just could not thank them enough for the generous hospitality. Schwester Hilde, of course, noticed that we are vividly sleepy, and she left us with her kind remark that tomorrow we would discuss the details of our provisions. She also mentioned that Dr. Jürgen A. would expect to meet me tomorrow. Then she departed with her kind gesture and smile and wished us a "gute nacht," very good night.

We wanted to shed off our whole day dust and took our showers in a snow white bathroom, enjoying the fragrant soap and the soft, "turkish" towels. We quickly slipped into our pajamas.

We had only a small bite before we retired, but the lemon tea was refreshing. Before I went with Robert to our second room, we all kneeled down at the bed, where our baby, Patricia, was already dreaming her fairy tale, and Robert started to pray a short evening invocation he had learned from his Hungarian babysitter. As we were kneeling, our son, softly with piety, started to pray:

"Our Almighty Lord, good Lord,
While I softly close my gaze,

But your eyes are still awake
In our sleep, keeping us safe, Amen"

We were all moved; our eyes welled up with tears, thanking the Almighty that we had arrived safe and unscathed, without an accident on the long journey.

Then we jumped into our snow white beds with soft pillows, seemingly filled with white snowflakes, while the cuddly comforters hugged our tired, battered bodies as we fell into well-deserved sleep, dreaming about "Hans and Grätel" of the Grimm Brothers in the free Western world.

Fig.1. The Heart Institute for Children - "Slovensko"

Fig.2. The Crest of the John Harvard University: "Truth".

Fig.3. Essential English for Foreign Students.

Fig.4. The "Alhambra" show and entertainment.

5.Fig.5. Kurt Jürgens, actor and singer.

Fig.6. My professor with the author.Rome,1967.

Fig. 7. Alexander von Humboldt,german scientist.

Fig.8. My family on the banks of the river. Patricia is trying to snap the clasp of my sandals, instructed by her Mom, Robert our son has his mustache from Nutella chocolate-hazelnut spread.

Fig.9. Our car "Bobby" a Renault CV4 model.

Fig. 10. The city of Szeged-Hungary, its cathedral and his open air theater.

Fig.11. The park Kalemegdan- Belgrade-Yugoslavia.

Fig.12. The resort of Budva on Adriatic.

Fig.13. The Island of Saint Stephan on Adriatic.

Fig.14. Cavtad - Mausoleum by sculptor Ivan Meštrovič.

Fig.15. The bay of Boka Kotorska on Adriatic.

Fig.16. Dubrovnik, perl of the Adriatic

Fig.17. Tübingen on the river of Neckar -a view. Germany

Fig.18. Tübingen- the old town and the main square.

Fig.19. Idyllic view of the river Neckar.

Fig.20. Wurmlingen and its chapel on the hill.

Fig.21. My dear Mom, 81 years old.

Fig.22. The wooden cover of our crate with our brick-a brack, delivered to the harbor of Bremen, Germany for shipment to US.

Fig.23. The Cathedral of Köln, Gemany

Fig.24. The Island of Manhattan, view from the air.

Fig.25. The Statue of Liberty, NewYork Harbor

Fig.26. The view of Boston, Massachusetts .

Fig.27. Children's Hospital Medical Center,Boston.1969

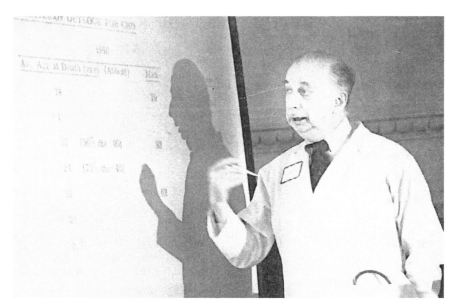

Fig.28. Dr. Alexander S. Nadas.

Fig.29. My wife and the two children,
Robert and Patricia on the banks of Atlantic, Boston.

Fig.30. "The Capitol" in Boston, the seat of the Government.

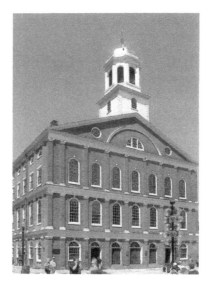

Fig.31. Faneuil Hall, Boston

Fig.32. A "look alike" picture of an "art nuovo" building
of the "House of the Good Shepard" in Bratislava, Slovakia.

Fig.33a. The entrance gate of cast iron to the University of John Harvard.

Fig.33b. John Harvard in the court of the University

Fig.33c. The Memorial Hall.

Fig.34. The Massachusetts Institute of Technology- M.I.T.

Fig.35. The Punch bowl with cups.

Fig.36. Our first Christmas in Boston 1969.Robert and Patricia.

Fig.37. Father Francis Venutta a Moravian priest with Patricia.1969.

Fig.38. Our son Robert at his First Communion.Boston.1974.

Fig.39. The Medical School of J. Harvard University, Boston.

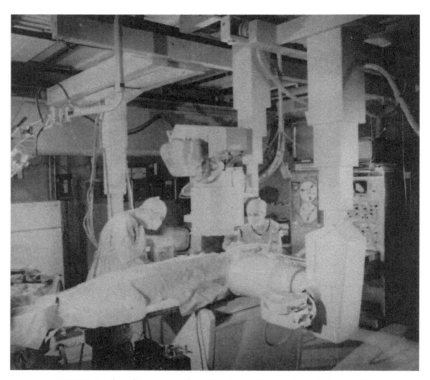

Fig.40. In the diagnostic lab. Boston, The author is in front .

Fig.41. The members of the Department of Pediatric Cardiology, 1970
The author is in second row, third from the right.

Fig.42. Dr. Alexander S. Nadas and the author
at the conference in New York, 1973.

Fig.43. The "rent truck" Ryder. 1973.

Fig.44. City of Buffalo, a view.

Fig.45. The Niagara Falls.

Fig.46. Statue of the Slovak writer Martin Kukučín (Dr. Matej Bencúr),
by sculptor Ivan Meštrovič. Galt, Canada. 1974.

Fig.47. Bethlehem, ceramic from Slovakia, Modra.

Fig.48. Our daughter Patricia at her First Communion in Buffalo, 1974.

Fig.49. The Verrazano Bridge in New York Harbor.

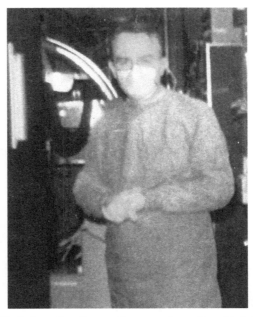

Fig.50. Before the diagnostic procedure. New York.1975

Fig.51. The church of Saint John of Nepomucene, the main altar, New York, 1975.

Fig.52. The Heart Center of Saint Francis in Roslyn New York.

Fig.53. Our house in East Hills, Roslyn, New York.

Fig.54. The wife of President Ronald Reagan, the First Lady Nancy Reagan expresses her thanks to Zoltan G. Mesko M.D. for his unselfish professional work for the children with heart disease from the whole world.

Fig.55. The children from South Korea are returning home after their successful heart surgery. In the background Sister Mary Gobel, a nurse from South Korea and the author.

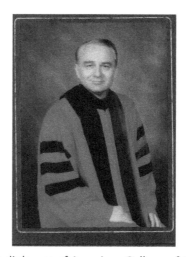

Fig.56. Author-a diplomat of American College of Cardiology.1989.

"Give hope and new life to a Slovak child with heart disease"

Fig.57. The Bulletin of the "Heart to Heart" Foundation of SACC in New York. 1990.

Fig.58. With the delegation of the World Congress of Slovaks, welcomed by the Prime Minister Dr Milan Číč, the author is the fourth on the right.

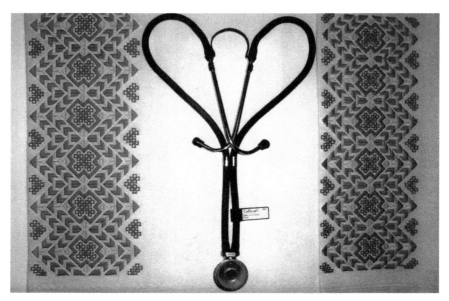

Fig.59. My stethoscope or "ears" for the heart.

Fig.60. With my wife in my office at The Heart Center of Saint Francis Hospital.

TÜBINGEN

Tübingen is a lovely and colorful town of half-timber houses (Fachwerk-haus) looking like gingerbread houses — only Little Red Riding Hood is missing. The town is wedged into the mound of the "Schwabiam Alb"(mound) south of Stuttgart in the state of Baden-Würtenberg. It has been known since the Romans settled there in the first century of our times. In the sixth and seventh centuries, the tribes of Alemanni settled there, and in the eighth century, the Dutchy of Würtenberg was established. At the beginning of the first millennium, Hugo the First, the magnate of the town, built a fortress: Hohen Tübingen (high). In the fifteenth century, the Cathedral of Saint George was built, and in 1471 the renown University of Carl Eberhardt was established, the oldest in the middle of Europe.

After the Reformation, Tübingen turned to a center of Lutheran Protestantism, but in the eighteenth century, the town was overrun by the Catholic Liege. Eventually the town returned to its Protestant and pietist traditions with their frugality, sobriety, order, justice, and meticulous cleanliness. In the nineteenth century, Tübingen belonged to the Kingdom of Würtenberg. After WW II the town turned to be part of the Federal Republic of Germany. The town is settled in the valley of the picturesque Neckar River, which cuts through its center, and along it the platan trees created a colorful alley. Since the ages, this lovely river offers its charm for the oarsmen and fishermen and for the university students' competition in kayak or scull. Even today you can hire a scull and glide on the charming river with the help of a student and his rudder for a few euros (Figure 17).

Tübingen is an "old town" with a majestic town hall, with a lively market and the adjacent Collegiate Church. Above on the Schlossberg (castle hill) resides the fortress of Osterberg. The architecture of the town exemplifies the typical half-timber houses (Fachwerkhaus) of craftsmen, shopkeepers and other citizens built in the sixteenth through eighteenth centuries. Their wooden frames are "filled in" with red bricks; thus the whole town has a uniformity of the houses. Some of them are embroidered with gothic or renaissance ornaments. It is a very nice and neat town, which offered us its hospitality for almost a year (Figure 18).

After a good night's sleep, the whole family took the elevator and went down to the dining room of the hospital. As kind of "Martian newcomers," revealed by our unorthodox and different appearance, which did not belong to the locals, we took our place on the side of the dining room amid many curious looks. As we learned, the physicians had their breakfast in the comfort of their homes with their families in that society.

Then we had the luxury to choose from a wide variety of food and drinks. There was milk, cocoa, and, of course, coffee and different juices as well. A variety of crunchy buns, golden "kaiser semmel" (emperors bun), or croissants with butter, honey, and different kind of marmalades in glass jars were available. Also hot frankfurters, scrambled eggs, cheese, and sliced ham were offered. We were in quandary indeed, what to choose, but we all had a sumptuous and scrumptious breakfast.

I went to see Schwester Hilde in her office afterward. She welcomed me with a wide and warm smile with her "guten morgen" (good morning). I asked first about the customs of our daily board for the family. She suggested, as for our provisions of food, that we should be satisfied with two daily tickets for the whole family, since the portions were quite large. She offered me two aluminum lunch boxes for food, which we should put to the kitchen window and the servers would do the rest. In our rooms, we had an electric heater to warm up the food, if needed.

The care for the provisions I delegated to my wife, and she took care of it daily at lunch and dinnertime. She took our children down to the kitchen window every day as she presented her tickets and the lunch boxes to the servers for lunch and dinner. Our little girl, Patsy, was still small, and her little nose was just at the level of the counter, but her vivid eyes curiously followed what was going on.

My wife noticed right away that the whole kitchen staff — the serving girls and the cooks — were communicating in a Slavic, Serbian tongue, as they were from Yugoslavia as Gastarbeiters (seasonal workers). The news that the hospital had new refugees from Czechoslovakia, a physician and his family, spread down to the kitchen as well. My wife in her communications with the staff, as she was not speaking German, addressed the girl in our Slovak tongue. Somehow the young girl understood that we are actually her Slavic brethren. From then on, the service girl who supplied us with the food jammed so much food to the lunch boxes that we were not able to consume it. In reciprocity, my wife thanked the girl in Serbian, "chvala" (thank you), and we always were well-supplied.

At 9 A.M. I arrived at the office of the division of Pediatric Cardiology and presented myself to the secretary, Anne-Marie. The head of the division was a known specialist in pediatric cardiology, trained in Göttingen by Professor J. Beuren, who learned his craft in the USA. I was glad that I would be able to work at that renowned and specialized center.

The young professor was a classical blue-eyed blond, good-looking German, probably my age or perhaps a bit younger. He welcomed me kindly in his rather small office with an official "bon ton," shaking my hands but remaining somehow reserved. We sat down, and he politely inquired about the well-being and condition of my family and if we were content with our accommodations and lodging. I, of course, thanked him sincerely and praised his generous help and concern and all the arrangements he had made in our favor, as the warm welcome of Schwester Hilde as well. All the conversation was in German.

We switched then into the medical sphere when he inquired about my medical school, my training in general pediatrics, and, of course, pediatric cardiology at my academic university hospital, and my board in pediatrics and pediatric cardiology. I presented him with the list of my fifteen publications, two of them abroad, and it satisfied him as far as my professional background.

The professor then portrayed my responsibilities at the Division, on the patients floor, and in the outpatient department, and he was obviously most interested in my experience and skill in the technique of diagnostic catheterization of the heart, that is, advancing a plastic tube into a patient's heart and arriving to a correct diagnosis in the diagnostic laboratory.

At about 10:30 A.M. after our professional exchange ended, he called upon the secretary of the professor and head of the Children's Hospital. The professor wanted to introduce me to his boss and pay him an official call with the new member of the hospital.

Just before our departure to the head of the hospital, Dr. Jürgen A. presented me with a check for my stipend. While the award commenced from July 1, 1968, I was surprised to receive a stipend for three months retroactively from the Foundation in their exceptional generosity, as they were informed that I was a refugee with my family after the Russian invasion into my native country. The board of the foundation obviously wanted to help me in my unexpected predicament. I thanked Professor Jürgen A. for his thoughtfulness graciously. Suddenly I felt that I was a millionaire.

We proceeded then to the elevator and went to the third floor to the Chairman's office. Professor Johann Bierich was a handsome, tall athlete with black hair and blue eyes, who in his white coat welcomed me with a pleasant smile and cordially shook my hand warmly. "Schön willcomen, colleague" (welcome colleague). The professor offered us to be seated into his beautiful, leather easy chairs in his elegant office. On his table in a crystal vase, fresh-cut flowers gave a pleasant smell, and an ornate background filled in the room with some colorful oil paintings. The professor was very kind and glad that I would fittingly complement the team at the Division of Pediatric Cardiology. He also inquired about the well-being of my family and their satisfaction. I was, of course, profusely thanking him for my acceptance into the hospital staff and all his support at that trying time for me and my family.

After about fifteen minutes, we returned to the office of my immediate superior.

The team of the Division of Pediatric Cardiology was rather small but efficient. There was a rotating resident, Dr. J. Schulte, who was a very pleasant fellow, with whom I bonded very easily. The secretary of the Division was Ann-Marie, a taller, very pleasant young lady with bushy, chestnut-colored hair and warm, brown eyes, wearing golden-framed glasses. She was a kind and warm person, always ready to help. The other nurse-technician was Helga, a rather cocky girl with her rusty-colored hair in a short cut with piercing, blue eyes, who from the beginning seemed to project her German superiority vís-a-vís a Slavic newcomer. That first impression of mine was later on validated by her sticky daily conduct with me. We had also a young but efficient X-ray technician with whom I developed a good rapport and an assisting middle-aged lady, who was also very nice. The professor formally introduced me to all members of the team, and I had to develop a positive and constructive relationship with all, which was not a problem for me, except the cocky Helga.

My professor took me now into the diagnostic laboratory, where he showed me his advanced technology, mainly cinematography, that is, a high speed camera, which in two perpendicular views was filming the interior of the beating heart chambers after a contrast dye was injected into it with the help of a catheter (plastic tube). That was the main strength of this laboratory with its more modern technology, which was not available in my hospital in Bratislava.

After we finished our review of the facilities, I mentioned to the professor that we barely had arrived to Tübingen with some engine problem in my car and would have to see some repair shop. The professor picked up the telephone and called upon a colleague who also owned a Renault French car even though much bigger than mine, a later model. A tall, blond athlete showed up in a few minutes, Dr. Fred Tossberg, who was kind enough to take me right away to his Renault car service.

In the afternoon, Dr. Tossberg took my sputtering little car with me to the service station. I explained to the technician that the car did not seem to have its previous pull and power, especially going uphill. The technician restarted the car, went under the hood, and, after a short inspection, he made the diagnosis of the problem that the engine was running only on three cylinders and the fourth one was blocked. I was quite shocked by that revelation, meaning that during the majority of our trip, we were running only on three cylinders and were very lucky to have made it. Of course as a technical ignoramus, I did not have a clue what was wrong with my car during our trip.

The technician relieved my anxiety with his nonchalant, "No problem, sir. In two days, the car will be okay, humming like a bumblebee, and everything will be fine."

Indeed in two days, I picked up our Bobby. As I turned on the engine, indeed it had a spritely and happy sound and was purring like a little kitten. As I started to drive the car, I noticed right away the power and pull of the engine, and the car was running vigorously as a well-oiled machine.

The next day I had to go through the administrative and legal procedures of every refugee in Germany. I went, escorted by Ann-Marie, to the police station to report that my family had arrived in the town. I had to fill out a couple of pages of questionnaires, and I was happy to have Ann-Marie's help at my disposition to fill in properly the correct answers. After that we went to the Office of Labor and asked to have a working permit. This procedure in that office I had to repeat every three months. I was also required to present a copy of my medical diploma and present the index from my medical school that listed all lectures I had attended in Bratislava. Later on I had to present all those documents at the Ministry of Health in the capital of the state Baden-Würtenberg in Stuttgart.

Following those rigorous requirements, I had to call up my sister in Bratislava and ask her to send me the notarized copies of those documents from my cabinet in my study. During this rather emotional call, I did not forget to send my love to my beloved mom and sister.

The papers arrived in two weeks in a registered letter, and the next day we drove with Ann-Marie to Stuttgart to the Ministry of Health. There again I had to fill out many questionnaires and paperwork while the civil servant registered my medical diploma and the index of attended lectures at the medical school. In a few days, I received from the ministry of health a reciprocation of my medical diploma with permission to practice medicine. The German system was meticulous, well-wheeled, and efficient. The first weeks of my work was hectic and demanding, and it was a welcomed solace to receive an invitation from my professor and his wife to come to their house on Saturday afternoon for a café and kuchen (coffee and cake). It was a quasi-classical expression of the German hospitality and Western culture.

The professor lived with his family in a garden part of the town in a two-story house. We fetched our best attire for our first social event even though our outfits quickly revealed our meager, if not impoverished, conditions as refugees.

At the gate of the manicured garden of the house, the lady of the house was welcoming us very graciously and with a warm smile. She was a pleasant young woman with hazelnut-colored eyes and a rich auburn coif. Behind her her husband greeted us with his German "schön welcome" (a nice welcome) and shook our hands. Over a few steps, we entered a foyer full of flowers and then into an elegant living room with appealing Scandinavian teak furniture and heavy-leather, beige-colored easy chairs and a nice, elongated coffee table. There too flowers were everywhere, obviously a forte of the lady of the house. Suddenly two typical German blond ("burschen") boys showed up, looking like their dad with their typical "puben" (boyish) haircut even though they had the nice, brown eyes of their mom. The older was about seven years old, the younger was four. After they introduced themselves with a bow, they were chaperoned by their mom to the children's room, and she took a friendly embrace with our kids as well. After some mutual obligatory courtesy and expressions, including our thanks to the couple, the lady of the house presented, on a silver plate, an ornamental pitcher of china with a coffee, Eduscho, with its inviting aroma. She brought then another plate with a fresh, homemade cinnamon roll sprinkled over with a laced vanilla sugar. It looked all very appetizing and savory. The children received the same cake but with tea served on a small service cart. Our kids enjoyed this "rolling service" since they were seeing that novelty for the first time.

Everything was perfect; the cinnamon role was moist and fluffy, revealing the art of backing by the lady of the house, and the Arabian coffee with whipped cream was exceptional. During our conversation, I was doing most of the interpreting even though my German was still rocky. I had to answer all the questions of our sudden, unexpected emigration and our long and arduous trip to Tübingen in our malfunctioning car. How did we decide or manage it all with two small children? There was no satisfactory answer to our decision-making process and to our escape, but many good, generous people had been very helpful in our precarious predicament. We were eager to decompress our angst to people who seemed to be genuinely interested in our unexpected saga.

Then the lady of the house invited my wife to show off her beautiful house as well as the colorful flower garden. My wife had taken a few years ago some private lessons in German; thus there was some "feminine" communication and interaction between the two.

While I was sitting on the sofa amid conversation with the professor, he came aside me, and from an adjacent cabinet, he pulled out a photo camera. I *thought* that he want to do some pictures of our families. Instead he came close to me and started to take pictures of me from close- up, from the front, from my side, and from a distance. I was quite surprised by the turn of the events, as it was rather unexpected and made me quite uncomfortable. It crossed my mind that he was taking the pictures perhaps for the police, just in case I turned out be an impostor. It suddenly spoiled the whole friendly atmosphere, which remained frozen and flawed and sowed seeds of mistrust that remained with me during my whole stay in Tübingen. He, of course, never asked permission to take my close-ups in his German upper-hand way of thinking. I never learned what the purpose was of his unexpected photographic "assault."

Suddenly the two ladies were just returning from the perusal of the garden and the house while from the children's room, large bursts of laughter were coming out, suggesting that everything was in order and the two "foreign camps" were having a good time.

Yet the time was running fast, and we were trying not to impose on the hospitality of our hosts, as the dusk was seeping in earlier in the fall. We thanked them for the memorable afternoon and their hospitality and returned to our new home in our well-recovered car. During our ride home, I told my wife about the picture-taking incident, and she was surprised as well by that unexpected and unusual event and was disquieted and uncomfortable as well. What does this mean? was our question. We never learned the answer.

The next week, I was expected to demonstrate my skill in the diagnostic laboratory, mainly the introduction of the catheter in the vein of the groin without a surgical cutdown. Schwester Helga, a young, German amazon, stood by me and demanded that before the procedure, I scrub my hands at least fifteen minutes "punctum" (on the dot). She remained beside me all the time while I quietly sniggered under my mustache with some disdain over this German punctuality and overbearing of a nurse. But when I introduced skillfully a catheter into the vein in the groin with a new, nonsurgical technique by the Swede Swen Seldinger, then my professional stock rose exponentially, even in the eyes of Schwester Helga. That was a new technique in this laboratory. The boss was satisfied.

I, of course, learned from the professor the evaluation of the cineangiograms, or movies, during the examinations of the hearts in children born with heart disease. Those movies were the backbone of the correct diagnosis of the patient. As days went by, a productive professional cooperation and symbiosis developed between the professor and me. On a personal level, our relationship remained reserved since the picture-taking incident. My German communication skills improved quickly and significantly in leaps and bounds, thanks to some basics of German in my early childhood and eight years of German in the high school. In two months, I was able to dictate into a Dictaphone my findings from the outpatient clinic to the pediatricians and the diagnostic conclusions from the diagnostic lab. If I made a mistake or slippage in my German, Ann-Marie innocuously corrected my imperfection. Obviously not every German girl behaved as a Teutonic amazon.

In Tübingen we were not the only refugees from Czechoslovakia. I met here a lecturer of Marxism-Leninism from Charles University in Prague who quickly changed political color and melted into the society. We met once or twice, cursing Leonid Brezhnev profusely. As the Latin saying goes, "Tempora mutantur et nos mutamur in illis" or "As the times are changing, we are changing with the times as well."

Somehow, out of the blue sky or through human "wireless," we were invited for a lunch by the famous professor of biology, Dr. Johann Kretschmer from the University of Tübingen. He and his gracious wife were extremely kind and humane and hospitable to our family. After the sumptuous lunch amid vivid discussion with a give-and-take of questions and answers, they offered us their help anytime we would have a problem. We were extremely thankful for such humane and psychological support and a boost in our predicament from that elderly, very friendly couple. Of course, there was no picture taking from close-up or otherwise. We left with deep thanks and were inspired by those two magnanimous people, real "Menchen" (humans).

74

During the weekends, we slowly explored and got acquainted with that historic jewel and university town, built up by colorful, red bricks, and visited the cathedral and the Catholic Collegiate Church as well. We used to go to that church every Sunday to get some solace or guidance as it slowly dawned on us that Tübingen would serve only our temporary "landing" in our quest for our permanent home.

Along the Neckar River (Figure 19), a lively alley wound along. On the river, we could see to glide small punts, pushed with a long rod by a university student for a few marks. Our children could freely run around and play in this lovely and peaceful autumn.

In the early weeks of our stay, Schwester Hilde, our guardian angel, came to my wife with a practical suggestion that perhaps our children could attend the local nursery school. If we would agree, she would be glad make arrangements for it. We, of course, found that suggestion sensible indeed, where our children could learn the language and my wife could have some rest and recover her energy.

The next day, my wife and the two kids were marching with great expectations to the nearby nursery, which was led by a pleasant and kind principal nun. She assessed our two cute and attractive children with her experienced eye and was satisfied with their appearance and manners. She then explained to my wife that she would take the five-year-old Robert, but Patricia was not yet three years old, and consequently she couldn't take her. The nun took the hand of our son, but suddenly Patricia released the hand of her mom and ran over to Robert. She crossed her hands over her chest and defiantly made her point, that she wanted to be with her brother. My wife and the principal were taken by surprise by this "revolution," a first in our family, and it seemed that we were going to have an unwelcomed argument. Then, to the surprise of my wife, the nun's face changed to a warm smile as she remarked, "Well Patricia is almost three, and so she can stay," to the great satisfaction of my wife and a victory for our daughter, and her face beamed from her triumph.

During the week, the children attended the nursery for five days, where they had their lunch and in the afternoon a catnap, and at 4 P.M. my wife picked them up and brought them home. In her morning free time, my wife could get acquainted with the old town, and as a woman, she was interested to browse through the rich farmers market in the middle of the town. There was a plentitude of greeneries and vegetables of first-class quality, all kinds of fruit and bananas, and an assortment of appealing meat products in a special truck with an automatic counter on the side with different fresh sausages, frankfurters, bacon of different kinds, and liverwurst as well. It was a real "abundanza" (plentitude) compared to the measly markets in Bratislava.

While in Bratislava, bananas were a precious and expensive item, and our children used to get two or three pieces from my sister, Catherine. These were exclusively only for our children. As my wife offered mashed banana puree to our baby daughter, not once was she dreaming for a bite of banana.

In Tübingen there was a plentitude of bananas, and she could enjoy them and bring a bunch of them home any time. One Saturday we were just strolling lazily through the center of the town. I knew that my wife had an old, ugly, Russian-made wristwatch marked "pobeda" (victory). It was a typical crude, Russian product that frequently and unexpectedly stopped. Suddenly we paused before an elegant watchmaker store, "Uhr house Hahenstroh's" (House for Watches), where I bought a beautiful, delicate, golden-plated wristwatch for my wife. She was overjoyed by that precious gift and wore it for many, many years. Of course right away she got rid of the Russian monster as a kind of a nightmare from the times of socialist years.

As the time was advancing and galloping forward toward Christmas and I got acquainted with the German academic system in the hospital, it dawned on me more and more that in that German class system, I would be unable to hope for any academic position or any upward movement in it as a foreigner, and at best I would be delegated to an assistant-doctor position for years to come.

Just to be sure and to have the right information about the academic matters, I learned through the "wireless" communication between émigrés that a Hungarian pediatric cardiologist, Dr. László Marcsek, had emigrated to Hamburg after the Hungarian Revolution of 1956. Eventually I located and called him up, and he was very open and friendly regarding his position in the last twelve years at the Children's Hospital as an assistant doctor. He confirmed to me that for a foreign doctor to get into the ranks of the German academic system was a pipe dream. Even though he had published a book of pediatric cardiology as the leading author, his boss and professor piggybacked his name to the title without any hesitation and any quandary. Even with such association with his professor, he had no chance to get to the academic ranks of the hospital. Later on I learned that, after some years, László left Hamburg and went into a private practice in the eastern part of Germany in Regensburg.

That information was quite sufficient for me, as fifteen years after my graduation, I did not want to lose additional years without some advancement in academia. I was not in the mood to play second fiddle for good. In November 1968, I wrote a letter to Dr. A.S. Nadas at the Children's Medical Center in Boston, and I described for him my predicament as an émigré after the invasion of the Warsaw Pact Armies led by the Red Army into Czechoslovakia. I let him know that thanks to the stipend of the A. van Humboldt Foundation, I was working at the Children's Hospital in Tübingen for a year. I asked him if it would be possible to renew or reactivate his invitation of 1965 for a fellowship in his hospital. My hope was small, but I dreamt that my "blue fairy" would again make a miracle and bring me luck and offer me such a privilege.

Toward the end of the November, Schwester Hilde came to see me and gently conveyed to me that the directorate of the hospital would suggest that from January 1, 1969, I should find and rent for me and my family an apartment, as the hospitality of the hospital — after three month of accommodation — will end at that date. This was, of course, foreseeable, and the hospital generously offered me a bonus premium to supplement my modest stipend for a family of four. Definitely we did not want to take advantage of the generosity of the hospital and give an impression that we were some kind of freeloaders.

Suddenly in the early days of December, the first snow showed up, and we had to pull out the overalls for our children and get some warm overcoats. I was working full speed, and I hoped and prayed for some kind of miracle from Boston, as a gift, by the coming birth of Jesus. My wife took very good care of the family, chaperoning the children to the kindergarten, providing us with our provisions from the kitchen of the hospital, and taking frequently our kids for fresh air at the snowy banks of the Neckar River for a stroll or bantering.

Schwester Hilde prepared for us and the children a lovely surprise when, the day before December 6, Saint Nicholas Day, she brought us some chocolates and gifts into our shoes as a morning surprise. We adults had to refresh our memories from our own childhood and recall the story of the Bishop Saint Nicholas from Izmir, Turkey, who was, after WW II, replaced in Soviet Bloc countries by Dedo Moroz (Father Frost). Consequently, many years before we had, with all the children of Germany, polished the shoes of our children and put them in the window in hope that till the night was over, Saint Nicholas would bring them some generous gifts or surprises. Before falling to sleep, our children said a short prayer to Saint Nicholas, hoping for some surprise gifts or goodies.

And indeed Saint Nicholas was very generous with his gifts and filled the shiny shoes of Robert and Patricia with chocolates, nuts, figs, and dates. The children were joyous about the morning surprise and the gifts in their shoes and never learned about the Russian Father Frost.

About a week later in the early morning of December 13, at 6 A.M. when we were perhaps turning on our other side in the bed, like in a dream or perhaps it wasn't a dream, we heard some faint, subtle voices, like those of angels from heaven. We just could not imagine — were we dreaming or were we hearing some angelic voices that, there on the third floor under the roof, were faintly resonating, or rather floating, in the air.

Unbeknown to us, there in Protestant Tübingen, just before Christmas, the feast of Saint Lucy was celebrated, who as a martyr in times of Emperor Diocletian was carrying food to the hiding Christians into the pitch dark catacombs of Rome, and she held a shining candle before her path to see the people for whom she had brought her gifts. She was named, therefore, Saint Lucy, or carrier of light (lux in Latin).

As we cautiously stuck out our heads from the door of our room, we could see in our disbelief a group of nurses dressed in snow white robes — as angels — with golden crowns on their heads, holding candles in their hands, with their gently flickering flames in the dark, as they glided smoothly around the round staircase and, in faint sopranos, were piously singing a ballad to venerate that martyr of light, Saint Lucy.

The whole procession of these "angels" glided around and along the corridors on the whole third tier level, almost levitating above the floor. We were looking at this "miracle" bewilderedly, but as we were looking at these "angels" as they were passing by, some of them winked at us, the foreign refugees in our nightgowns and pajamas. At the end of the procession, our "archangel" Schwester Hilde, in white robe, was passing by and singing, yet she still made a mischievous wink to the members of her adopted family.

It was a beautiful, pious event of that Advent, commemorating Saint Lucy bringing the light to the persecuted Christians. As it was so early in the morning, we still returned to our beds for an additional catnap, during which the angelic choir and their subtle voices were still resonating in our minds. From then on, every December 13 we light a candle in our home to venerate Saint Lucy and commemorate our morning "dream" in Tübingen.

During those days, we were in full throttle, searching for an apartment to rent for our family. Somebody mentioned that in the neighboring small village of Hirschau, a family had built a house, and they were trying to rent out a fully furnished basement with two rooms and a kitchen. We indeed went to visit that picturesque village, then in her white "costume" of snow, about five kilometers (three miles) from the hospital. We met the owner and his welcoming wife, a pleasant brunette, and we liked the neat premises and right away made a deal at a reasonable price, starting to rent it from January. We were very happy that we had found that apartment not far from the hospital. The couple had a little girl, Rosina, who was like our Patsy, which was an additional social bonus for us.

As the Advent dawned on the town of Tübingen , it was richly decorated in the center and along the main avenues with many coniferous pine trees with their cones painted gold, with leaves of periwinkles with their ruby red berries and yellow green leaves of mistletoes with their pearl white berries. The market was full of freshly cut pine trees with their penetrating aromas of pine resin, some of them already decorated with colorful ribbons and tinsel. They were fresh, colorful and lovely; one of them with a silver star on its top was to our liking, and we bought it right away.

On the bridge in the shape of an arch over the Neckar River, there was a kiosk full of little gifts and bric-a-brac for Christmas. We noticed a golden-plated bell, about three inches high. It could be wound up to play the pious and mellow Christmas classic, "Stille Nacht, Heilige Nacht" or "Silent Night, Holy Night," composed by Francz Gruber and Joseph Mohr in a godforsaken Austrian village.

That little bell, then already with its patina, for over half a century has remained a centerpiece on our Christmas Eve table and reminds us of our first rather lonely and emotional Christmas in the first year of our emigration in Tübingen.

Our Christmas Eve was still lovely. Most importantly we were all together, and my wife made miracles with fluffing up the Christmas tree with some tinsel, colorful glass balls, and mistletoe on the Christmas table, which was always part of my Christmas in the house of my parents. The presents were small but heartfelt as a gifts from the first-born Jesus. We parents did our best to project for the children a merry and joyous Christmas even though in our minds, we were "at home" with our dear parents. At our Christmas Eve prayer, we tried to suppress our tears, but our eyes, nevertheless, turned wet. We were, in our minds, humming the well-known Christmas ballad:

> "I'll be home for Christmas,
> If only in my dreams."

During the evening, we were dressed up in our festive Western attire — Patricia in a sky blue, knitwear robe, Robert as a student in a navy blue jacket with light gray pants, black shoes, and a red bow tie. My wife wore a lovely, cinnamon-colored knitwear, very elegant, and I followed in the sartorial attire of my son.

Our table was covered by a snow white damask with decorated small fir branches along the edges, and the Christmas china and silver was supplied by the kind Schwester Hilde. In the middle of the table, a white candle gave us an intimate light and hope as we said our prayer before the meal.

"Bless us, Lord, and all these gifts we are going to receive
In the name of the Father, Son, and the Holy Spirit. Amen."

We could not have our traditional sauerkraut soup with its porcini mushrooms and its biblical overtones of its tartness or bitter touch. Instead we had a tasty chicken soup with floating angel hair, which was very tasty indeed. At home usually we would have fried fish, obligatorily the famous carps of Bohemia, a symbol of Christianity. Now a fried local flounder was on our menu with potato salad with mayonnaise, and the children were happy with the boneless fish. We had a cooled, golden Riesling with a beautiful bouquet and an appealing taste to splash down the delicious fish, while the children had an ice-cold soda. The dinner was "crowned" with a chocolate Black Forest cake with whipped cream. The dinner was indeed festive, savory, and sumptuous.

The evening was quickly advancing, and at 11 P.M., warmly dressed, we departed into the white winter land and were treading through the snow, kids jumping happily around into the nearby Collegiate Church for our first midnight mass in our emigration.

The church was full to the last spot while the organ was improvising in a chromatic prelude the Christmas tunes and carols that were well-known in all of Europe. We were seated by an usher, and in our souls we were greeting and celebrating the birth of the little Jesus in Bethlehem and pleading for his help to keep our nuclear family together in our struggle to find our new shelter or home, of which just a few months ago we had tragically lost.

In my own mind, my thoughts were swirling like in the cloud of a maelstrom. What would the new year bring for us in our uncertain future? The holy mass ended with a world-known, virtually eternal song, "Silent Night, Holy Night," and the whole crowd of the faithful sang it in moving piety while the organ, in its majestic, chromatic accords, underlined and colored the festive atmosphere. At the end of the mass, all the faithful joyously wished to each other, "Fröhliche Weihnachten" (Merry Christmas)!

After we returned home from the church, a Christmas stocking was hanging on our door handle with a message of "Merry Christmas," with chocolate candy for the children from Schwester Hilde, who was like a mother goose to our children. She had a kind and big heart, and she liked to surprise us in her generous affection.

In a week, on New Year's Eve, the town welcomed the new year with celebrations and grand, boisterous balls, while after our subdued dinner, we quickly retired into our dreams.

The next day, January 1, 1969, was also a holiday. We went for the morning mass while the town was lazily waking up from last night's celebration. For us it was the day of our moving out from the protective premises of the Children's Hospital. With some trepidation, we quickly packed up our belongings into our small car, and in two rounds, we transferred everything we had into our new home in the village of Hirschau.

Hirschau was a small village with about three thousand inhabitants on the small arm of the Neckar River. In difference to the town of Tübingen, which was overwhelmingly Protestant, Hirschau was a Catholic settlement, as we later learned. The village had only one main street, and from this central artery, many small lanes branched out with numerous family housings. In the center of the village, a tall bell tower of the church stood out like an exclamation mark. In one side street of the village stood the house of family Eisner in the middle of a well-kept garden, with surrounding hedges demarcating their property. The landlord was a technician in the neighboring factory, and his wife, Frau Eisner, was taking care of the household of her husband, their daughter, Rosina, and some chickens in a small coop in the back of the garden and the ubiquitous hound around the house.

The vicinity around the village was bucolic, indeed, with farmland and vineyards, and above the village a half mile was a small hill, like a sugar loaf, then snow white, where a small chapel — the chapel of Wurmligen — was subtly wedged into the hill, extolled and praised in the cants of German poets (Fig. 20). The local poet Ludwig Wieland, like a minstrel, sounded his acclaim in a short poem:

> On the top of the hill, stands a small chapel,
> Peacefully, looks she down on the luscious green valley,
> And around the blooming meadows and streams,
> A young shepherd is cavorting around, happily.

Our landlords were very pleasant and welcoming people. When they noticed our hodgepodge luggage and the other bric-a-brac, they realized that we didn't have anything and that, indeed, we were real refugees.

We quickly settled in the modernly furnished apartment, which was nice and clean, and we were happy that somebody had accepted us and offered us temporary lodging. The rent was paid regularly to the landlord wishes. The small village had an elementary school and nursery as well. Every morning Rosina and our two children strode step by step, one with Frau Eisner and the others with Frau Mesko. The village had a grocery store as well, where my wife was a regular customer and quite esteemed by the owner, who cared very much that Frau Mesko had fresh bananas, her idiosyncratic fruits from the times in socialism. There the old custom was still common that "our customer was our lord."

The times were passing fast even in that small village, which was then all white, but the main roads were paved clean in the morning dark. I did not have any problem driving into the town in the winter even though my tires were worn out and my car sometimes slipped, but I did not have the means for new ones.

In early mornings in that wintertime, we were frequently woken up by a local, small plow, pulled by a mini-tractor that clattered briskly as it cleaned the sidewalks. At 7 A.M. the sidewalks were clean for the children pacing into the school. Again the German fondness for "putzen" (cleaning) was well-visible before every entrance of every house, which was squeaky clean.

In my work, the time was advancing in steps and leaps. My responsibilities were increasing, and on the morning "journal" of the entire department of pediatrics, I was intertwined with the whole team of doctors, about twenty-five of them, as an integral member of the Department. They were all very friendly and kind to the new refugee.

At the beginning of March 1969, I received an envelope from the USA with the carmine-colored crest of John Harvard University on it and the logo "veritas, truth." My pulse instantly quickened and rose. I abruptly opened the envelope, and I just could not believe my eyes. Professor Dr. Alexander S. Nadas had sent me an official invitation and appointment at the Children's Hospital Medical Center in Boston starting on July 1, 1969, as a Fellow in pediatric cardiology. Enclosed was a small envelope of heavy-duty cardboard. As I opened it, I found two green cards, one for me, the other for my wife, indicating that from the day of my appointment we would be residents of the USA. I was quite surprised by this unexpected development and was extremely happy. It seemed that my "blue fairy" again offered me her miraculous helping hand. I called up my wife right away and revealed to her the good news. She had to sit down in her unexpected astonishment.

The letter stipulated that I had to contact the U.S. Embassy in Frankfurt am Main. Both of us would have to go through a screening, or "vetting," to fulfill all the requirements to be accepted on U.S. soil. The letter also called to our attention that we were responsible for our transportation, or flight, to the USA.

When I drove home to Hirschau, all kinds of thoughts and concerns were boiling in my head. How was I going to fulfill all those administrative requirements and financial ones as well. I virtually blasted into our home while handing the envelope and two green cards to my wife! Two weeks later, I received another envelope from Boston, where the Children's Hospital Medical Center welcomed me and my family to the privileged International Fellows Program, and an identity card was enclosed.

Simultaneously I was informed that the program would be at my assistance and would help me with our accommodations and lodging, thus our adaptation into the American way of life would be a success. It was a great relief and appreciation that such an exceptional program would be at our assistance. The wholesome care for a member of a hospital was something totally new to me. I was happy to read that such a human concern and organizational structure for Foreign Graduates, let alone émigrés, was in assistance, that "somebody" would care and was indeed concerned.

In my hospital, I did not mention that I had received a Fellowship in Boston yet. I did not wanted to project that I was unthankful for all the care and opportunity I had received from the hospital. I continued to work hard in the diagnostic laboratory, where all the work was virtually on my shoulders. In ten months, I had performed close to one hundred workups for our patients.

In April, which was quite rainy, I drove to Frankurt am Main, which was about two hundred miles from Tübingen. During my trip, the heavy rain was sharply striking the front window of my small car. Hence I chose the slowest right lane of the highway. It was about noon when I arrived at the U.S. Embassy.

I was seated by a concierge in a nice and warm waiting room till a member of the embassy invited me into his office. There I presented to him my passport and the letter of invitation from Boston. As he was reading the letter, his expression and demeanor softened. Probably not to many people presented themselves with a letter of invitation from the University of John Harvard.

During the two-hour screening, we went through all my ancestors and the history of my education and employment in the Children's Hospitals in Czechoslovakia. Those diplomats were well-informed about our compulsory membership in the

State Unions (controlled by the Communist Party). They looked with great suspicion for such a membership; hence I was probed further about what it meant to be a member of those unions even though they were automatically compulsory. Of course a membership in the Communist Party would automatically disqualify my entrance to the USA. The officers knew that some people were concealing their past memberships in the Communist Party. Thus to this point, the vetting was quite thorough.

After the screening, I was escorted to the X-ray lab for a chest X-ray as a screen for tuberculosis. After that test at 4 P.M., I drove home, where I arrived at 8 P.M. quite exhausted.

A week later, I repeated the trip with my wife for her vetting. There I was also the interpreter and translator for her answers to the officer of the embassy. Fortunately everything was in order to the satisfaction of the consular officer.

For the screening and chest X-ray, a nurse picked up my wife and escorted her to the waiting room of the lab. There the nurse offered her a white, paper gown, under which my wife was supposed to be naked, except her panties. That was, for her, something totally new, unexpected, and uncomfortable. In the waiting room, there were about five or six German girls with golden blond hair, with heavy makeup and ruby red lipstick. They were the girlfriends or fiancées of American GIs who were returning with them to the USA. They underwent the same vetting of their professional pasts. My wife, as she looked at those startling blonds, mulled over in her mind, could they be some kind of prostitutes? But she quickly reproached herself of her unjustified suspicion.

Those girls went to the X-ray lab one after another. After the last one, my wife sat alone in her paper gown, and she was with her back toward the lab. Suddenly a technician showed up and called out loudly, "Judy." My wife continued to sit peacefully, and she did not respond to the call since the name "Judy" did not mean anything to her. The technician repeated the call with an increased crescendo: "Judy." My wife looked around, but she did not see any Judy and she continued to sit nonchalantly. Eventually the technician called out the third time: "Frau Mesko," and she spritely answered, "Yes, that is me," and followed the technician into the lab. Later on we had a good laugh about that encounter.

After that "achievement," we descended to the basement of the U.S. Embassy for a small lunch, and there we got our first taste and impression of the American and Native culture.

At the entrance, a wooden arch was supported by two huge totem poles, where a head of an Indian was carved out with a black- and red-colored mask with a frightening look in his eyes and a black-and-white-checkered mosaic on his chest. At first it gave us a scare, seeing it as a guard with a menacing impression, like one to the entrance of a prison. It made us, people from behind the Iron Curtain, somehow uncomfortable. But farther in, the cafeteria was quite inviting, especially seeing a counter with a rich assortments of different meals and a pleasant smell. There we saw, for the first time, a juicy hamburger! We chose the more familiar frankfurter, or "hot dog," wedged into a soft bun that tasted, to us, like compressed cotton compared to the crunchy "keisersemmel" emperors bun or a slice of rye bread. The piquant Heinz ketchup made up for the taste, which was, in this composition, quite appealing. We skipped the liquid and suspicious-looking mustard, which gave us an impression of Montezuma's revenge. We splashed down the lunch with a refreshing Coca-Cola and had a nice percolated coffee with its pleasant aroma, even though, for our taste, the coffee was a bit watery. To the Eastern foreigner, at that time, nothing was quite perfect! In the middle of the table stood a crystal-glass sugar bowl with a tin cup and opening, which somehow mysteriously was offering a tablespoon of crystal sugar. All over we were very happy with that new and welcoming hospitality.

Afterwards we went home as fast as we could since at home our children were waiting for us impatiently.

Then we turned to a Catholic charitable organization in Stuttgart, recommended to us by the local chaplain from the Collegiate Church. The organization was helping us arrange our transport by air, that is, to get our airline tickets from West Germany to the U.S. It also arranged to receive permission to enter the U.S. based on our green cards. A lot of paperwork followed, and it gave me plenty of entertainment in the evenings to come. We received a lot of instructions, like how much luggage we could carry. We could also send a wooden crate with all our bric-a brac, like kitchen wares, clothes, shoes, and all my new books, which would come in handy to be used in our new home. It was a lot of homework for a few weeks to come.

In the middle of April, with great anticipation we were expecting to see my dear mom, whom I had not seen in over a year. She came escorted with my sister Margaret to see us and her grandchildren, who called her the old fashioned way, Ó ma, before we departed for our great journey over the ocean to the U.S. The children were excited to see their Ó ma and Auntie Margaret as well, with whom they had a very close and warm relationship. At that time, the borders from Czechoslovakia were somehow "porous," and the authorities, to our great surprise, issued visas for my mom and sister to visit their relatives in West Germany. We were all excited and thrilled, not knowing when the political wind would change and concerned that I would not see my mom, and the children their Ó ma, for a long while. We secured a comfortable hotel for our loved ones in the middle of town.

On the day of their arrival, we went to the railroad station in our festive attire, as we would expect an eighty-one-year-old "queen." And queen she indeed was for all of us!

My mom still kept her ramrod posture, and she was mentally always honest, straight, and decent in her "old-fashioned way." Our children arrived at the railroad station with two small bunches of snow whites, one for Ó ma, the other for my sister.

We were all waiting with excitement on the platform, and I immediately approached the door of the coach, where my sister was waving with her handkerchief toward me, while my wife kept the children tightly at her side.

I jumped up to the coach, and I embraced my dear mother, and we were both sobbing tears of joy that we could see each other again (Figure 21).

Then I hugged my sister through my tears, and I was quickly helping with the luggage, and at the stairs I supported my mom so she could safely descend to the platform. Suddenly the two children got loose, and Robert and Patricia were running with joy to their Ó ma and auntie with their bunch of snow whites, hugging and kissing them both. My Judy was the last, who embraced warmly her Ó ma and Margaret amid her sobbing and copious tears.

It was really unbelievable that, even though the country was still occupied by the Red Army, permits were given to travel to the West till the fall of 1969 and the infamous "normalization" was draconically introduced.

My mom and my sister were very happy with their accommodation in this classical town with their gingerbread-like houses, and we spent together a happy ten days. It would be another ten years before I would be able to see my dear mom in Budapest, Hungary.

It was a great advantage that my mom was fluent in German since her mother had her roots in the capital of the Silezian Dutchy, Troppau (Opava), where she was raised till her mother died. My sister was quite sufficient in her German as well, and the two could communicate easily with the local people.

The authorities in Czechoslovakia were very stingy with the Western currencies and allocated only a few German marks for my mom and sister. In her wisdom, my mom had reached into her jewelry box and taken a few diamonds with her that she could easily exchange for German marks. My mom liked to be independent and march to the drumbeat of her own drummer and have her affairs in her own hands.

She also brought, or smuggled through, an exquisite and delicate necklace that was braided from human hair the color of linen, originating back to the times of Austria-Hungary and Emperor Franc-Joseph. The individual fibers of the hair were braided together into ellipsoid links in the shape of a dogberry, where each segment was linked together with a golden clip. It was a historical piece, which I saw for the first time. The jeweler was taken by surprise by the exceptional beauty of the necklace and immediately purchased it.

While I was working, my wife, with the two children, escorted my mom and sister through the beautiful center of the town and the colorful farmers market with a plentitude of enticing local products. Judy took the family to the beautiful alley of weeping willows along the Neckar River, which were just starting to go to their full golden bloom. Judy, very generously as a host, invited our guests for a sumptuous German lunch. In the afternoon, shopping was on the menu at that exceptional occasion in the West. The fine department store offered beautiful merchandise of any kind compared to the bric-a-brac available behind the Iron Curtain. My sister bought some necessary items that were not available in her home. Eventually my mom and my sister came to see our apartment in Hirschau and how we lived in emigration in the West. Everything was rented and rather modest. My mother just looked in her bewilderment around, and on her face we were reading her thoughts: So this is what my son was able to achieve? A teardrop showed up in her glistening eye. We quickly aborted that visitation of our émigré display and misery.

At the same time, the days were running fast in which the family could be together. My mom, of course, knew that we would go over the "big lake," as the Atlantic was called. In her foresight and love, she sewed for her two grandchildren two small pillows from white and light blue striped fabric that they could rest or sleep on during the long flight to the U.S. It was her expression of her deep emotional connection to her only two grandchildren. Those two pillows remained as a precious relic in our family for many years to come.

When I first saw those two lovely pillows, they reminded me of an emotional ballad from our native land:

"She is sowing my shirt, while thinking of me,
And praying to the Almighty:
Give me back, O Lord, give me back my beloved son."

Those were very difficult times for me. The parting from my dear mom was difficult, painful and very "wet." As we said our last goodbye, all of us were sobbing profoundly. To this day, I have the picture of my dear mom etched in my mind as she was standing, stoically and motionless, at the window of the departing train. Her face was resolved with the reality. The only thing that remained to be done was to bid farewell to her dearest by waving to them her love with a snow white handkerchief.

In early May 1969, I received an official letter from the dean of the medical school in Bratislava with his ultimatum that if I did not report to him in fifteen days, I would be dismissed from my position as an assistant professor of the medical school. I did not respond to this authoritative letter; consequently I was kicked out of the University Medical School.

In the middle of that month, a Congress of the European Pediatric Cardiologists convened in the city of Zürich, Switzerland, only two hundred miles from Tübingen. I was interested to go, to tank up on new and relevant information in my specialty before I went to the U.S. My professor was in agreement with my attendance at the Congress. With the help of Anne-Marie, I received a visa to Switzerland, still with my Czechoslovak passport.

I had a premonition that it just could be that my professor from Bratislava would attend that Congress, as she had attended a similar Congress with me in Rome in 1967. My premonition was correct, and indeed the name of my professor was on list of the attendees.

After the tragic invasion of Czechoslovakia in August 1968, six senior members, four of them cardiologists like me, had left the Children's Hospital in Bratislava and emigrated to the West. It was a tremendous loss in knowledge and experience for the hospital, from which it did not recover till 1990, after the fall of the Soviet Union and the Iron Curtain. In 1990 professional training in the U.S. was offered through the Foundation of American-Slovaks in New York with additional help from the Agency for International Development from Washington. That training helped to rebuild the professional strength in cardiology and cardiac surgery when a children's heart center was established at the Children's Hospital where I worked as a key member of the team for six years. In 1967 I was the backbone of the diagnostic team, and my emigration was a fundamental blow to the hospital.

During that Conference in Zurich, I welcomed my former boss and professor and greeted her with warm friendship and was happy to see her again, escorted by a younger lady doctor. My friendship was mutually reciprocated, and she was visibly happy to see me as well, warmly shaking my hand. During the Conference, we met repeatedly, exchanged courtesies, and discussed the presented lectures. A decisive "confrontation" came on the last afternoon of the Conference when she let me know that she wanted to speak with me "eye to eye."

We sat down — three of us — in a comfortable box, and I ordered coffee and biscuits for all of us, and the professor was thankful for my hospitality since they were short on Western currency. Then she told me face-to-face, looking straight at me, "Look, Dr Mesko. I was the pediatrician who was caring for the two children of the head of state, President Gustav Husak. I can guarantee you that nothing will happen to you if you return home. I will vouch for you, and you can return to your former position." It was a serious offer worth considering, but I was very concerned and doubtful that the political hacks of the Communist Party would respect her guarantees.

I thanked her very much for her forthrightness and willingness to help me, but I had to reconsider the whole thing with my wife. I did not reveal to her that I already had a fellowship secured at the Children's Hospital in Boston and couldn't let pass that unique opportunity — the only one in my life. What will happen afterwards, I will leave to God Almighty.

We departed with a friendly goodbye. It will be another ten years until I would meet her again in 1978 in Budapest, Hungary, at a similar Conference.

At the end of May, unexpectedly my best friend showed up in Tübinhen. We had been friends since our early childhood when in the grammar school we sat together from the first year on. He was an architect and somehow had made contact with a Czech architect in Tübingen, who invited him to work for his company as an assistant. It was for him a new professional experience to work in the West and an opportunity to earn some Western currency as well. Eventually he remained in Tübingen till his visa expired in fall of 1968. He was considering remaining in the West, but because of his aging mother, he eventually returned home.

We were very pleased by Oskar's arrival, and after his work, he was our everyday guest, as he was alone. We spent many evenings together when he came to our home at Hirschau, discussing, pondering, and wracking our brains about what was going to happen to all of us and our families after the invasion in that political cauldron that had developed in our native country. We did not have any realistic answers or solutions for the future. One Sunday afternoon, we were invited to the house of the Czech architect Mr. Kolenda. He was very welcoming to all of us as his countrymen. His wife was a fetching young woman with her pitch black hair in large chignon and black eyes as well, looking more like an Italian southerner. As a German lady of the house, she was obsessed with the order of things. The couple had two nice children, a girl and a boy, and they played nicely in the surrounding manicured garden with our Robert and Patricia. Unfortunately for Patsy, suddenly Mother Nature had a calling. When she did not know where the toilet was, she solved it in her own practical way and crouched behind a bush and simply peed there. Unfortunately that was noticed by the lady of the house, and she went really apoplectic that somebody had committed a sacrilege in her manicured garden. Her husband intelligently turned the whole episode into a joke, and the following scrumptious cake and aromatic coffee smoothed over the social catastrophe. The conversation at that time again swirled around the political misfortune of our country and its suffering people, in or out of their native land.

At the end of May, it was inevitable that I would have to inform my professor and reveal my cards. I asked him for a formal meeting, where I informed him that I had been invited to be a Fellow at the famous Children's Hospital Medical Center in Boston. Consequently I would be unable work for him from June 1, 1969. The professor was greatly surprised by the unexpected information. He could not imagine that an Eastern refugee would be awarded such a prestigious position at the University of John Harvard. By his expression, it was visible that he was not thrilled that he would lose an experienced associate, but eventually he congratulated me on my professional fortune. At the end of our conversation, with a shy smile he invited me and my family to his house for a farewell afternoon coffee and cake.

At that time, I obviously sent a letter of my gratitude to the Alexander van Humboldt Foundation, where I thanked the Foundation for their generous support and stipend and that, on June 1, 1969, I would be leaving for further specialization in Boston.

In the first days of June, we transferred our wooden crate with all our belongings to the Catholic Association in Tübingen (Figure 22). They were very cooperative, and they sent the crate to the harbor of Bremen and then by ship to the USA at their own expense. A few days later, the Association forwarded to us our airline tickets by TWA from Köln to New York. The tickets were charged to our account.

In middle of June, I parted from my professor with cordiality and his small team as well. I had achieved there a professional and human respect and appreciation for my work, and "eventually" I was adopted into that small community of good people. At the end, Schwester Helga abstained from pestering me from washing my hands before the diagnostic studies for a total of fifteen minutes "punctum," precisely!

Eventually we went to see and express our thanks to the professor and his gracious wife, who was always very kind to our family. Her husband was now magnanimous as well and wished us good luck in the U.S.

With heavy hearts and a lot of tears, we said goodbye to Schwester Hilde, who was our guardian angel and a second mom to our children. We were all very close to each other, and she remains in our heart to this day. To our landlords, we announced that on June 15, 1969, we would leave for the USA, but we would pay the rent for the whole month. Those good people then understood why we hadn't bought any furniture or curtains or other things for our apartment. Our parting was very cordial, with our children parting from Rosina with hugs and kisses as well, with whom our kids could communicate in broken German. At that time, we did not imagine that after twenty years, we will have a desire to come back to Hirschau to express our thanks to the Meissner family, that they had accepted us and gave us shelter in our most difficult time of life.

The most difficult time came when we had to part and say goodbye to our small car, Bobby, who was really our savior from the time our emigration had begun. We could not even imagine how our emigration could proceed without that most important "member" of the family. His warm, soft beige color gave us a soothing feeling, and his purring was always reassuring, when he was in his "neutral" soft buzz, that everything was in order. And when push came to shove, our Bobby was able to transport us even on his three cylinders, and we were able somehow to make it from Belgrade to Tübingen. What an Olympic achievement! His picture, along with my wife's, is the most precious adornment and testimony decorating my working desk to this day. Dear Bobby, wherever you are, we will cherish you in our memory forever as our savior at the time of our greatest peril. Your forever thankful, The Meskos.

At the end, the harsh reality kicked in. The car was in excellent shape with only twenty-five thousand miles on its speedometer. A German man purchased him for seven hundred German marks, probably almost for nothing.

On June 12, 1969, I ordered a black Mercedes that took us and all of our luggage from Hirschau to Tübingen. There we picked up our friend Oscar, who came with us to the Stuttgart railroad station for our farewell. We were all anxious before the awesome, historic trip, and in Oscar's mind, the idea of staying in the West resurfaced again. We purchased our tickets and went all to the appropriate platform for our train, with all our battle-proof and beaten-up cheap luggage. We certainly could pass as a picture of the wandering gypsies. But the arriving train sounded its sharp and forewarning whistle for the passengers to be carefully off the side and off the tracks.

My parting with my best friend of forty years was highly emotional and rather dramatic. As two mature men, we embraced each other in a spastic convulsion and clenched teeth with glistening eyes while tears poured over our face. We kissed each other on both cheeks, like in a Russian fairy tale. My wife was profusely crying; she loved Oscar very much, and he gave only fleeting kisses to our children, and abruptly, emotionally distraught, he left. The train was already there, and we had to quickly climb the steep stairs to the wagon and find our place in the comfortable and clean compartment. The children waved a short goodbye to Tübingen and, our fateful trip across the ocean eventually started, a trip about we never ever had dreamed! After an hour, the train stopped in Frankfurt am Main, where our friends from Bratislava — now refugees as well — were waiting for us. For years I was the pediatrician of their two children. They had settled in Germany in the nearby town of Hanau. Our friends could not believe that we had mustered our courage to go to a very far land, "over seven seas." Just a few words of bewilderment from our friends, but the dice were already cast. We had a quick embrace on the platform, and as the dispatcher already had given the green sign for departure, we quickly climbed up on the train to continue our trip to Köln.

In the famous northern city of Köln, the Catholic Association reserved for us a comfortable hotel for two days close to the center of the town. It was well-located in the historic town, which gave its name to the famous "Eau de Cologne" and his perfume 4711, the number on the street where the chemist concocted that fragrance. But the city's real jewel was its majestic gothic cathedral (Fig. 23), which we visited the next day. There we thanked the Almighty for His protective hand over our family and prayed that He would guide us on our adventurous journey of emigration. We prayed for His further help and blessings in our pilgrimage.

The shopping center was quite close, and from our savings, we dressed up our children and my wife with a beautiful, knitted outfit in cinnamon color and a light beige, "chic" overcoat. The quality and cut of the clothing were first-class. I was already well-dressed from Tübingen with an elegant, light gray striped attire, right out of a textile factory where the suit was tailored for me. I just bought a pair of fancy black shoes. We had to also purchase a new suitcase for our recent acquisitions.

The two days passed by quickly, and on June 16, 1969, we ordered a cab, which took us to the airport and to the TWA reception desk. There we presented to the receptionist our tickets, our Czechoslovak passports, and our green cards and handed over our suitcases.

At the entrance into the huge turbo jet, the stewardess immediately took care of our two small children and escorted all of us to our assigned seats. The outfit and the environment on the jumbo jet was all very new for our children and very appealing. The kids, while giggling, were patting the elegant and soft upholstery of the seats, and they liked the clasp on the safety belts as well amidst all the new fun for them. My wife then pulled out from her sack two delicate, small pillows, the masterwork of my dear mom. They were very handy during the long trip for our children.

In a short while, with a lot of noise, rumbling, and shaking, somewhat scary for our little daughter — but the reassuring smile of her mom calmed our Patsy down — the huge "silver bird" took off and took the direction toward our new refuge of freedom: the USA.

My practical wife was well-prepared for the trip with toys and, for Patsy, her doll, which she kept in a tight squeeze during the liftoff. Robert was busy with his colorful book of American Indians and their famous chieftain, Winnetou. In a while, the stewardesses served us some soft drinks or different juices, followed soon by a sumptuous lunch. An eight-hour flight followed. We reclined the seats for the children for their rest and sleep on the soft pillows of their Ó ma. As the "big bird " was humming monotonously, the children fell quickly asleep into their dreams. With my wife, we had our exercise books of English, which we studied compulsively to "polish" our English.

As we were closing in toward New York at the sundown of the day, we spotted the emerging Manhattan through some clouds, with all kind of skyscrapers that stood upright as different type of stalactites — tall and small, slim and stocky — holding up their heads and spires toward the golden rays of the glittering sunset (Figure 24). It was a fascinating overview of the island, presenting itself like magic in a spectacular show-off to the viewers from above. We were able to spot the glittering spire of the Empire State Building and alongside the blue ribbon of the Hudson River and the two elegant corrugated Twin Towers. Oh, and look at the Statue of Liberty welcoming us now as well, standing tall on a small, isolated island facing New Amsterdam (the original name of New York). There she had stood proudly since October 8, 1886, as she welcomed millions of refugees and émigrés, these "wretched masses" under her protection (Fig. 25).

Since 1903 on the plaque of her pedestal, a poem by Emma Lazarus, a refugee of Sephardic, Portuguese roots is etched, on which she eloquently utters the last stanza:

"With silent lips: give me your tired, your poor.
Your huddling masses yearning to be free
The wretched refuse, your teeming shore,
Send me, the homeless, tempest-tossed to me,
I lift my lamp, besides the golden door!"

We landed at John F. Kennedy airport at 5 P.M. local time, and we were escorted to the hall for the control of our passports. We walked along the hall in lanes, and as we passed the formalities, to my astonishment, I saw a gentleman with a sign "Mesko." I could not fathom who could wait for us in New York since we did not know anybody in New York. The gentleman approached us and addressed us in our native language, saying, "Welcome to New York, doctor," with a smile. He passed a small bouquet of flowers to my astonished wife. As it transpired, the gentleman was the uncle of my former patient — a small boy — whom I had cared for and his heart problem many years ago when I was a Resident at the Children's Hospital in the eastern metropolis of Košice. I was really astonished when I learned that the father of my patient had learned somehow through the "human wireless" that we would arrive in New York. The father of the patient called up his brother in New York, who turned to be the gentleman who had come to welcome us at the airport. It seemed to us that the thankfulness and humanity of some people just does not know borders. The gentleman then gave me his business card, wishing us all luck, and departed.

In the next days, I sent to the gentlemen a thank-you card with our heartfelt gratitude for his gracious welcome. I also asked him to convey our eternal thanks and appreciation to the parents of my former patient and to my patient as well, who now was a healthy youngster and had not forgotten his "doc." At the exit of passport control, we were greeted by a member of the Catholic Association, who escorted us to a minibus to be taken to the nearby hotel at the airport, where we spent one night.

The next morning was June17, 1969, the sixth birthday of our son, Robert. We prepared for him, of course, a small gift and congratulated him with all our love and asked the blessings of the Almighty in his new life and wished him the first American "happy birthday to you."

Then we descended to the dining room in our European and festive attire for the day, somehow to celebrate our arrival into our new country and home. The waitress welcomed us with her professional smile and seated us in a box where the children could see the departing airliners. For breakfast we were directed to the ready-to-eat hot counter. There in a line of silver containers, different food was offered as we lifted the silver lids. We never had seen anything like that, but it sure looked very practical. Leaving our children in the box, we took two trays with four small plates, and using a large, silver spoon, we placed on each plate a spoonful of scrambled eggs, small sausages, and nice, warm buns as we came to the end of the line. As we returned to our table, the waitress offered black coffee in porcelain cups with milk and cream on the side. The children were presented with two tall glasses of ice-cold milk with floating ice cubes. We looked at each other and the ice-cold breakfast: so what now? Was the milk served icy because of the summer heat? The children were puzzled as well, as they never had gotten an icy breakfast. We asked the waitress if she could bring for our children two glasses of warm milk. Then the surprise was on her side, as she quipped, "Warm milk?" I quickly jumped in and replied, "Perhaps a warm cocoa?" She gave me right away her charming smile with her happy reply: "Yes," and presto, the warm cocoa was right on our table to the relief of all of us. Our first American breakfast was delicious indeed!

BOSTON

After the breakfast, we had to pack up quickly, as the minibus was waiting to take us to the airport. After a short flight of fifty minutes, we landed at Logan Airport in Boston, our final destination. Just before our landing, we could see from a bird's-eye view" the city of Boston spread on the two banks of the winding blue "ribbon," the Charles River. The city itself was indeed wedged into the delta of the Charles River as its waters were virtually sucked into an embrace of the Atlantic. We could also see the skyscraper Prudential Building, a landmark in Boston, on the right side of the river, while on its left side the sprawling buildings of the town of Cambridge and its universities of academics and research, most prominently the University of John Harvard (Figure 26). Boston is a historic city with an eclectic character, founded by the first Protestants, the Puritans, who in the year 1620 landed on the famous Plymouth Rock as they were escaping religious persecution in England and the Netherlands.

On the neighboring peninsula of Shawmut in 1630, the town of Boston was established. History was etched there from the beginning into the land of America by its historical prologue of The Tea Party, an uprising of the citizens of Boston against the taxation of imported tea, organized by the Sons of Liberty in 1770. That was followed by the Massacre of Boston, when British soldiers killed five of the uprising rebels claiming their liberty.

The first convention of the American Congress convened in September 1774 in nearby Philadelphia with thirteen participating colonies, and the seeds of revolution were sown into the fabric of Boston citizens as well, followed by the battle on the neighboring Bunker Hill.

Boston is an important international seaport and center of outstanding and re-nown schools and universities, established by initiation of the "Boston Brahmins" in the seventeenth through nineteenth centuries.

Boston also started the abolitionist movement (1831) for liberation of the slaves. In the nineteenth century following the Potato Famine, Irish emigrants came in droves, and later Italians and other papists, Poles, Slovaks, and Hungarians showed up. In the early years, these "foreigners" had difficult times and were persecuted as religious minorities.

The first Latin school was established in Boston in1636, and later in 1861 the University of John Harvard and Boston University were founded. Today Boston is educating 250,000 students a year, and dailies such as *The Boston Globe* and *Boston Herald* are among the most prominent and influential newspapers in the U.S.

But look, we were just landing at Logan International Airport, where in the exit hall our sponsor, Dr. Frederica P., was waiting for us with a lovely bouquets of summer flowers. With a warm and welcoming smile, she handed over the flowers to her "krasna" (beautiful) Judy. Dr. Frederica P. had come to the airport with her friend Jody, and so two ladies were welcoming us and our two children. It was a joyous reunion with many hugs and kisses, as our last meeting with the doctor had been about eight years ago in Slovakia. Our children, in their fashion-able European attire, were the centerpiece of attention of those two childless ladies. Frederica was still very crispy at her age, and she took command of our disembarkation. Eventually we took by an airport trolley our luggage to her Ca-dillac, and she drove as to Brookline, the first suburb adjacent to downtown. She lived there in a nice, two-story, Victorian house, surrounded by a small garden, where she settled and had her private practice as well. We were taken to her ele-gant living room and to a dining corner where a prepared dining table was ready for our first American lunch. She had a female servant and cook, who was assisting us during our lunch.

Frederica could not believe how Robert our son had grown up to be a hand-some boy. She had not met our daughter Patricia while in Slovakia in the mid-sixties, but Pat's nimble disposition and vivacious smile and her lively, hazelnut eyes enchanted our hosts.

We spent a couple of hours with our most esteemed and dearest friend and enjoyed her after-lunch coffee and cake. We shared with her and Jody the high-lights of our story, or odyssey, of our emigration from Belgrade to Boston. Around 4 P.M. we had exhausted the particulars of our story and answered all the questions regarding our misfortune, and great luck as well. Then Frederica took out from her desk our dossier with the communications between her and my professor at the Children's Hospital, my future boss. She already had all the documents and information about my family and myself within the framework of the International Fellows Program and that we would be living with the families of two physicians from the Children's Hospital Medical Center. That stay should introduce us and should be instrumental with the uneventful accommodation to the American way of life. It was a well thought out arrangement that would help us to get accustomed to that new way of life, especially for us coming from a country behind the Iron Curtain, where the Cold War was still raging on full throttle.

We returned to the Cadillac loaded with our belongings, and Frederica drove us into one of the side streets off the main artery in Brookline, the famous Boylston Street. A green streetcar was just passing by, and we noticed its unusual shape and a singular antenna, again a new novelty for us. Frederica drove us to the entrance of the huge family home of Dr. Richard Feinbloom and his wife, Debby, and their three children: Joshua, Aaron, and a daughter, Deborah.

From the house, right away a young lady of the house sprinted out — Debby — a tall, pretty brunette with hazelnut eyes and a large chignon of dark brown hair and a svelte frame. Right away she cordially embraced my Judy, our two children, and me as well with a cheerful "Welcome to our home!" Debby introduced herself to Frederica as well and thanked her that she was so gracious to bring our family into her home. But Frederica did not come in with us inside the house, as she amicably said her goodbye to us and handed over to me her business card and remarked, "I will call you tomorrow."

The house of the Feinbloom family was spacious and looked huge in our "eyes of refugees," with a half acre of luscious, green garden. In the back of the house was a large patio with a tile floor and a set of comfortable rattan furniture. The main space was for the children's playground with a slide, swing, and a path of sand for some creative play or a lark.

Debby took us right away inside and to the second floor, into "our" two rooms, with beds for all of us and a bathroom. What a luxury, the thought passed through our minds.

We tried to master the two intriguing telescopic windows, which ended with a bump on my head. We had indeed a large space available and all the comfort, where we could at least, for a week, unload all our traps and bric-a-brac, the hallmark of haunted refugees.

We refreshed ourselves and washed our hands and then climbed down to a large living room on the first floor, which had a dining area and a social corner with a large, leather sofa and matching easy chairs. From the nearby kitchen, equipped with all its Western technology, an enticing smell was emanating toward us rather encouragingly.

Debby guided us and offered me and Judy an easy chair, and the children were entrusted to their oldest son, Joshua. He took Robert and Patsy first to the garden, but with the heat of the day, the children returned to the air-conditioned children's playroom with lots of toys and enormous chaos. Our children — as we learned later — were astonished and did not know what to do in the pandemonium of things. But as children always do, they managed to develop a nice friendship while playing with Joshua, Aaron, and Deborah as well, despite all the tumult of toys.

In the living room, we offered Debby a beautiful, handcrafted, wooden fruit bowl with a copper intarsia mosaic pattern with inlaid copper wire around the edges of the bowl. It was a masterpiece of our native folk culture from the high mountains. Debby took the bowl and put it, with nonchalant indifference, on the dishwasher grill and said, "Thank you very much." My wife and I looked at each other, but there was not a hint of derogation in Debby's gesture, rather a hint of unfamiliarity with the function and value of the precious and esteemed European artifact.

Debby offered for us different types of drinks or cocktails, like a Bloody Mary, gin fizz, or gin and tonic — a "terra incognita," or an unknown territory, for us — served in crystal glass, either on the stem or in a wide tumbler. Those drinks were then in social vogue in that society. We squeamishly asked for only a drop of whisky with soda, and then we clicked our glasses with Debby, and she again warmly welcomed us into her home.

Suddenly in the afternoon, her husband, Richard, showed up — a tall athlete with a generous, rusty brown tuft of hair, dark brown eyes, and a warm expression of his demeanor and welcoming smile. He greeted us into his house very generously, and we tried to reciprocate his appreciation and his welcome with our deep thanks to both. We were thankful of their generosity, as they offered us their hospitality and home in our precarious predicament. Richard quickly poured himself a large shot of whiskey and took a big gulp following his busy day.

We had to then again repeat our story of our flight, or emigration, to Richard, since he was interested in more details of the invasion of our country and the unforeseen political collapse of the regime with "a human face." I tried to be specific as much as I could to satisfy his curiosity. He expressed his astonishment. How had we managed to face all the unexpected hurdles after the invasion in August 1968? It looked so that we received from him an enormous acknowledgement for our courage and struggle for our future freedom.

At that moment, the domestic gave to the lady of the house a sign that dinner was ready, and Debby invited all of us, and the children as well, to the festive table, where the children sat on the lower end of it. The dinner was really a feast. It was our first juicy, American rib steak prepared on a barbecue grill, a novelty again. It was really a great culinary treat for the hungry stomachs of the émigrés. We had to be able to adroitly handle the special sharp knives, which looked to us like daggers. Yet these "daggers" cut easily through the thick steak as its tasty juice poured across the cut. The juice was sometimes bloody, another rather unusual first. My wife cut some well-done pieces for the children, as they were somewhat bewildered by the unexpected bloody exhibition. A soothing coleslaw followed, complimenting the piquant steak very well. A spectacular Idaho potato, with its elongated shape and baked in its skin, was served in tinfoil, slashed along its lengths in its "fly" and primed with a dollop of thick sour cream with chives. Another wow! There were also some other vegetables available, but we just stuck with the potato — yum, yum. As the Irish, the potato was also a Slovak main staple on our dinner table in our native land. The children had their soft drinks, and we were offered an American Budweiser beer. In a while a dessert followed, the quintessential brownies, with a dollop of ice cream, a treat that our children enjoyed enormously. Coffee followed amidst lively conversation, where I was the main speaker and interpreter while the pleasant smile of my wife was a complementary and charming ingredient. It was a great dinner, a Lucullan feast indeed, as it was called in Roman times.

The children went to the playroom with Joshua, Aaron, and Deborah to have some fun in a menagerie of new toys while we went to the living quarters, where the practical Richard portrayed for us the real reality we would have to face.

We had two weeks as a family to make all the arrangements so that on July 1, 1969, I would be able to report to my new chief, Dr. Alexander S. Nadas. Dr. Nadas was well-known as the "boss" who steered his Department of Pediatric Cardiology as a "military battalion," and I had to be ready as his new "fellow soldier."

First of all, we had to find an apartment for the whole family — something new, quite unusual, and unfamiliar — in a foreign country. Yet I had to have a base for the family so that I could concentrate on my new job in a different language and a new "modus operandi" in medicine. We would have to have an apartment and purchase some furniture, and Richard suggested that I could purchase some used furniture from the departing fellows who just had finished their training. He suggested to go to the tall building adjacent to the hospital, where the residents resided, and they advertised on a bulletin board at the entrance of the building the available furniture. It was all new for me, and weird as well, to have to chase some used junk. There was yet no time for tribulation or procrastination, and I had to dive in straight ahead into the "new ocean" and its practical matters and start to swim under my own banner. I had to roll up my sleeves, clench my teeth, and fight for my family and myself and assert myself in a new world.

It was obvious that we would need a car to commute to the hospital and drive to some supermarkets or stores.

Fortunately I had my international driving license from West Germany, which was validated by the Department of Motor Vehicles in Boston. A millstone fell off my mind.

The next day, we left the children at home under the supervision of the domestic. Richard went to his work at the Hospital, and Debby rolled out her Cadillac from the garage, and our odyssey to find a real estate agency began. It was a rather bewildering experience for me and my wife. We had saved some money in Germany for unforeseen expenses; unfortunately the exchange rate in those times was four German marks for one U.S. dollar. Consequently our savings shrank to a quarter of what it had been. With Debby's help, we eventually found an agency that gave us its advice to go to the suburb of Brighton to an agency that was renting apartments for physicians and their families from surrounding hospitals. Indeed, Debby took us to the neighboring suburb of Brighton, where the agent took us to a small but nicely secluded park, where four two-story houses stood and were available for families. The agent showed us a nice, two-bedroom apartment on the second floor, with a sizable living room, a smaller bedroom, and a small third room — an alcove for the servant with a nice view to the green garden.

There was a fully equipped kitchen with electric stove and oven and a washing machine and drier. Wow. Surely we never had had or fathomed to have such a technology. Right away we rented the apartment for one year. The next day, I was chasing for some used furniture, and I purchased from a fellow a king-sized bed. Then, with some luck, I purchased from a Resident a used but nice Danish set of furniture, that is, a sofa with two nice easy chairs and a beautiful, oval-shaped coffee table of teak wood. With Debby's help, we transported the furniture with her Cadillac in two rounds to her garage. In addition we purchased for Patricia a baby bed at Sears and some other items for our household, chosen by my wife.

Since the apartment was empty before the date we would move in, the agency gave us permission to move in our furniture before our move in on July 1, 1969.

At the end of that tumultuous week, a large Cadillac with its back open showed up at our house, and somebody rang the bell. For some mysterious reason, I went to open the door, and to my surprise, I was now facing a smiling, blue-eyed, enticing blond lady, who introduced herself. "I am Prue Rosenthal, and I came to help you to transport your furniture to your new apartment in Pama Gardens in Brighton." I was speechless in that unexpected situation, and in my embarrassment, I invited the lady into the house as the best solution to clarify the unforeseen matter.

Prue was the wife of an Attending in Pediatric Cardiology at the Children's Hospital Medical Center who later turned out to be my good friend. At the Department, the news had spread through the human wireless that I would be a fellow at the Department, an émigré from Czechoslovakia who could need some help.

Prue offered her generous help as a "biblical Good Samaritan," as she just had shown up at the Feinbloom house on her own initiative. We were really moved by her generosity, as she never had heard about us till then, and she had offered us her unexpected assistance. I quickly introduced Prue to Debby, but the two "doctor's wives" new each other. They rolled up their sleeves and, to our bewilderment, started to transport our luggage and bric-a-brac to her Cadillac. We joined them immediately and loaded the car and transported all our belongings to our new apartment in Brighton. We returned to the Feinbloom house in an hour, and Debby invited Prue for a coffee and a friendly chitchat. With Prue and her husband, Ami (Amnon), we remained good friends for years to come.

On the last day of our sojourn with Debby and Richard, we departed with feelings of eternal thanks for their warm welcome to that new world, their unselfish and generous help, and their advice and introduction to the American way of life, which was totally different, like in an "upstairs-downstairs theater," from our life behind the Iron Curtain.

Debby was very kind and took us for the second week to live with a second family, where we would stay a week before getting on to fly on our own wings and be literally on our own.

The family of Dr. Richard Robb was of Irish descent. Richard was the Physician in Chief and head of the Department of Ophthalmology at the Children's Hospital. They lived in Brookline as well, not far from the Feinblooms' house.

At the entrance of the house, we were welcomed by a tall, slender, blue-eyed, quite fetching young woman, with a short cut of black ebony hair. Lucy looked very appealing, being about the age of my wife. Her husband, Richard, was at home on that Saturday, a handsome, tall athlete with black hair and eyes. He welcomed us with a friendly smile. The couple had three children: the youngest, Erica, was about the age of our daughter, and the boys were somewhat older. We lodged on the second floor as well, in two rooms and a spacious bathroom with all its amenities for comfort.

After the initial welcome and expression of our sincere gratitude and their goodwill to accept four émigrés from a different world, we presented them with our small gift: a beautiful ball carved from a light wood with an ornamental copper hem on the edge of the artifact. Lucy and Richard were thrilled by the enchanting piece of art, and they placed it into their glass vitrine.

We were happy to see their appreciation and visible joy for the present of an original woodcarving of our native folk art.

As we were seated in the living room, we had to repeat again our gruesome story, which, to our own disbelief, had started almost a year ago. The Robbs were well-informed about the invasion of the Warsaw Pact Armies into Czechoslovakia, but they had not fathomed that 150,000 citizens turned out to be political refugees. Lucy and Bob were shocked by our story and expressed admiration for our temerity to leave our home and our country and strive for our freedom.

At the dinner, the conversation was vivid, full of questions regarding the narrative of our odyssey, and they could not fathom facing such a grim turn of events. Richard then asked me about my academic qualifications and was quite impressed that I had been awarded the Alexander van Humboldt stipend.

The whole next week was quite hectic — what to procure or buy for our new "home sweet home" and at the lowest price possible. I will start my job in few days, and I wanted to have my family secure and comfortable. But what about my transportation to the hospital?

Then again Frederica came to our rescue. One of her patients, an older lady, wanted to sell her used Cadillac. Her son, a middle-aged gentleman, showed up at the Robbs' house with the car. When I looked at this huge car of dark green color, I was quite intimidated by its size. The car had an automatic transmission, of course, and the gentleman put me right away behind the driving wheel, but I felt quite uncomfortable with the monstrous machine. Yet the gentleman prodded me and showed me the gear lever and explained the letter D was for driving forward, P was for parking or neutral and R was for reverse. Quite simple but totally new for me. He continued, "Why don't you try it, doctor?" My adrenalin shot up with my blood pressure. I put the gear lever to D, pushed the gas pedal, which was also enormous, and we moved forward. It seemed to go well for a while, but at the first corner, I almost hit the edge of the pavement and almost scratched the car. My instructor was jolted in his seat at that moment and was concerned that I would damage the fine car. We continued to drive the car for a short while, and then we returned to our home. I thanked the gentleman for his help and patience and remarked that I would let him know about my decision. The price for the car, well-kept by the old lady, was only five hundred U.S. dollars, very enticing indeed.

The next day, I called up Frederica and thanked her for the unique offer of the car, which was in excellent condition and had an enticing price. Yet as a "greenhorn" in the U.S., I was afraid to drive such a huge car, and it would give me quite a stress driving every day to my work, with some risk as well, to face such an everyday task. I thanked her for her care in such a generous way!

The next day, we drove with Lucy in her Cadillac to an agency with smaller, perhaps European, cars. It was an Italian allegedly respectable dealer who had been in business selling cars for over twenty years. There I accidentally noticed in his parking lot a Renault 16 sedan in beautiful Bordeaux color, which I'd seen in Germany. It was love at first glance. The car looked brand-new — at least for me — with a nice, black upholstery. It had an automatic transmission and a rather large trunk. The dealer claimed that the car was brand-new, as the speedometer indicated only a few miles. We agreed on the price, and with the purchased car, I followed Lucy in her Cadillac to her home as a proud owner of the car. Coincidentally it was the same brand of Renault our beloved Bobby was; thus my bias was self-evident.

Later I went to the official Renault dealer for its six-month checkup. After the checkup, the technician informed me that I had purchased a used car and the speedometer had been rewound to zero by somebody, probably the dealer. The car had been used already for five thousand miles. It looked as if an émigré would not take advantage or cheat on another émigré unless he was from the Italian Calabria.

One afternoon, still as guests at the Robbs', I took a quick shower. Around the bathtub, a plastic curtain was hanging. As I started to take the shower, I placed the curtain on the outside of the bath tub. Suddenly my wife ran up to the second floor and started to pound on the door of the bathroom. I did not know what was going on, but she yelled at me that the water around the tub was seeping down into the kitchen. Oh you "dumkopf" (dummy), but it was obvious that my intelligence and the law of gravity had totally let me down. I was very embarrassed by the accident, and I am sure that Sherlock Holmes would have sarcastically quipped in his reprimand, "That is elementary, Watson! How come you did not know that?"

It was again a new experience, since we were used to taking a bath in the tub and not the shower in my native country. But Lucy was very forgiving, and she just took a "port-wish," wrapped a towel around it, stood on a chair, and wiped off the water from the ceiling. She patted me on my blushing cheek and just quipped, "Forget it, Zoltan. Everything is in order." Perhaps I was not the one and only who had that faux pas.

On Friday evening, Robert came home from the hospital in a mischievously good mood. In the large dining room, the dining table was prepared for our farewell dinner. The children were dining in the neighboring room. The next day we had to move into our new apartment, to our new "home sweet home."

A New England surprise was prepared for us, and a huge lobster from Maine was the main course. We regarded it as an expression of their magnanimous hospitality and their warm friendship in our precarious predicament.

As we were seated around the dining table, Lucy, with her charming smile, tied around our neck large, paper bibs to protect our clothing or neckties. On the bib, a large, red lobster was prominently printed. It was a real novelty for us and the first lobster for us in our lives.

Suddenly Lucy showed up from the kitchen with a small serving trolley, and on it were the large, flat serving plates for the humongous red lobsters that were rolled in as well and served for everybody. Wow! We never had seen such a monster! In my youth, I had seen only small crayfish, which my cousin pulled out from the holes on the banks of the Rimava River in Slovakia. But these? They were the really monstrous cousins of the small midgets of which I was acquainted with.

Every one of us was served with a huge lobster and, on the side of the plate, special cutlery, or perhaps special "weapons," were available that should help us get to the choice meat from the claws and tail of the huge lobsters. A pair of heavy scissors or pincers were available with a special, narrow fork with three prongs and a small hammer to crush the claws of the beast. On the front of every plate, a small, crystal bowl was filled with a golden, melted, salty butter, into which the bites of the lobster should be dipped, to appeal or "bring out" its taste.

On another large plate, golden-colored corn cobs were offered. A special fork had to be thrusted into each end of them, which served also as a holder of the cobs. In the middle of the dining table, a delectable wicker basket was filled with rolls of golden cornbread, with their mild sweetish taste, indeed delicious. We just did not know where to look on that picturesque, culinary "abundance." Wow!

In elegant crystal goblets, a golden-colored, light chardonnay from the vineyard of Saint Michel of Washington State was served. It had an enticing, lemony bouquet and a very pleasant taste. To start the dinner, we clicked our glasses for our better fortune in the future, full of hope and happy cheers. In the midst of a cordial conversation with those friendly and pleasant people, we forgot for a moment all our concerns and tribulations. Then Lucy and Robert had to show us their "forte," technique, and experience of how to use all those utensils to attack the large claws and tails of those humongous lobsters. Fortunately we were rather adroit students, and following their advice, we broke the shells of the claws, and with the slender forks, we redeemed the pink, jelly-like meat, dipped it in the salty butter, and tasted it for the first time in our lives. It was indeed a choice delicacy, tender and delectable. In combination with the corn rolls, it "tickled" our taste buds, giving us a symphony of sweet and salty savory perception. It was really something special! A cool Chardonnay was an appropriate compliment to the delicacy. Very soon we were greasy from ear to ear, to the amusement of our hosts. Yet we continued in our "fight" with the corrugated tails of the magnificent beasts, rewarding and tasty morsels which we indeed enjoyed. All along in a uplifted mood — mediated by the Chardonnay — a vivacious, cordial conversation blossomed during the memorable evening. It was a magnificent and enjoyable dinner, and its memories are still dear to us.

The next day with heavy heart, we had to say goodbye to our dear friends amidst of lot of hugs, tears, and good wishes. With their help, we packed up our last bric-a-brac and moved into our new apartment, where the used and battered-up furniture was starkly staring at us. As we suddenly remained alone in our "new home," the harsh reality hit us right in our stomachs. When we looked around and saw the heaped-up and battered furniture, worn-out luggage, and all the shabby bric-a-brac, my Judy started to bitterly cry in her desperation and grief as she recalled our brand-new condo with our elegant furniture in our native land. The children were bewildered as well, looking at their distressed mom, and I had tears in the corners of my eyes as well when I realized that we were indeed looking like some gypsies from Romania.

I embraced my dear wife and tried to calm her down, and as the best solution to the drama, I packed up my family in our new car and took them for a Sunday lunch at the neighboring McDonald's. The juicy hamburger with the refreshing Coke and a dollop of ice cream seemed to do the trick, and our mood somehow improved. A timid smile showed up on the face of my wife, and the children chimed in.

On return to our new home, we had a pleasant surprise in the afternoon when our guardian angel Frederica and her friend Jody showed up and brought for us a standing lamp for our living room, which had a nice umbrella with some spring flowers on it, and some useful pots and cutlery as well, and some nice blankets from Mrs. Fleischner, so far unknown to us, the wife of a professor of radiology at Beth Israel Hospital in Boston. The two ladies offered us their time and help as well to take us to some department stores to purchase some necessities for our new home.

I jacked up my courage, and we all went on that Sunday afternoon — quite bizarre for us — to the Sears, open on Sunday afternoon. We needed a bed for me, so we purchased for my small room a Castro Convertible folding iron bed and a small writing table for "my study!" If the Emperor Franz Joseph could sleep whole his life in an iron bed, so could I! The iron bed had just one major drawback, that my knees frequently hit the sharp iron corner of the bed and triggered tirades of choice cursing in my native language, which fortunately nobody understood. There were some items for the house as we finished our shopping spree with the ladies.

In the bedroom, we had "inherited" a king-sized bed that my wife and our son, Robert, could squeeze into. We had no bedside tables or night lamps, and the new baby bed was set up on my wife's side. I was in my cubbyhole with my iron bed next to the kitchen.

In the living room, we were facing a shabby sofa and two easy chairs covered by a worn-out beige fabric. The oval coffee table of teak wood was well-preserved and the "jewel in the crown."

It was now very handy for us that the stores were open on Sundays, and on weekends we could purchase some blankets, sheets, pillows filled with plastic foam (we used to have down), towels, or whatever else was needed, and my practical wife was in her element as the commanding captain. Of course, everything was very spartan, modest, and explicitly "proletarian."

Finally we had to fill up our fridge and the cabinets in the kitchen for a week, since my family, without a second car and without a driver's license for my wife, was "grounded" from Saturday to Saturday.

My wife tallied all of her necessities and ingredients on a list, and we drove to the closest Stop and Shop and purchased all the groceries and needs for our first dinner in our new home.

My wife could indeed make miracles, and in a short while in her culinary sorcery, she could prepare a tasty and scrumptious dinner. We were dead tired, depressed, and ate mechanically and in silence. Only our faith and hope gave us strength for a better and brighter tomorrow! Nevertheless, before our bedtime, we thanked our Lord for all the gifts and blessing we had received and tucked in our children for our first night. The soothing and blissful night and the subtle breeze from the garden took us to the realm of our dreams, that we were in a promised land where the impossible would turn into possible.

The next day, a bright and shiny Sunday woke us up. The sun enticed a happy smile on our children, and everything turned out to be happy. They were in their new pajamas, happily stomping and bouncing around only as innocent children can.

My wife was quickly on her feet, and soon the enticing smell of ham and eggs electrified everybody around the table in the kitchen. Wonder bread did wonders for the children with its soft texture with a blueberry jam — yum-yum — followed by warm cocoa. A strong American Folgers coffee was the high point for our first breakfast. Everybody was now ebullient and happy after the cheerful breakfast when the family was together, and in the bright sunshine, our confidence and hope readily bounced back. Not far away from our house, about a half a mile, stood a beautiful, neo-Gothic shrine, almost a miniaturized copy of the French cathedral in Chartres, which in its almost white sandstone glared its beauty in the morning sunshine.

We came to this cathedral as refugees from a very faraway land to express our heartfelt thanks and gratitude to the Almighty for his protection on our first holy mass in the U.S. We wanted to give thanks for all the unforeseen and unexpected help from strangers as human beings, totally unknown to us, who, guided by Him, offered us their unselfish help and solace and were at our assistance in our time of deep distress. Yet our hearts were still heavy, longing for our parents, the dearest ones, for their love and support at that heavy time, when we felt lonely and rather alone.

Despite occasional despair, the most important thing was that the whole family was together and healthy and blessed and that we would be able to lay the foundation to our new home and future. With great humbleness, we tried to put down our roots into this land of freedom, and this shrine remained our important scaffolding and spiritual support during the whole year we lived in Brighton.

On July 1, 1969, in the morning I drove with my new car to the Children's Hospital Medical Center, as it was officially known, on Longwood Avenue in Brookline. It was an integrated institution of the University of John Harvard (Fig. 27). In the basement of the hospital, I parked my car.

The Children's Hospital was one of the best and most renown hospitals for diseases of children in the U.S. and in the world as well. Originally it had been established on July 20, 1869, by a military surgeon from the Civil War, Dr. Francis Henry Brown.

Two years before establishing the hospital, Dr. F.H. Brown traveled crisscross Europe and gathered the newest information and the best advancements in medicine from the top-graded hospitals and institutions in continental Europe. He then transplanted that knowledge and experience to the U.S. to the so-called "South Boston" on Ruthland Street, where he opened up a Children's Hospital with twenty-two beds. In 1903 the hospital was integrated to the University of John Harvard (established in 1636) as its teaching institution for pediatrics, pediatric surgery, and other subspecialties. The pioneers of the institution evolved to be the surgeons, as William Ladd and his chief resident, Dr. Robert Gross, in 1938 performed the first heart surgery in the world on a child, who tied off the so-called "ductus arteriosus botalli," a congenital remnant or connection between the left pulmonary artery and the aorta, the main vessel of the body. Dr. Sydney Farber was the first in the world to treat childhood leukemia, and Dr. John Enders received the Nobel Prize when he isolated the virus of childhood poliomyelitis, followed by vaccination of that debilitating disease. Other Nobel Prizes followed by Dr. Daniel C. Gajdusek (1923), whose father originated from Slovakia (Smrdaky) and his mother from Debrecen, Hungary. He graduated from the medical school of J. Harvard in 1946, and from pediatrics he switched to study the mystery of slow viruses, like kuru, which brought him the prestigious award.

I entered that "sanctuary of medicine and science," and the elevator took me to the third floor to the Department of Pediatric Cardiology. There Peggy, a middle-aged, tall, blue-eyed and blond secretary, welcomed me and escorted me to a small, neighboring lecture room, where the fellows now sauntered in, one by one. These were the "chosen" physicians who had been accepted for training in pediatric cardiology for three or four years of training. For each academic year, a group of about five fellows was regularly assigned.

Suddenly the door opened, and into the lecture room entered *the* Dr. Alexander S. Nadas and his associate, Dr. Donald Fyler (Fig. 28). The "boss" was a tall, somewhat-corpulent man in his late fifties with a prominent Roman nose, penetrating, chestnut brown eyes, and on his scalp, his hair was somewhat thinning and getting gray at his whiskers. We all rose from our seats as he greeted us with a smile and his "welcome, fellows." In short he briefly outlined for the following year the program, where the beginners, or the "greenhorns," like me, would start our training from scratch. In each year of the training, the fellows rotated in different subspecialties of the program, like clinical patient care of the Department on the floor. That followed the training in the diagnostic laboratory — cardiac catheterization — or the division for irregular heartbeat or arrhythmias, succeeded by the department of cardiac pathology of congenital heart diseases, led by the world-famous Dr. Richard Van Praagh, and then training in the research lab on animal models, usually dogs. It was a time-honored, complex teaching program, with its emphasis on the teaching within the departments, led by the experienced teachers of the individual programs.

I was the only one from Europe, especially from Eastern Europe or, more specifically, from the Soviet Bloc countries. It was obvious to everybody in the group that I was a refugee from Czechoslovakia (by the way, where is the country was the obvious question) after the invasion of the country in August 1968 by the Red Army. That, of course, was my private matter! I had the impression that, in age, probably I was the oldest among the "greenhorns."

After about an hour of instruction with Dr. Nadas — as everybody addressed him — he pointed out that our assignments were listed on the bulletin board in the secretary's office.

It was well-known that the professor had had to struggle hard through his own thorny and difficult trajectory as an émigré in the late thirties from Budapest, Hungary, till he achieved and reached that prominent and unique pedestal of his, as one of the founders of the specialty of Pediatric Cardiology in the USA and in the world. He led, or perhaps commanded, his department as a "Hungarian captain," as his style of "reign" was marked by his heavy Hungarian accent, even being in the U.S. for over thirty years. At work, everything had to work and be snappy — no jokes unless they were witty and to the point.

At the end of the conference, I was the only greenhorn to be invited to the small office of Dr. Nadas. There the main wall was decorated by a copy of the graphic of Pablo Picasso's *Don Quichote de la Mancha*. The choice of the *Don* was not incidental, but rather intentional and was related to the "Don" of that office, a Don of a new age, represented by the "hidalgo" or lofty knight in his kingdom, where he did not have to fight (he already had) with the formidable — real or imaginary — windmills.

Dr. Nadas invited me to his office with a cordial, "Welcome, Zoltán." (He was the only one who pronounced my first name with a prolonged á, as in Hungarian.) He let me sit down in front of his large desk, full of papers and books. On the side, there was a sofa of leather and two easy chairs, mainly for guests, while by definition, I was only a trainee or Fellow of his Department. He was very friendly and first asked me about the condition of my family and our accommodation and inquired about the story of our tortuous emigration. Perhaps it reminded him of his own flight from Budapest in 1938. He quickly switched then to impersonal and professional matters. He kindly and calmly explained to me, in his heavy-accented English, that according to his best consideration and judgement, he decided that I would spend a year in the cardiopulmonary research laboratory, doing research in pulmonary circulation in children with congenital heart disease. He argued, appropriately, that I had to improve and polish my English, with which I wholeheartedly agreed. He further explained that in all U.S. hospitals, all communications were conducted in medical jargon or their abbreviations or parlance, which, at that time, I would be unable to master. Such a mismatch could cause some stress and misunderstanding, and I could jeopardize the smooth conduct of the Department and make it less effective.

I was somewhat taken by surprise by this development and felt disappointed or let down, since as a "real Slovak," I thought that after my yearlong experience in West Germany in a pretty good center, I knew "almost everything" in pediatric cardiology. As I learned later, I did not! Or perhaps he wanted that way to challenge my potential or intelligence. I never learned what was on his mind.

Following that discussion, Dr. Nadas expressed in great sincerity that he and his wife, Elisabeth, would be honored if we accepted their invitation for lunch next Saturday, and he passed me his business card. I realized that the exceptional invitation was perhaps related more to my exceptional predicament as an émigré and coming from the neighboring country to his native land. I regarded it as an honor and a gesture of his humanity and perhaps a psychological encouragement or underpinning, since he knew well and was well-aware of the dicey, insecure, and precarious frame of mind of a refugee. I expressed my sincere gratitude for his magnanimous kindness for me and my family.

Yet all our discourse remained always on a strictly professional level and all in English, and he did not utter a word in his native Hungarian even though he knew that I was fluent in it. Our personal relationship remained on a professional level as well during my all four years in Boston.

When our conversation in his office came to its end, Dr. Nadas called on his secretary and asked her, "Peggy, please take Zoltán to the cardiopulmonary laboratory." There everything had its order, and it was snappy. The professor shook my hands and wished me good luck in my work.

I departed with a lot of misgiving and insecurity. Peggy, a kind and professional woman, gave me an encouraging smile while we trotted to the first floor of the neighboring, red-brick building. There she introduced me to the head of the lab, Dr. Mary-Ellen Wohl, an Assistant Professor in her academic rank. She was a real professional and good theoretician in the field of pulmonary circulation.

Mary-Ellen, as everybody addressed her, was a tall, rather stocky woman in her forties, a daughter of a professor of medicine. She had a broad, oval face with soft, blue eyes and an open, welcoming expression, and a large chignon of light, hazelnut-colored hair. Her family was of German origin. She presented herself as kind and a matter-of-fact professional when she offered me a seat in her small office on the side of a large examining hall, full of different machines and contraptions rather unfamiliar to me. At first glance, it looked all too technical to me.

Mary-Ellen presented and projected for me the research program of the lab, where she studied the circulation of the blood in the vessels of the lungs. The heart was actually an intimate bedfellow of the lungs, she explained, "embraced" by them from both sides in the chest, where the heart offered its propulsive energy to the blood flow across the lungs while the lungs, in their breathing cycle, sucked in the vital gases, such as oxygen, and exhaled the ghastly carbon dioxide, thus the body could function. Hmm, I said to myself, such an intelligent and lucid interpretation of such a physiological "intercourse" of these two organs (except the reproductive ones) I never had heard.

My intellectual curiosity was certainly stimulated by this nimble and masterful presentation of her program. After a half an hour of presentation, Mary-Ellen rose in my eyes and was elevated at least to the "third floor" of my assessment. I realized, and it was obvious to me, that my previous European training in pediatric cardiology was shortsighted or limited in its scope and was rather mechanical, oriented only on the heart. Indeed the field of pulmonary circulation was an unknown territory, or was rather Greek to me. The only task for me was to get immersed into the physiologic relationship of pulmonary circulation and its intimate symbiosis with its pulsatile pump, the heart. It looked to me that we from Europe were rather narrow-minded regarding the symbiotic conception of the heart and the lungs.

The lab itself was a rather large hall, like two joined classrooms, full of different machines, as spirometers of different kinds and many rubber hoses attached to different bombs filled with oxygen, nitrogen, and helium. Only the exercise bicycle was familiar to me.

Three technicians were working there under the supervision of the chief tech, Mary, a young, nice blond with blue eyes and a very pleasant and cooperative disposition. The other tech was Eleanor, and the next was Ann, an adroit black girl with round, dark eyes, full of wit and ready for mischief or a good laugh. All the girls had a bachelor's degree and Mary a master's degree in medical science.

It was obvious that I was the only "apprentice" there, and I would have to learn a lot, but fortunately I was eager to do so. All the girls were ready and willing to share with me their medical and technical prowess and knowledge, and each of them had some special knack in the field, ready to share.

The Department had a young secretary, Janett, a cheerful blond, who organized and planned all the examinations and tests of patients, and she typed up the results of the tests on her Underwood typewriter and expedited them to different divisions. Her office was frequently the center of conversation, banter or gossip, in our free time.

We were examining the abnormal distribution and exchange of the ventilation in the lungs of children with different congenital (born) abnormalities of the heart. With different flowmeters and spirometers, we examined the volume of the ventilation and their proportional gas content and their flow through bronchial tree (windpipes) with the help of inert gases such as nitrogen and helium, which did not mix with oxygen or carbon dioxide, but labeled them in proportion to each other.

We also measured the so-called alveolar ventilation of lungs in these children, that is, the ventilation in the smallest unit of alveoli, where the respiratory gases were exchanged. We used for that the so-called "body box," where the patient sat and breathed in a closed space: a box. By using an oximeter attached to the tip of the finger, we assessed the oxygenation of the blood in cyanotic, or "blue," patients at rest or exercise. The Department had an excellent professional standing and was visited by a number of respiratory physiologists from other countries as well, like Dr. John Pheelan from Australia, who spent some time in our laboratory.

In 1970 a new chief took over the department, Dr. Denise Strieder of French origin and temperament with solid professional credentials. She was the wife of

Dr. John Strieder, who in 1937 at Massachusetts General Hospital, performed the first heart surgery, the ligation of open ductus botalli (a vessel-connection between the left pulmonary artery and the aorta, which had not closed at birth) on an eight-year-old black girl, who unfortunately died of infection in the era when penicillin was not available.

In the research lab, I spent a whole year enriching and polishing my English and enriching my vocabulary, but most importantly I published with Dr D. Strieder two professional research papers in two peer-reviewed journals, the *American Journal of Physiology* and the *European Journal of Physiology*, about the gas exchange in "blue" children with right to left shunt (abnormal mixing of blood through a hole in the heart).

That year was, for me professionally, easier without night-call duties. and my weekends were free. We used that free time to enrich and improve the quality of our family life in our living quarters. In the department store Lechmere in Cambridge, we purchased a beautiful music box of a fine German trademark Grundig with a radio and record player that could automatically change the records. The frame of the music box was from a fine, red-brown cherry tree, which to today serves us with its music and is an ornament in our living room. We also purchased our first-ever color TV of RCA brand, which enriched our vocabulary and the cultural content and pleasure of our family. The children enjoyed and had great pleasure from programs like *Sesame Street* and *Mr. Rogers Neighborhood*. The evening news enriched our English and polished our articulation and pronunciation. It also started our trajectory and narrative of American democracy, our education of virtues of a free citizen in contradistinction to the indoctrinations in Marxism-Leninism in our native land, after the WW II part of the Soviet Bloc.

We were living rather modestly but in freedom, and we were content and rather happy. Nobody was breathing down on our necks with some kind of ideological mantra, and we weren't being pressured by some secretary of the Communist Party. My yearly salary was small in 1969, seven thousand dollars, and my "boss" gave me one thousand more than the other fellows, as I had a family and was a political refugee. It was the lowest salary I ever received, but I was part of the "eclectic elite," or chosen minority, of physicians at Harvard, where any fellow would work for half of it if he or she could.

Saturdays were also the days for grocery shopping, as we turned to be part of the American consumer society. We crammed our one and only car went to the First National supermarket. Our weekly budget for groceries was twenty dollars, and a gallon of gas was ten cents. My *very* practical refugee wife listed all the items necessary for her kitchen and household. One time we saw a peculiar-colored item in a jar labelled Jif. Yes, it was the quintessential American peanut butter. As we learned by experience, the most important feature of it was that it stuck to your teeth and palate. Hence you barely could swallow it. Our children were the first pioneers who liked it on the soft Wonder bread with Welch's purple grape jelly. We also learned that the "goo" was highly nutritional with its high protein content and was very healthy. My wife soon followed, but I was the last apostle who eventually liked very much that "stuff."

Fortunately my wife was an inventive and excellent cook, who during our time in socialism, had made culinary miracles almost from nothing. Here she had the choice and plentitude of items, and we were all very happy that on our dinner table, our native and familial dishes were served.

We liked to live in a neat environment, and our present milieu needed a lot of upgrading. On an early weekend, we all rolled up our sleeves, and with sandpaper and scraper, we scratched off and removed the old, dirty polish from the parquet in our living and bedroom, and on the cleaned floor, we applied fresh beeswax, with it pleasant fragrance and color. Hence it made the rooms look like new.

My wife was displeased by the worn-out upholstery of our sofa and the two easy chairs. We went to the local Sears department store and purchased an elegant fabric for the upholstery, with a checkered pattern of patches of sea-sand alternating with light brown stripes. It was a very appealing decorative design. My Judith, in two weeks, changed the upholstery on the sofa and the two easy chairs with the help of our four-year-old daughter, Patsy. The result was an unbelievable, picturesque beauty and pleasure. We had now a brand-new Danish set in our living room, with a polished teak coffee table. I was very proud of my wife and little daughter.

In September our son, Robert, was matriculated into the prestigious Mount Alvenia Academy, a private Catholic school where, according the customs in New England, all the students had to wear a uniform of blue jackets, light gray pants, and black shoes. A checkered tie was mandatory. For us as refugees, the yearly tuition was reduced to half. Every morning a small minibus came to our house at Pama Gardens in Brighton to pick up our boy. We were very happy that our son could attend such a prestigious primary school.

As the fall sneaked in with its many-colored foliage of New England, we tried cautiously to make short trips to the nearby Blue Mountains — our first expedition to the countryside — for some outings for our children. We drove also to the beach at the beginning of Cape Cod, where on sunny days our children could play in the sand or run and stomp around (Figure 29).

Out of curiosity, we started to slowly put out feelers or search in Boston or its vicinity where perhaps there was a "lost soul," or a refugee from our native country. Through the church, by accident we learned that there was supposed to be a priest around from the old country. The word of mouth went both ways, and one day somebody knocked on our door, and in the door stood a young priest with a wide and cheerful smile. He was a handsome lad with chestnut brown, curly hair and vivid blue eyes. He suddenly introduced himself, "I am Francis Venutta from Moravia, a westward neighboring land to Slovakia."

He was a researcher of tropical diseases at Boston University Hospital, who had previously spent some years in Africa, where he got infected by malaria, which was now under control. He remained our esteemed friend for all the years we stayed in Boston.

Another weekend Frederica came to check on us, and she brought her friend, Mrs. Fleischer, the wife of the professor of radiology from Beth Israel Hospital. She brought us a large strawberry sponge cake, for the children some toys, and also some used pots for our kitchen and two bedside lamps. She was a very gracious and cheerful gray-haired, brown-eyed older lady with roots in Vienna, Austria. She had emigrated from Austria in the late thirties with her husband. She suggested that her husband would be interested to meet me. Indeed I visited the huge neighboring Beth Israel Hospital, where I met the professor. He was glad to see me, as a kind of a "messenger" from the old country of his, which was just a stone's throw — across the Danube — to the neighboring Slovakia, my native land. We remained in a cordial conversation for over an hour, and he wanted to know "everything" that was happening around his native Vienna. He handed over his business card and offered me his counsel if I needed anything. We said goodbye to each other, or "auf wieder sehen" in his native German. I did not impose on him but was heartbroken to learn that the kind gentleman died suddenly of a heart attack in his swimming pool.

Once in a while on a weekend, we took the streetcar on the neighboring Boylston Street, and we rode on a rickety green streetcar to the center of the town. For the children, it was something new and great fun. In the Downtown on Beacon Hill, we could admire the majestic and glistening golden dome of the Capitol, the seat of the commons of the state of Massachusetts. Since 1798 it had been the seat of the government and the Supreme Court. It was a commanding, historic building in the style of secession (Figure 30).

Not far away since 1743 stood the famous Faneuill Hall, built in Victorian style. It was first a market, then a place for congregations of citizens, where they presented their civic and political views and concerns regarding the city of Boston (Figure 31).

The children wanted to see the famous museum of Mme Tussaud with all their replicas and statues of political and civic figures, such as George Washington, Abraham Lincoln, and the other Founding Fathers, all life-size. It made a great impression on our son.

In a neighboring exhibition hall, there was an exhibition of an artist who displayed his pictures made out of fabric from textile. We were very impressed by this original, delicate, and subtle technique and the mode of presentation of that kind of art, which tried to display a colored version of the theme in textiles of different colors, like in a painting.

Suddenly I was startled and took a pause before a picture, and in my surprise, I stood there almost petrified. The picture seemed to present a copy or seemed like a twin picture of a Renaissance manor house in Bratislava, the capital of Slovakia, called *The House of the Good Shepherd*, standing opposite of Saint Martin Cathedral. I was mesmerized and could not resist having this picture, which reminded me of my city, my land, my former home. It was an emotional rapture at first site. I rather foolishly, on the spur of the moment, purchased the picture in a fit of nostalgia, to the surprise and amazement of my wife. I wanted, needed, or yearned for a piece of my past in my new home. This picture, *The House of Good Shepherd* remains a precious relic in our home to this day (Figure 32).

In my present assignment and work at the cardiopulmonary lab, I was not isolated from the main group of the fellows. Dr. Kalim Aziz from Pakistan likewise spent a year in the lab and then joined the regular clinical fellowship program. He was a very bright and intelligent fellow, and the next year, when we worked in the clinical part of the program, we published together a research paper in the prestigious *British Heart Journal*.

During that first year, I participated regularly in the weekly diagnostic conferences of the Department in conjunction with the cardiovascular surgeons. Before the surgical intervention or correction of a heart problem of the patient, all the diagnostic findings were presented by a fellow, and after an animated discussion, the decision was made about the best surgical approach and solution of the problem. It was a totally new approach in the training of budding cardiologists and was impossible to receive in Europe. My intellect was like a dry sponge that eagerly sucked in all the new information and novel approaches in diagnostic and surgical solutions of the presented problem. The fascinating advantage of those intellectual interchanges was that it was an absolutely democratic process where a student of medicine, a resident, or a fellow had an even and open forum and appreciation for his question, view, or contribution.

On another weekend, we went to see Cambridge, the "Mecca" of scientific research. We visited the Harvard campus, entering through its famous and orna-mental wrought-iron gate, behind which, on a pedestal, sat John Harvard in time-honored attire, and close by was the Memorial Hall of the university (Figures 33 a, b, and c). But the whole campus was a huge one, and we could only track through part of it. We also visited MIT (Massachusetts Institute of Technology), founded for technical research in 1861 at the beginning of the Industrial Revolution (Figure 34). Then we strolled through Cambridge and its red-brick buildings on a sunny Saturday, and on the main square in a delicatessen store, we noticed in a shop window an advertisement with a picture of mountains, entitled "Tatra bryndza," a soft sheep cheese from Slovakia. We could not believe our eyes!

As we later learned, you can buy everything in America — you just have to find it. We hastily entered the store, and right away we bought a full carton of our "bryndza," right out of the mountains of the High Tatras in the middle of Slovakia. My wife prepared for us a wonderful and tasty dinner of original dumplings with our native bryndza. That night everybody was really happy!

Slowly but surely, the colder fall furtively lurked into our neighborhood despite the mostly sunny days. On many leaf-covered trees, such as the appealing maple trees and their pentagonal leaves, the sun sparked of a golden pigment that started to penetrate into the fabric of the green base of the leaves, which slowly, imperceptibly, began to change to golden and rusty streaks, ending in a carmine or ruby red cover on the corona of the trees. The change was gradual and dispersed, and in the golden sunshine, the whole tree displayed a panoply of bright colors of foliage so well-known in that part of the land on the East Coast. A load of visiting tourists came at that time to New England to be delighted by the symphony of colors of the changing foliage at that time of the year.

We joined the crowd as well, driving from Boston along the sea to Cape Cod and its principal town of Princeton. While the picturesque foliage was enticing on the trees, in the surrounding huge fields of land, the pumpkins of different sizes and colors and shapes were becoming ripe, ready for their harvest.

We were coming close to the high point and the climax of the autumn sea-son with its harvest, at which time the farmer was bringing home all his colorful produce from the fields, with all his thanks to the Lord for the bounty of the year, to celebrate his blessings on the most important family feast of the year, the Day of Thanksgiving.

In our native land, we were familiar only with a pale tuber of squash at the end of the summer or a pumpkin similar in shape and size to its American cousin, but with a green, white-striped skin. It was used only for baking in an oven, mostly in winter as a delicacy.

The local pumpkins were in this land of freedom somewhat more upright, boisterous in their shiny skin of deep yellow, as if they had been dipped into orange juice. They were used for soups, sauces, or cakes, and the children could create a jack-o'-lantern ghost with a candle lit in it to be displayed in a window, or they could put the jack on a stick to scare small children. These customs were all fresh and new for us, seen for the first time by our children and us as well.

In another outing, we discovered a variety of other pumpkins, smaller in size, called squash. These could be lemony yellow or green with stripes and a pedicle on the top. Here the top could be circularly carved away, and the pulp inside the squash could be used for a tasty soup, spiced up with different seasonings. The soup could be served inside the hollow squash as a very elegant way to present such a delicacy. My wife was eager to try it out in our family and then for our guests.

Part of the autumnal ornaments of the land were also the grotesquely shaped yellow and green gourds, with their multitude of white "warts." These served as our picturesque decorations in our living room in the fall, placed into an ornamental wooden bowl from our native country, a custom we maintain today.

Almost at the beginning of the winter came the intimate and most celebrated day of Thanksgiving, the day when all families of the land gather together to give thanks for all the blessings and gifts they received through the year. We had to turn to quick studies of this celebration, connected to the Native American Indians, who helped the Pilgrims survive the first harsh winter. The Pilgrims came from England and the Netherlands, and some of them landed at Plymouth Rock in Massachusetts in 1620. These Pilgrims were not prepared for the harsh winter on this flat seacoast. The Wampanoag tribes were the ones who offered their corn, pumpkins, maple syrup, and meat from dear or boar, which saved from starvation these newcomers. Therefore, since 1674, the fourth Thursday of November was proclaimed as the day of Thanksgiving in the land of George Washington, and in 1941 Congress confirmed it.

About a week before this day of festive celebration, we received a telephone call from an unknown gentleman, who introduced himself as Mr. Chisholm from Wellesley. He surprised us with his call and invitation, by which his family would be very happy and honored if we could accept their invitation to celebrate Thanksgiving in the circle of his family. We were taken by surprise by this unexpected invitation, as without it we would just have spent the day like any other day, in our humble apartment. We never learned how Mr. Chisholm learned about us, as the "new pilgrims" of this blessed land.

On that very day of thanks, we drove to Wellesley and arrived in front of an elegant, one-story building, or perhaps a manor house, with a line of columns at the entrance, surrounded by a manicured garden with trimmed shrubs and some white birch trees. In the entrance, Mr. Chisholm himself showed up in his genteel disposition with his warm welcome. He was a middle-aged man in his mid-fifties, lean in his physique with heavy glasses, soft, brown eyes, and well-groomed hair with a gentle parting on the left side. He cordially smiled, coming up to all of us. He was flanked by his younger, fetching wife of blond coif and hazelnut-colored eyes, who right away hugged my wife and our children while we shook hands with our host. We were dressed still in our festive European attire, at the beginning perhaps a bit formal, but we quickly felt at ease. Our hosts invited us to their living room, where we met their three children, somewhat older than ours. Robert, our son, who was attending school, was already fluent in English, and Patsy, his sister, was not much behind. Hence the communication between the kids was perfectly smooth. The lady of the house called on her housekeeper, who escorted the children to their quarters full of toys and books.

We were seated in the elegant living room of the local banker and were offered an aperitif of whisky and soda. On an elongated, oval coffee table in a large, flat bowl, large shrimp were presented, hanging on the rim of the bowl, which was full of ice cubes. In a side dish, a scarlet red, bright Heinz ketchup was inviting us to dip in the shrimp and try a new delicacy called shrimp cocktail. It was really a tasty hors d'oeuvre of the New World, especially liked by my wife, but I never fell in love with these sea "beasts."

Simultaneously the conversation was vivacious and *again* with many questions regarding our dramatic and adventurous flight or emigration. I repeated the story so many times that I could recite it even in my dreams.

But our hosts were very interested in the many details and minutiae of our unforeseen adventure. The lady of the house was very interested in the resilience and the tenacity of our children. How had they really coped when they suddenly had lost the safety and the warmth of their home? All were very good questions, but I don't really know if I satisfied our generous hosts with my sometimes-perplexing answers.

In a while, we were invited into a large dining room, decorated around the large dining table, and on the walls were yellow and orange garlands and festoons, and the vases in the room were filled and embellished by the flowers of the season, like mums, matching in color the decor of the room. The dining table was covered by an ornamental tablecloth of damask and delicate china and silver. Intertwined between these, neatly scattered fruits of the season decorated the tablecloth, like dainty berries or hazelnuts and a few colorful maple leaves touched by the rust of the changing season and some little gourds as well. The whole dining table in the living room gave the impression of a colorful, rustic reflection of the autumn family feast. Around the table, all the members of the two families were seated — the smallest, our daughter, was flanked by her mom just in case help was needed.

The housekeeper showed up with a large, oval tureen of fine china with an ornamental cover and a large, china ladle as well.

Mr. Chisholm took the hands of his wife and offered his other one to me. His wife took Judy's hands, and we all joined our hands in a ring, or wreath, of the whole family. Then the landlord bowed his head, and everybody joined in while in a pious voice, the landlord expressed the Almighty his thanks for all the gifts that his extended family were going to receive and thanked us that we could celebrate that Thanksgiving with his family. It was a very moving experience for our first Thanksgiving and was not without our wet eyes. That expression of deep humanity and hospitality toward us, an unknown family, at those trying times for us, gave us hope that we should continue in our toil to establish our new lives in this new country of opportunity and freedom.

At the end of the prayer, we shook hands, the ladies exchanged hugs, and we wished to each other a happy Thanksgiving, amidst the cheers and giggling of the children. Now the banquet could begin indeed.

After a tasty pumpkin soup with croutons, which warmed up our tummies and tickled our taste buds, it raised our appetite for the next course as a short pause followed. Then the housekeeper brought in a huge, golden-colored turkey on a large, porcelain plate — the first one we ever had seen in its shining and glistening glow, that is, in its full "beauty." We were all astounded by its majestic size and "grace." As we learned, the turkey had been roasted for couple of hours, repeatedly basted with aromatic gravy, and its temperature controlled by an electrical thermometer, which was announcing by red light that the turkey had an ideal texture and was ready. Indeed the crust of the turkey was golden brown and its skin delicately crunchy. From its outlet, the fluffy stuffing was bulging, composed of grounded giblets and soaked croutons in the gravy compounded by green celery and parsley to give rise to its piquant and earthy taste. Around the centerpiece of the turkey, a large plate of mashed potatoes was presented, and in smaller bowls, different condiments were offered, such as baked yams, green peas and beans with cracklings, pearl onions, cooked corn, and cranberry jam and relish. In a wicker basket, squares of golden cornbread were available with their pleasant, sweetish taste. A gravy boat of china offered additional gravy for each portion of the turkey. What a feast!

It was a view and a picture for a painter to depict, this rich, multicolored feast, like the Roman Lucullus table. We just did not know where to look at this portrayal of a gourmand's "abundanza."

At that almost majestic moment, Mr. Chisholm stood up and, in silence, pulled out a knife, almost a short sword, ready on his side and plunged it into the breast of that golden beast along its breastbone and cut a slice of white meat for everybody's plate, followed by a cut of dark meat from the plump thigh of the turkey. It was almost like a spectacle on the scene of a theater, where a Biblical lord was breaking and giving a portion for his disciples. Everybody sat in silence and followed that time-honored ritual of the family, like a votive offering. It was really a festive celebration and expression of thanks and received blessings of that family, which on that day gave its embrace and love to a nuclear family tossed out of its home and native land by a wicked event of fate.

Now the real banquet and happy dining could commence, where everybody could help themselves to complement the turkey with its tasty stuffing, poured over with the thick sauce from the gravy boat. And, of course, all the other side dishes were available, like mashed potatoes, a favorite of our children. All this went on amidst vivid and amicable conversation and cheers between old and young.

The crystal glasses were filled by our host with a pleasant and crisp white wine, advancing the mutual talk and amusement. The children were happily sipping their apple juice or a soft drink of their choice.

After an hour of mastering and enjoying the turkey and other goodies, we took a small pause from this magnificent feast. Then the housekeeper exchanged the plates for the presentation of autumn desserts, which she rolled in on a trolley (another wow for our children), like the classical pumpkin pie with a golden crust and its creamy stuffing, waiting to get a dollop of whipped cream. There was also a fruitcake available, and for the children, the time-honored brownies were the ultimate enticement, perhaps with a dollop of vanilla ice cream!

On the corner plate of the trolly in a bowl, a wild green jelly was offered. We learned that this was the classic American mint jelly, which was supposed to be the endpoint for the taste buds of the palate after the variety of sweet desserts. We looked with suspicion on this unknown mystery, and at least for now, we avoided it.

An aromatic "caffe arabica" joined this symphony of desserts, which at least for us was the climax of the magnificent dinner. Liquors or cognac were offered as well, but we graciously declined.

But the time was innocuously advancing, approaching almost 10 P.M., and it was time that, with a heavy heart, we had to say goodbye to this lovely family. Our hearts were full of enormous gratitude and thanks, as we had enjoyed our first thanksgiving in the U.S. amidst this welcoming family. Between many hugs, kisses, and handshakes, we left the house with great gratitude and a feeling of hope amidst this exceptional sign of humanity.

The next day, we did not forget to send a thank-you card to the lovely family for the beautiful celebration of the day, on which we were an integral part of their family. It remains a memorable jewel in the annals of my family, fulfilling Matthew's dictum (25:35-40): "I was a stranger, and yet you welcomed me."

After the last week of November, unexpectedly the first snow showed up when Richard M. Nixon was our president. December started boisterously in that Christmas season with great exuberance, something never seen in our land. Suddenly it dawned on us that it was a different Christmas season from the European "Advent" of piety and expectation of the birth of the baby Jesus. The season revealed the richness of the country and almost a hedonistic and boasting presentation of the affluence of a society never seen before. The stores and their shopwindows were packed with exquisite merchandize and ornaments full of glittering garlands, stars, jingle bells, and artificial snow, with the ever-present Santa Claus with his glittering sleds in tow with Rudolph the Red-Nosed Reindeer, who lit up the road for Santa's sled with his shining nose. The children were elated and joyous by the celebration of the season, but my wife and I were puzzled and somewhat confused. We were looking for the creche and the little Jesus in his cradle, which we could find, rather hidden, only in a corner of our church. Most importantly we couldn't really find it and adore it! The difference of societal, cultural, and religious values dawned on us with its full weight right then.

In our hospital during the season, there was an explosion of Christmas parties. I had never seen anything like that. In every Division on a different floor, there was a party prepared by secretaries and the nursing staff as the day was coming to its end. A classroom of the Division was always made available where the tables were shoved together for a long line, covered with white bedsheets, and on the top of the long table came the exhibition of all different delicacies, prepared at home by the ladies of the staff. There was fried chicken, wing or thighs, fried shrimp, and a plate of Virginia ham, where the marinade had also some sugar, making the taste of the ham more enticing. On the other plates, there were little cocktail frank-furters and spicy meatballs with toothpicks and ketchup alongside. There was a plate of different kinds of cheeses — a block of French brie, cheddar, gouda, em-mental, and others.

In the center of the display was large crystal bowl (Figure 35) filled with punch, a mix of champagne, white wine, and cranberry juice. After a cup or two, it was able to give you an awesome and memorable punch to your head. The guests were now roaming in and out in groups, singing and whistling "Merry Christmas" with lot of hugs and kisses between friends, and after tasting some of the goodies or having a drink, the groups could move to another party. When I saw that joyous and cheerful pandemonium, I thought these people were crazy or had lost their senses! Actually they just were having a very good time during that merry season.

For December 20, each Department received a special invitation for the Christ-mas celebration of the hospital from the physician in chief to the large amphitheater of the hospital. About two hundred doctors from all over the world who were there for training or research and all the physicians of the staff were invited. The "boss," Dr. James A. Janeway, who was known colloquially as Dr. Charlie, was the most respected and revered physician, with his Anglo-Saxon upbringing and his stellar professional career. He was a rather slim, medium-height, blue-eyed, and salt-and-pepper-colored hair gentlemen of a pleasant disposition. He was the quintessential gentleman of New England, and he had everybody's respect. Dr. Charlie was merrily swirling between his "flock," and to all the physicians, he expressed his wishes of a Merry Christmas.

I came to the lecture room somewhat late but with joyous expectations and curious excitement. The doctors, with their glasses in hand, were merrily buz-zing like in a beehive, and the mood was festive. On the top of the lecture room, there was a podium and a huge blackboard, which was filled with expressions of "Merry Christmas" in different languages. As I was walking toward the podium and mixing with many known and unknown colleagues, suddenly and unexpectedly Dr. Charlie himself appeared before me, and I was startled. He had a piece of white chalk in his hand, and with his inviting smile, he said to me, "Colleague, would you be so kind and write a Christmas wish on the blackboard in your native language?" I was surprised by this unexpected task, but I was looking into a warmly smiling gentleman's face. I quickly collected my faculties, took the chalk from his hand, and courteously replied, "Of course, Professor Janeway!" I approached the blackboard, and in my native language, I wrote in capital letters, "Prajem Vám veselé Vianoce," or I wish you a Merry Christmas. I returned to the professor with the chalk, and he smiled at me and remarked, "Thank you very much, colleague."

It was and still is an unforgettable event in my professional life, which I cherished as a precious little diamond in my years to come.

During that Christmas season, our first in Boston, I did not forget my professor and colleagues at the Children's Hospital in Bratislava behind the Iron Curtain, and even though my salary was rather meager, I sent the hospital a volume of *Pediatric Clinic of America*, which was concisely addressing the newest information in Pediatric Cardiology, thus they could beef up their theoretical acumen. This Christmas custom of mine I repeated for the following fifteen years, when every Christmas a package of a book was sent to my professor. I tried to recompense the department of pediatrics for the tragic loss of myself and other members of the team in cardiology.

As Christmas arrived, Boston was covered with fresh and crispy snow, and the shopwindows of the stores of the town, with their glittering jingles, projected a joyous, exuberant atmosphere. The happy and merry mood was in the air, and everybody was nice and jolly at that time.

In that season, the generosity of the people and neighbors was exceptional. My wife was surprised when a unknown lady rang the bell at our apartment and offered a gift for the children or a beautiful fruitcake. As it eventually turned out, it was the spouse of a colleague from roentgenology, who occasionally dropped off her baby for babysitting in our house. And other known and unknown ladies showed up and brought some goodies or toys for our children! We were astonished by the kindness of these people as they "loved thy neighbor," an unknown experience in the society behind the Iron Curtain.

Eventually my wife and I started to prepare for our first American Christmas in this new land of ours with some anxiety and unease. Christmas Eve was, in our family for decades, the holiest evening of the year, when we celebrated and anticipated the birth of the little Jesus. I purchased a smaller Christmas tree and decorated it with colorful and glittering glass balls, noticing that they were made in Bohemia (today the Czech Republic). We usually used candles of different colors for our tree, where the "dancing " of their flames gave some intimacy or mystery to the evening. Candles were forbidden, and we used colored, electric lights, which were more glittering and appealing. A particular ornament, a candy wrapped up in glittering foil, was an obligatory part of the decoration, which was commercially available in Europe. My wife was able and eager to skillfully improvise. She wrapped around the candy a fine, silky, white paper, three inches long. In the middle, she wrapped the candy in its white cover into a glittering tinfoil, which she twisted tightly around the two ends of the candy. The ends of the white wrapping were fluffed up with scissors like an open flower. It made the impression of white snowflakes scattered over the tree. When I came home, I could not believe my eyes.

My wife was able, by some magic, to prepare our traditional sauerkraut brine with dry mushrooms, with its tarty taste reminding us of the biblical exodus and its bitterness of slavery and life without Christ. She procured the pricey dry porcini from Switzerland, as these were our traditions. As a side dish to the sharp brine, the famous boiled Idaho potatoes were served.

The Christmas table was covered with a tablecloth with ornamental patterns of the pine tree and its branches. In the middle, a red candle was prepared to bring the Christmas light into our family.

On a small table, all the sweets were displayed, thanks to the generosity of our friends, known and unknown. My wife also prepared our own biscuits, made of yeast-leavened dough sprinkled with sweetened poppy seeds, according to ancient Slavic pagan customs. A bottle of white wine from the known winery of Mount Saint Michel was cooling in the fridge. Christmas Eve happened to be on Friday, and I was somewhat busy at the hospital. I was leaving the research lab at 5 P.M., and the snow just had started to fall in large flakes, descending on the festive town.

I was trying to find a fish for the Eve, a symbol of Christianity. In the old country, it was usually carp, raised in large lakes in Bohemia, which so far we were unable to procure.

I was feverishly circling with my car at the dusk of the white Brookline and went from fishery to fishery, but it was too late, and those shops were already empty. But I had to find a fish at all costs for our Christmas table on that first eve in our new home! In my anxiety and unhappiness, I got into an emotional spell and was almost panicky as I was chasing the fish, as the snow was heavily falling. In my desperation, my emotions took me over, and my eyes welled up with tears while I banged on the steering wheel. I had to find "that beast" for our first Christmas eve! In some remote corner of Brookline in a small fishery, I find a small, quivering sea bass. I grabbed it, paid for it, and ran out of the store. I returned to my car almost shaking, and my nerves just had given up. I started to sob in my car in my relief of my incomprehensible distress. In spite of all my wretchedness, eventually I was relieved that still we will have this symbol of Christianity on our festive table. That was my own dramatic beginning of our Christmas in that new country of mine!

I quickly recovered as I was driving home rather fast at that late hour, and coming home I was still somehow shaky, yet victoriously I presented my wife with my Christmas "catch," no matter what kind. My wife noted my emotional upset, and she tried to calm me down, patting me on my cheeks: "See, you found your fish." A glass of Budweiser calmed me down eventually. My wife then quickly fried the tiny pieces of that fish, a portion for each of us, and as a side dish, a choice potato salad was prepared and on the table, with a beautiful, freshly baked challah ready as well. The feast was almost all set to start Christmas Eve.

I took a quick shower, and we all dressed up in our festive attires — our nuclear family — and sat down around the festive table, where the flame of the red Christmas candle was gently flickering and glowing around us, and the little, golden bell from Tübingen started the holy evening, tenderly intoning, "Silent night, holy night, All is calm, all is bright…holy infant so tender and mild, Sleep in heavenly peace."

A short poem that I remembered, I recited in a trembling voice:

"On the glorious feast of the birth day of Christ, our Lord,

I wish all of you my dearest from God:

Happiness and abundant blessing of his Almighty!"

Our tears, my wife's and mine, were amply flowing over our cheeks, and our small children were baffled seeing the distress of their beloved ones, but a warm smile from their mom eased their anxiety.

At the same time, my wife and I were, in our minds, in our "old home" with our parents in the old country and the old lyric, "I'll be home for Christmas…if only in my dreams" resonated in our tortured minds (Figure 36).

We realized then very well that we were on our own, four of us in our small ship on a huge ocean.

Just before we started our festive meal, I quickly thanked God for all the gifts we were going to receive, in the name of the Father, Son, and the Holy Spirit, and the celebration of Christmas Eve could continue.

The first course — warm, tasty sauerkraut soup with mild, boiled potatoes — lifted our spirits. The fried fish, with a golden-brown crust, was very tasty even though everybody could enjoy only a small piece of it. It was well-complemented with the piquant potato salad, which gave the satisfaction of a homey taste and brought satiety for all. The light white wine, with a pleasant, fruity bouquet, lifted our mood; the children had their bubbly soft drink and were delighted by all the sweet delicacies and the expected gifts wrapped in ornamental paper. Those were, of course, rather modest. Patsy received from an unknown benefactor her first Barbie doll and Robert some exciting books about the first Pilgrims. I surprised my wife with a bottle of perfume, and a colorful necktie was my surprise. We were all thankful that we were all together, healthy, and the gifts were an additional bonus of trimmings. During our merry and joyous Eve, we were all happy that we had found our new habitat and enjoyed our intimate environment with our lovely children. As the intimate family time in our happiness was passing quickly, at 11 P.M. we dressed up into winter clothes and boots, and through the snow-covered suburb, we trudged to our nearby cathedral for our first midnight mass in America. The holy shrine was packed and in a festive mood. The altar was quasi-embraced by fresh, green Christmas trees spreading their fragrant aromas of their resins. The pine trees were richly decorated by stars from dry, woven straw, and their golden hew was emboldened by the yellow glow of the flickering lights of the snow white candles. The white chrysanthemums on the altar underlined the beauty of this eerie and festive presentation.

The church was brightly lit, full of the faithful in festive and mysterious expectations of the celebration of the birth of Jesus, symbolized by the presence of the ornamental creche on the side of the main altar. It was icy cold; everything around was white, majestic, and somehow eerie.

The mass was ostentatious, with the congregation of the group of priests in their golden attire and a flock of altar boys in their crimson robes. The faithful huddled together, singing with joy the beautiful Christmas carols that we were hearing for the first time in our lives. We could actually follow the lyrics from a sheet as they were celebrating the birth of the Good Shepherd, just like in the old country. It was heartwarming to have a common thread and a spiritual consonance with our new fellow parishioners. The whole church was quivering from the chorales of the faithful in the harmony of the joyous carols. The last song was the ever familiar *Silent Night, Holy Night*, and the old tune summoned a joyous smile on our faces, like meeting an old friend, while the chromatic chords of the organ gave a subtle background to that Christmas anthem.

It was a moving finale of the celebration and mass. The faithful were happy and joyous as the biblical profession was fulfilled; hence the people were hugging each other — known and unknown — and wishing each other a very merry Christmas. It looked to us that amidst all those people and their goodwill, we were now part of that flock, and we had found our community and home. After the mass, our children wanted to pay homage to the newborn Jesus, and we took them to the manger and the scene of nativity. There they could see the baby in the manger with Mary and Joseph on his side as a donkey and heifer kept him warm with their exhaled heat. The shepherds were coming down from the mountains, singing, "Jesus Christ was born. Alleluia!" Our children were joyous and happy to see the enlightening scene of the nativity with the baby Jesus. We gave them some quarters for their offerings to the church. As the coins dropped into the metal box for the collection, the coins clinked loudly, to the amusement of our kids, and piety got intertwined with the joy of a child.

We were soon tracking home after the midnight mass through the snow. Fortunately our Pama Gardens were not far. The night was peaceful and white, and we soon fell into a sound sleep while dreaming of our Christmas in our native home.

The next day, we invited our Moravian friend, Father Venutta, to spend the day with us and bring his blessings into our new home. He was happy to accept our invitation. After that nice young man knocked on our door, he entered our home with his enticing smile, wishing us a blessed Christmas for our whole family. We welcomed that first guest of ours in our home and warmly shook his hands (Figure 37).

Father Venutta brought some small gifts for the children: a book about the first Pilgrims for Robert, and Patricia received a red hat, like Little Red Riding Hood, and matching warm, red mittens.

My wife was busy in the kitchen, trying to please our precious guest. The festive table was ready with a fresh tablecloth, embellished with green twigs on it. We all took our seats, and the Father began with his prayer and his blessings for our house and our nuclear family. Soon in the large bowl, the aromatic chicken soup, with its steam, was spreading its inviting smell while the golden rings of chicken grease were swirling enticingly on its surface. The delicate angel hair were floating underneath with the colorful rings of carrots and green leaves of celery. Everybody was cheerful from that tasty introduction, which fostered a vivacious conversation with this pleasant fellow.

As a main course, my wife prepared for Father Venutta a classical Wiener schnitzel fried to an golden crust, which the father had not seen for ages. He was very surprised and pleased by the delicacy, giggling in joy with a happy smile. As a side dish, homemade potato chips were served with fresh slices of cucumber salad, "blessed" with red, Hungarian paprika and speckled by black pepper, giving the salad its piquant zing. The cool chardonnay was already decanted in the glasses, and we happily clinked them for a happy "cheers."

The Father was elated by the Lucullan feast and the schnitzel, which reminded him of his home in faraway Moravia. The Father narrated his experience in African Congo as a missionary and physician, and the children were listening in awe. The cooling wine was a pleasant stimulus to the storytelling of the African adventures of the Father.

In the afternoon, we moved to our "rejuvenated" living room, where the renewed upholstery of the chairs, with their elegant beige cover, gave high marks to the "master upholsterer," my wife! Then the father, in that intimate ambiance of the family, on his own started to read the everlasting and timeless Christmas stories of the Christmas miracle while the children listened in transfigured attention to those eternal events of ancient times.

In that cozy family atmosphere, I was recollecting in my mind and recalling that many, many years ago, my dear dad used to read those stories to me and my sisters in that holy season.

It was really an intimate family ambiance in the presence of that servant of God. We had to realize and admit our tremendous fortune as a gift of destiny, that we had a roof over our heads and were lucky to find some new friends — even from the old country — and were getting part of a new community, which welcomed us in it with great love.

After a short while, my wife offered the guest a tasty coffee arabica and cocoa for the children with whipped cream available as well and different kinds of cookies and cakes from our friends. Our conversation continued about the destiny and misfortune of our old country. After a while, at dusk the father thanked us for our invitation and hospitality during the season, gave us his blessings, and departed with a cheerful smile and goodbye. We remained in touch with the Father for all four years we stayed in Boston.

On the first floor of our building lived the family of a physician from Japan who was also a fellow at the Children's Hospital, but at the department of dermatology. We met occasionally in the morning when we were rushing to the hospital or in the evening when we came home. The family had two handsome boys of similar age as our children. The children were the first to break the ice of communication, as they played nicely together in the garden. In the new year, there was tremendous amount of snow, so Satosi and Snow — as their names were — started to build a snowman. My wife offered a pot as a hat for the snowman, to the great joy of the boys, and a large carrot in his mouth, and the fun was universal. Suddenly the two boys pulled out a small sled from the shed, and the children pulled each other amidst of lot of fun, where Patricia turned out to be the main coachman.

Hence a friendship was born between my wife and the lady from Japan, a slender, pleasant woman with dark eyes and black, braided hair in a coif. She invited my wife for a "tea ceremony," when the green tea was served in a terra-cotta pitcher and cups.

It was for my Judy a new experience and a new meeting with the Far Eastern culture even though the two ladies communicated between each other mostly by hands and in some broken English. But the chemistry between the two ladies from two different parts of the world was positively enticing. A problem developed when my wife noticed that her friend could not pronounce the vowel "r," which sounded like "l." One day Michico invited my wife for a tasting of her Japanese rice, which was pronounced like "lajs." My wife looked up quickly in the dictionary and looked to the word of "lice" and was somewhat perplexed: "But we don't eat lice in our country!" When Michico offered her a ball of rice, the surprise was now on my wife's side. She apologized and took the rice home for her close "inspection." She soon realized it was rice cooked in simple, salty water, which was not to our liking and customs. She thus took the Japanese rice and unceremoniously dumped it into the dustbin.

But my wife, as a "real Slovak girl," wanted to show off to Michico our "lajs," that is, the "real McCoy." So she cooked our "lajs" in rich milk, placed it on an ornamental plate, sprinkled it with melted, golden butter and crumbs of dark, swiss chocolate, and with great pride, she offered it to Michico.

By chance Judy looked out through the window later, and in her bewilderment, she noticed that Michico had thrown out our choice "lajs" into the garbage can as well. After this cultural and culinary "exchange," the two ladies stuck to their broken conversation or gestures and a cup of green tea.

A pressing issue for us was a driver's license for my wife. Her teacher of English was mostly our son, Robert, who was now already fluent. He read and translated for her the driving manual, and Patricia pitched in as well. My wife improved her English and her communication skills through our friends, like the wife of a radiologist who had surprised us at Christmas with her fruitcake, as Judy had taken care of her son Daniel, where our Patricia was helpful as well. Those meetings of the two ladies ended up in daily conversations, very useful to my wife.

I was relentlessly working hard in the research lab and examining the children's pulmonary function tests from the department of cardiology, culling that data together and preparing them for my first publication.

While in daily contact with the team of colleagues and friends, I just by chance learned, to my astonishment, that if I wanted to stay in the U.S. and practice medicine, I would have to pass a licensure examination. I almost fainted hearing that stunning news. I also learned that every medical student who completed his studies and received his M.D. diploma had to prove his ability to practice clinical medicine to the state board in the state where he would practice his craft by passing a licensure examination of the state. That was all new and Greek to me!

The only solution was to roll up my sleeves, acquire all the books from general medicine and its subspecialties, and prepare myself for the exam in the state of Massachusetts. The exam was, as far as its content, similar to the ECFMG exam, which I had passed in Prague in 1967, but it was more comprehensive and detailed in its context. The examination also lasted twice as long as the one in 1967 — that is, it lasted whole two days. My friends who had passed that exam of "torture" earlier were very instrumental and helpful with their seasoned advice. It meant that after I returned home and had dinner and a strong espresso to give me a mental kick, I studied every day till midnight, at least for a year.

At the end of my first year, we decided to move closer to the hospital in preparation for me to work in the clinical part of cardiology with its night calls. At the end of June, we moved to a more spacious apartment on Saint Paul Street in Brookline in a nice house with a Victorian facade. The apartment was a modern, comfortable, two-bedroom apartment on the second floor. Behind the building, there was a luscious, green garden to play in for the children, and the street was well-kept and clean. On the corner of the street, there was a parish of Saint Paul with its church and school, which was very convenient for the children.

At the end of the month, I rented a pickup truck, and we loaded all our trappings and bags, and with some heavy hearts, we moved out of Pama Gardens, our first "encampment," and to our new home.

That spring our son, Robert, received his first communion, together with his whole class (Figure 38). It was a festive day for our family, and the church was embellished all in white, filled with parents celebrating that memorable day in the lives of the children. Our son followed in the footsteps of his father, now in the free world, where the faith of everybody was his free conviction and not his liability, as behind the Iron Curtain. There was no cover-up needed to hide going into church, as was the case with his parents, who were forced to be married in a church in secrecy in Budapest, Hungary. Our son, Robert, was baptized in secrecy as well, in a small, godforsaken church in a small town, and likewise our daughter, Patricia, was baptized under the cover of darkness in the Blue Chapel in Bratislava. Now in this county of freedom, everybody could freely practice his religion, without any cover-up or dire consequences.

From our new apartment, I had the definite advantage that I could walk across the luscious greenery of the park to the hospital on Longwood Avenue, where nearby the Harvard Medical School and its Countway library were located. It was only a fifteen-minute walk from our place across a bridge over a small brook in those idyllic and scenic surroundings (Figure 39).

About the same time in spring, my wife crammed her knowledge for the driver's license exam, a basic need in our circumstances. She took the streetcar on Boylston Street, with her two children as her "advisers," to the Department of Motor Vehicles. After her identification and filling out the necessary forms, she took a seat in a special, for her awkward, chair with a small, oval desk on its side. The children tightly clung to her from both sides among the crowd of people. Robert was her main translator, but Patricia pitched in as well. When Judy, my wife, was not sure of her answer, she turned to her daughter. "So Patsy, where should I put the cross for the correct answer?" She had a lollipop in her hand, and with its stick, she pointed to the right answer. "Here, Mom!"

The result was unbelievable, if not miraculous, as my wife received her driver's license, a great help for the life of the family.

On July 1, 1970, I entered the "promised land," or the "Mecca" of pediatric cardiology, under the command of Dr. Alexander S. Nadas (Fig. 28), who was really commanding his department like a Hungarian brigadier. Everything was running like a Swiss clock, and everybody had to be in "attention," not physical but intellectual. Each of us were one of the cogs in that no-nonsense cogwheel, where jokes were out of the question unless they were witty and to the point. If one of the fellows was interfering in the smooth cooperation of the Department, his fellowship was terminated at the end of the academic year, as it happened to a fellow who had come to the Department as a captain in the U.S. army after his assignment in Vietnam. There were no exceptions, and the working process had to run impeccably.

During the academic year, the fellows, after three month on the clinical floor with night calls, switched, at least some of us, to the division of pathology of congenital heart problems. It was led by the world-renown Richard van Praagh and his wife, Stella, who was of Greek origin. Those two eminent scientists established there an "exceptional museum," or collections, of hearts with different anatomic entities or diagnoses of the heart, and the specimens were kept in large buckets, immersed in formalin. It was something unheard of or unseen, at least for me. It was probably the best collection of these specimens, and it was also one of the most interesting rotations of the fellowship, which was fittingly complemented by the somewhat peculiar, if not bizarre, disposition or eccentricity of Richard.

With some excitement, I was looking forward to the diagnostic lab for cardiac catheterization, where I felt that I already had some fairly solid experience after two hundred studies in Europe.

The next rotation, for three months, was in the experimental lab, working on the samples of heart-lung specimen of a dog set up as a pumping machine. I never had had the opportunity to participate on such an "in vivo" lab work in my native land; hence I was somehow reticent or uneasy during the first sessions of that experimental work.

The rotation in the Intensive Care Unit (ICU) following a cardiac surgery was dynamic and exciting. There I met the famous Dr. Robert Gross, a handsome man of athletic physique in his sixties, with chestnut-colored brown eyes and a well-groomed, brown hairdo. He was walking, or "levitating," through the ward as a surgical "God," with only a few words or a quip at some patients' beds. It was he who, in 1938, was the first surgeon to perform heart surgery on a six-year-old patient.

In the afternoon, we were assigned to work in ambulatory clinics under the supervision of a younger attending, examining patients referred to our clinic by regional pediatricians. It was a rational, purposeful, well-developed program by Dr. A.S. Nadas that gave training and clinical experience to fellows in all subspecialties in pediatric cardiology.

I started my first year in fellowship on the clinical ward, where Dr. Bill Plauth was in charge as our attending. Bill was a muscular fellow (tennis player) with black eyes and heavy-framed glasses. He was a little emotional and easily agitated — some would say a little neurotic — but he was jovial, good teacher. On the floor, there were also with us the Residents of General Pediatrics, who rotated in cardiology during their training. The team was composed of six or seven doctors. I was the only foreigner from the Soviet Bloc. Some of my colleagues had the impression that I was from Yugoslavia. Consequently I gave some geography lessons about Eastern Europe and Czechoslovakia to them. For most of them, my country was an unknown country with a cumbersome name, and for others, perhaps, it was somewhat suspicious as well.

With some time, I gained some respect with my theoretical knowledge and clinical experience as well. We had on the ward a three-year-old sick little boy who was cyanotic (blue) due to his serious heart condition, a blocked valve (tricuspid) in the right side of his heart. Suddenly he developed a tachycardia (fast heart rate) over 200 beats/minute. The boy was close to a low-output heart failure or shock. Bill tried different maneuvers and medications as well, but the rapid heart rate was just stubbornly resisting to respond to any medication and stop. Suddenly I blurted out, "Bill, how come you don't try the medication called methoxamine, which by pressure reflex to the aorta has a good chance to succeed and stop the fast heartbeat?"

Then Bill blurted out, "What? What medication? I never heard about this drug." Bill was my boss; he looked at me with a great deal of suspicion. What was this Eastern fellow blabbering about? But Bill was open-minded in that predicament and called up the pharmacy, which confirmed my information that it was medically sound, and the pharmacist sent up the drug right away. Bill told me, "Zoltan, show me how you would do it." I replied, "Okay, let's attach the patient to the ECG machine," and we mounted the leads on the extremities and the chest of the little boy. We were surrounded around his bed by a group of Residents and nurses as well. Bill was visibly uncomfortable and nervous. I introduced a needle into the vein of the patient and filled my syringe with the "miraculous" drug.

I started to run the ECG machine, and the tracing showed a very rapid heart rate over 250 beats /min. I took the syringe and slowly injected the drug into the vein of the patient. The tension of the observing group was palpable. The heart of the little patient was, for a few seconds, still running its course and beating fast, but suddenly the recording of the ECG showed only a straight line, indicating that the heart had stopped beating. Bill wanted to resuscitate the patient, but I held his hand and almost exclaimed, "Wait!" Suddenly after a few seconds, the little heart started to beat in a regular, sinus rhythm, about 100 beats/min, and the patient looked relaxed, and his shortness of breath was relieved.

Bill was astounded but relieved and happy that the "Easterner" had taught him a lesson. From that moment, I received the nickname Dr. Methoxamine. We remained friends with Bill for many years even after I left Boston, and we still exchange Christmas cards to this day. During that clinical rotation, I published my research paper with Dr. Kalim Aziz in *British Heart Journal* about the phonocardiographic (sound tracing) changes of the pulmonary valve after the pulmonary artery was banded, constricted. We remain good friends with Kalim since he spent a year in the pulmonary research lab as well one year before me.

The diagnostic lab for cardiac catheterization (advancing a plastic tube into the chamber of the heart) surprised me because I had to learn by a cutdown — that is, by a small surgery to isolate a small vessel-vein in the groin of children — even though I was familiar and had experience to introduce the tube without surgery — that is, by a percutaneous way, developed by Swedish radiologist Sven Seldinger. But the Chief of the lab, Dr. Donald Fyler, an excellent specialist of his kind and a good-natured Irish man, taught us, the new fellows, to introduce the catheter into a vein by cutdown. But in short time, the Swedish technique to enter the vein through a special needle gained ground, and I tried to facilitate the acceptance of that method (Figure 40).

The next rotation was in the division of pathology to study the anatomy of congenitally abnormal hearts with the world famous but exceptional Dr. Richard van Praagh. When he lectured or explained a problem or issue — very lucidly — his presentations were interrupted by sudden bouts or outbursts of an infectious laugh even though there was nothing to laugh about. When you met him for the first time, you were not only bewildered or amused by him, but it could crossed your mind that something was wrong with him. At the same time, he was a highly intelligent and superb scientist, one of the best in his field, who developed a simple, but easily understandable, interpretation of the structure of the normal heart, the so-called segmental structure, or arrangement of the chambers of the heart. The heart, according to his theory, is like a three-story building, where on the top were the atria, followed in the middle by ventricular chambers with their outlet, the great vessels.

The rotation with Dr. R. van Praagh gave me a totally new perspective of the anatomy and physiology of the congenitally deformed heart. He was an excellent teacher, and with him we reviewed many of his specimens of the malformed hearts with his lucid, even though peculiar, presentation.

He usually "fished out" a heart specimen with specific malformation from the big, plastic buckets, put it on a working desk, and along with his bouts of staccato-like laughs, he explained in great detail and with attention to minutiae the anatomical abnormality, and we listened with great attention to his matter-of-fact commentary. It was an exceptional way of presentation, but it was very effective.

It was not rare that during lunchtime — where "time" for Richard was an esoteric element in his independent mentation —he put on his rubber gloves, took a specimen, and put it on his working table, still wet with formalin, while on the side of his table, he had his lunch, usually a bowl of green salad. With Richard everything was possible! Then he took a tweezer, and with great nonchalance, he pointed with it to a particular detail of the heart. Then he put the tweezer aside, took his fork, and put into his mouth a piece of the green salad while his eyes were already smiling, and suddenly he burst into one of his legendary laughing fits. As a result, we fellows started to laugh as well, and everything was "comme ill faut," or in perfect order, for Richard and us as well.

From this rotation, which I repeated a year later, I worked on a research paper about the spontaneous closure of ventricular defects (a hole between the two ventricles of the heart) after a surgical intervention, when the pulmonary vessel was encroached by a band. My coauthor was Dr. A.S. Nadas himself, and the article was eventually published in the prominent peer-review journal *Circulation*.

I enjoyed the rotation in the Division of ICU, where all the technology of the sensors made us aware and promptly projected for us the dynamic and quickly changing circulation after the corrective surgery. We were vigilantly following the function of the heart by continuously monitoring the ECG, the patient's blood pressure, his urinary output, and the oxygenation of the body, and while the patient was on a ventilator, he had continuously an oximeter on his index finger. It was all exciting and educational for me, where the ICU nurse was in the first line of defense or the "guardian angel" of the patient as she followed her patient with an eye of the eagle. The team work between the surgical Resident and one of us from cardiology and ICU nurses was excellent, the best I have ever seen in my career. Over the whole ICU unit, the Head nurse, or "the Queen Sally," was in charge, known as the "battle horse of the unit." Everybody had to behave and be in a good relationship with Sally unless he wanted to endanger himself like the French at Waterloo.

For the last rotation of the academic year, I was assigned to the division of experimental cardiology, where, in the early seventies, the lab was working on the problems of transplantation of the heart in children. The physician in charge was the affable, somewhat bold Dr. Grier Monroe.

The bulk of the experiments on the dogs were performed by Dr. Grant La-Farge, a six-foot-tall, lanky athlete with a graying scalp of gently curling hair. He was a remarkably handsome man, like a French artist from Mount Martre in Paris, with his dark brown, inquisitive eyes and very friendly disposition. He was very proud that in his veins, the blood of American Indians was pulsating.

He was very dexterous and skillful to prepare a heart-lung unit from an experimental dog. On it we studied and recorded the response of the heart to different stresses or loads. In the first experiment, my stomach started to act queasy when Grant first had to clean out the heart from all the worms and parasites from the heart of those stray dogs. But he just took his tweezers and nonchalantly fished out all the worms, as he would pick up a cube of sugar from a crystal bowl. He then attached the breathing tube of the dog to a ventilator for the oxygenation of the heart and then started to test the function of the heart at a fast or slow heart rate, at high and low blood pressure, or increased or decreased resistance to maintain the cardiac output.

That part of the experiments were interesting, but I had grown up and been trained as a clinician. Thus this subspecialty did not gain my appreciation and favor.

It was yet enlightening and very didactic in following the physiology of the stressed heart and its adaptability to different loads and resistances. With Grant I remained in a very friendly relationship for many years to come.

In the afternoon, I had an assignment to the ambulatory clinic, where I worked closely with the young attending, Dr. Amnon (Ami) Rosenthal, whose wife had helped us move our belongings during the first days in Boston. Ami was a handsome, six-foot-tall fellow with pitch black hair and eyes and a slightly swarthy complexion. He was a pleasant and appealing man. He studied the changes in the composition of blood and red cells — in shape and number — in children with so-called "blue" heart problems where their oxygenation was compromised by admixture of the "blue blood" into the "red blood." I tried with him to do some research in those children where their number of red cells turned high and posed a danger of thrombosis. We tried to lower the number of the red cells with an experimental drug, but because of prohibitive side effects, we had to terminate our research project.

With Ami and Prue, we developed a long-lasting friendship, and in later years when Ami was appointed as a Professor of Pediatric Cardiology at the University of Michigan in Ann Arbor. My wife and I flew in from New York for his "gala evening" and chipped in for his Foundation a thousand dollars. Then we again re-kindled our friendship with Ami and his gracious wife, Prue.

During my first clinical year, I had to finish my preparation for the examination for licensure in the state of Massachusetts, in addition to my everyday clinical responsibilities. I had to study night by night while my wife kept the front of my family safe and sound.

In January 1971, I sat with a group of about forty physicians from all over the world for two days in the conference room of the State Department of the State of Massachusetts under the watchful eyes of a group of proctors who swirled around us. I was already familiar with the structure of the exam since my ECFMG exam in Prague in 1967. We struggled again through two sessions in a day, lasting about four hours, in the morning and in the afternoon.

After two days, I returned home in the evening exhausted and just wanted to go to sleep without dinner. I was really groggy. My wife put me quickly to bed under the covers, and I immediately fell asleep without feeling her tender kiss on my forehead. I slept till noon the next day. The house was peaceful, and the children were tiptoeing around their dad.

I was professionally well-prepared, and in March I received the good news and the diploma of my license from the State of Massachusetts. That license from the prestigious state of science had the advantage that it was acknowledged or given reciprocity in some other states. We were very happy, and at the Hospital, I received a warm congratulations from the fellows, as well as a tap on my shoulder: "Good job!"

During the three years of training and research, it was in everybody's interest to present to our "boss", Dr. A.S. Nadas, the results of our research as a corresponding complement to our clinical work. I presented the results of my research to Dr. A.S. Nadas about the unexpected, spontaneous closure of the ventricular septal defect (a hole between the two ventricles of the heart) after a small surgical intervention, a snarling of the pulmonary vessel by a band. The "Chief" mused and reflected for a while and then suddenly remarked, "Hm, this is quite interesting and new. Finish up your research, Zoltán, and you will present it at the yearly conference of the American College of Cardiology in Chicago."

It was an unexpected jolt but privilege for me as well, but if the boss thought that my observation was innovative, important, and worthy of presentation, then there was nothing more important than finishing my research and presenting my final results to him.

The results of my research were presented to the whole Department in the presence of the boss. An animated discussion followed at the conference, where I had to defend my research thesis, but the results of my research held the line, and I received universal approval.

In a few weeks, our small group indeed flew to Chicago to the Annual Meeting of the College. Peggy, the secretary, secured our airline tickets and hotel accommodation. As the day of our departure was approaching, I started to be somewhat anxious that I, from a country behind the Iron Curtain, should make a presentation at the gathering of cardiologists from the whole world. Certainly I could not imagine it a few years before.

The conference lasted almost a week. The day before my presentation, Dr. A.S. Nadas called upon me and remarked, "So Zoltán, tomorrow morning at 7:30, you will come to my hotel room and will present to me your lecture."

During that night, I slept like a watchdog, lightly and vigilantly. In the morning, I dressed up in a freshly ironed, snow white shirt with a spritely blue necktie, navy blue jacket, light gray pants, and lacquered black shoes and knocked on the door of the room where Dr. A.S Nadas sat in his pajamas on the rim of his bed, expecting his disciple to be on time. I never had seen my boss in that garment, so I had to suppress my chuckle. But he was nonchalantly pouring his coffee into his cup while Dr D. Fyler, who was lodging with him, was just sauntering around as his "companion-kibitz."

"Come in, come in," I heard the boss say, and he let me sit down in a comfortable chair and remarked, "So Zoltán, shoot!" I presented him my lecture, which I previously had crammed, and the boss occasionally intervened. "Make here a pause, put some emphasis on that, and finish it with an elegant conclusion."

The boss was content, and at my departure, he patted me on my shoulder. "You have to trust yourself!" he remarked. "When you present something new, the other cardiologists will not have knowledge of it." He finished with, "Good luck!" It reassured me — in my anxiety — that my boss was trusting me, and I couldn't disappoint him.

In the morning session of the conference, more than a thousand physicians were present, and my blood pressure was rising with the approaching lecture. Nevertheless, when the President announced our lecture, I spritely climbed up to the podium. For a moment, I glanced over the huge conference room with all the experts, perhaps hesitated for a flash, but then resolutely approached the microphone, adjusted it for my level, and started. "Ladies and gentleman," I said in a measured tone with distinct articulation — my best — and in regular cadence. I portrayed the idea and the substance of my research. I narrated the essence of the process and the methods, stopped and explained the figures, paying attention to the pivotal details, and continued to the next particulars, eventually summarizing the results of the research in an "elegant" conclusion. I ended up with the customary conclusion: "Thank you very much." I received an immense and long-lasting applause.

I was very happy and hoped that my boss would be happy as well. I owed him so much! At the same time, it was heartwarming that even as a member of a small nation, I was able to raise my intellectual acumen with the support of excellent teachers who were not only outstanding scientists, but also decent human beings, examples of integrity, interest, and care with a sense of "Aesculapian" physicians with Hippocratic ideals.

As I descended from the podium, many known and unknown colleagues were congratulating me, and my boss in the front row winked at me, that he was content with the performance of his European trainee, or "altar boy," and friend.

Suddenly through that small crowd of well-wishers, a young doctor from Poland broke through, Dr. Krystina Dymnicka. Perhaps my last name had attracted her attention, since it was similar to the name of the first Polish king, Mieszko I, from the Piaszt dynasty. She came from the northern city of Gdansk and was interested in the results of my research.

We did not wanted to disturb the proceedings of the conference, and we sat down in a small, neighboring parlor. When she learned that I was from Czecho-Slovakia, a country behind the Iron Curtain, she opened her heart full of lamentation about the deplorable conditions of medicine in communist Poland. We stayed in touch for years, and later in the eighties when I was an Attending at the Saint Francis Heart Center in Roslyn, New York, through our Gift of Life Program, we admitted about sixty children from Poland for diagnostic workup and surgical repair, all free of charge.

The next year, I was chosen for and had the privilege to be part of the group delegated from our Department for the World Congress of Cardiology in London. From my group of fellows, a friend from Chile was chosen as well, whom we called "Hidalgo," who was always ready and able and could easily raise his emotions.

That time it was all pleasure, yet we were obliged to attend the relevant lectures from pediatric cardiology and report in Boston all the novelties from the research of others. We were all happy and excited.

The Congress and its presentations were held in a huge complex of buildings, with many conference halls on the banks of the Thames River.

On the second day of the Congress, I stopped for a second and could not believe my eyes when I noticed the presence of my Professor and previous boss from the Children's Hospital in Bratislava. I immediately approached her, and she was pleasantly surprised as well. Our meeting was very friendly and cordial, as she was visibly glad, and we entered into cheerful conversation as old friends. She was in her seventies, still looked spritely and energetic with her lively, blue eyes of the blue forget-me-not. Eventually her good friend, a professor of cardiology, joined us in our vivid deliberation. We ended up in a side cafe in a box for a coffee or a bite. As we sat down, we had so much to say, as she was my favorite Professor, and she reciprocated my affection. She asked me how I was doing professionally, and as she knew well my wife, Judy, she asked about her and our children. It was a happy occasion when we could somehow pick up the pieces from where we once had left off.

Suddenly a former classmate of mine, now a professor, passed by. As he noticed me, now part of a delegation from the USA, he quickly advanced and bypassed our group even though he knew us all very well. My Professor noticed that guy and ironically remarked, "He is here to report on us to the State Secret Service." I did not react to that caustic remark, but I realized what I had avoided by my emigration.

In our free time, we had some time to browse through that magnificent city and its wonderful milestones and monuments, like Big Ben, listening to its sonic, baritone chime, and Westminster Abbey, the burying place of most of the British kings, and the neighboring impressive Parliament.

One evening we went with my Chilean friend Pedro to get some taste of London at night and took a classic black cab of the city to the Piccadilly Circus, with its flickering and blustering colorful lights and advertisements, for some evening amusement or shindig. We were lucky to get two tickets to the famous Palladium. It was a posh amusement theater with an evening show of dancing, singing, and acting of funny clowns with their hilarious skits. The main attraction was a beautiful girl with her mellifluous mezzo-soprano, her fancy dancing in solo or with her partner. At the end, amidst earthshaking applause, yelling, and stomping, she came to the front of the podium, and at the end of her last bow, she grabbed her tress at her nape, pulled off her wig, and the face of a man suddenly showed up! The whole audience was flabbergasted and went "gaga" in their unexpected astonishment and again started to clap their hands in high regard of this ingenious "schtick" and entertainment. In the early seventies, that kind of impersonation was in its inception. Nevertheless, we enjoyed that unbelievable evening and the fun of decadent London.

At the end of the Congress, some young scientists were recommended by the Board of the Congress to be accepted for a membership in the prestigious Royal Society of London. I was surprised, as I was one of them as well. I suspected that the recommendation came from my boss, Dr. A.S. Nadas.

At the end of each academic year, the whole Department of Cardiology and its members, and some of the secretaries and nursing staff as well, were invited to be part of the picture of the year. The picture was taken for the posterity of the Department (Figure 41). In the academic year of 1970-71, the professors sat in the first row, and in the second row, the instructors and the fellows were standing. In that row, the author stands as the third fellow from the right.

Almost simultaneously at the end of the year, an outing was organized for the whole group of the Department, with a trip to a seaside resort on Cape Cod, southeast of Boston, for a traditional clambake. The seniors and former fellows chose that peaceful settlement on the coast of the Atlantic to have some relaxation and fun after the successful year. All of us came by car in our sporty outfits and shorts to this seacoast resort. Different beach mattresses and blankets were spread out along the seashore on the fine-grain, pinkish beige sand. Anybody could stretch out and enjoy the sun in late May. Some of the more courageous put on their swimsuits or trunks and tried out the rather cold water of the Atlantic.

The leaders of the group purchased the clams from a local fisherman. The clams were really huge, like the palm of my hand. The clams were then put into large containers, which to me looked like garbage cans, and in them the clams were steamed on an open fire. We "juniors" were just wondering what would be the end of this whole gourmet cooking and the seemingly cobbled-up shindig.

When those "beasts" were fully cooked, everybody got one served on a paper plate with a small, warm doughnut and a small, paper jar with melted, salty butter. Then with a special knife, we had to split the clam, which was not always without a struggle, especially for us beginners. Then we had to bring the half shell with the clam to our mouth, and with a big suck, we should suck the whole clam into our mouth. During that adventurous endeavor, the juice from the clam usually sprinkled and soiled our shirts, and our hands were pretty greasy. We needed a lot of napkins to dry our hands and to save our shirts.

Following the ingestion of the clam, we dipped the doughnut into the salty butter as a complement to the clam and tried to enjoy that new culinary experience.

But a complication would develop when the wind from the Atlantic blew in and stirred up the fine sand onto all our plates with the moist clams. Hence every bite of the clam left sand in our mouth. Eventually I gave up that adventurous struggle and asked for a nice, juicy hotdog with a dollop of Dijon mustard.

After that juicy and sumptuous sustenance, splashed down with a refreshing beer, afterwards coffee or soft drinks were served. Our boisterous mood and energy sprang then into action, and we played volleyball like possessed or crazy people, while some of the braver nevertheless tried the icy waters of the Atlantic amidst a lot of cheering, laughing, and bantering during the memorable trip.

At dusk we packed up all the bric-a-brac and returned home to Boston with joyous and precious memories that are still fresh and alive in our aging minds.

Unfortunately every beginning has to come to its end. My four years at the Children's Hospital were coming very slowly, but irrevocably, to their last chapter. I was most fortunate to gain and absorb a tremendous amount of knowledge and information and adopt the philosophy of "evidence based medicine" with the help and groundwork of quantitative studies based on statistical analysis, instead of just subjective intuition. It was a revolutionary "revelation" in my medical reasoning and conclusions. That teaching gave me a tremendous advantage and an "American" professional kick to continue in those valuable footsteps. The outstanding academic environment showed me that the professional attitudes and scientific approach were the results of mutual interaction of facts and honing of scientists in an academic environment and not any kind of political ideology.

Our teachers, like the biblical rabbis, incorporated into us the principles of professional and personal honesty and honor, which was the fundamental intellectual scaffolding of any academic integrity. The professional and personal bar was at the top at that Harvard hospital.

With my new license in hand as a trained pediatric cardiologist, I had to face the reality that I was only one cog in the professional market of that specialty. It was something totally new, unknown and worrisome for me — how to look or find a new job.

In the socialist countries behind the Iron Curtain, there was always a government agency that would put you somewhere to work, whether you liked it or not. You were almost like "merchandise," where a commission for distribution of doctors decided your fate, according your political correctness and connections and not your qualification.

Now in this free country, I had to face the market forces of supply and demand and find myself a job. Without any previous experience of looking for or haggling, being a foreigner made me extremely uncomfortable and uneasy. My certificate of training in a Harvard-affiliated hospital was certainly an advantage. Yet I was not familiar with the concept of "hunting" for a job or its technique in that market of free competition, where according to theory of social Darwinism, a person with initiative and resourcefulness, who was clever and capable for himself, had a better chance to be successful. Unfortunately I had another disadvantage that was impossible to overcome. I was almost ten years older than my fellow friends in our group. It was understandable from the point of view of any institution that they would prefer a younger and trained "stallion." From our group of fifteen fellows, only two remained at the Children's Hospital, and one of them was the favorite of the deputy chief of the Department.

What now? Where to be or not to be was the almost Hamletian question. I needed some well-seasoned advice.

In March 1973, I asked for an appointment with my boss, Dr. A.S Nadas, and described to him my shaky situation as a foreigner, even though well-trained. I did not know how to proceed to get a job after my training. The boss understood very well my insecurity and precarious situation, compounded by the fact that I had a family as well. He knew well that my American colleagues knew the system and the ways and means — through advertisements in journals, word of mouth, or connections — of how to acquire a job.

My boss listened carefully and was well-aware of my predicament since in 1939 he had to overcome many almost insurmountable hardships in the beginning of his medical career. The boss then remarked, "You know, Zoltán, I will look around what can be done, and I will let you know. Come back in a week."

After a week, the boss sent for me and explained to me that he had consulted his good friend, Professor Dr. Ed Lambert in Buffalo, N.Y., and he informed him that he could offer me a position as an instructor or senior fellow at his Department of cardiology for a year, and then he would see how things would work out.

Dr. A.S. Nadas further explained, "Look, Ed Lambert has a solid team and an outstanding heart surgeon, Dr. S. Subramnian, who occasionally operates on children from Boston (information I was not privy of until then). As you know, Dr. R. Gross, in his advanced age, is not achieving optimal results with the newer forms of surgical technique in some lesions. Thus occasionally we transfer a patient to Subra (as Dr. Subramanian was known). Of course, this information is strictly confidential and is off the cuff!"

I had only a very faint idea about Buffalo. I knew only that in winter, it was usually hit with a heap of snow. With the portrayal of the professional profile and strength of the Department in Buffalo, it put the whole situation in a different light. I always cared for my professional advancement in my specialty. Hence that suggestion looked indeed enticing and advantageous. I thanked my boss for his nimble intervention on my behalf, and he replied, with a smile, "Okay, Zoltán. Good luck."

A month later in April, I flew to Buffalo in the northwest corner of New York State on Lake Erie, a stone's throw from the famous Niagara Falls on the Canadian border.

Dr. Ed Lambert was a six-foot tall, blue-eyed, blond gentleman with a smooth, sleek hairdo and a pleasant, halcyon-type disposition who cordially welcomed me in his office in a modern Children's Hospital located in a well-kept green park. We had a long, friendly exchange about my previous training before Boston in my native country and in Germany. After our deliberation, he invited me for lunch in the cafeteria of the hospital. In between he mused that I would have the responsibility of teaching clinical cardiology to the pediatric residents and fellows and be part of the cardiac diagnostic lab. I was very pleased by his suggestions and portrayal of my duties.

As we returned to his office, Dr. Peter Vlad, his associate and deputy, showed up. He was an outstanding cardiologist of Romanian origin. He was a tall, gaunt, gray-haired, athletic man with dark, penetrating eyes behind his heavy eyeglasses. In his mouth, he kept his pipe all the time, huffing and puffing white clouds of smoke of a sweet aroma around him, making the surrounding ambiance quite pleasant. When he heard my first name, Zoltan, presumably of Hungarian origin, his eyes seemed to nervously jitter, and perhaps he turned somewhat edgy. I knew that historically there was no love lost between Romanians and Hungarians, but when he learned that actually I was from Slovakia, he was able to give me a courteous smile. After those friendly deliberations, I made a verbal agreement with Dr. Ed Lambert, and I accepted his offer of a job for one year.

The Professor then called on his secretary, Mary, a lovely, warm, tall, black-eyed young lady with ebony hair, who supposed to be helpful to find an apartment for me and my family. And helpful she indeed was. She and an agent found for me an accommodation where the doctors of the Department were renting their lodging. The agent took me to a nice apartment building called Delaware Towers, in walking distance from the Hospital on the main street of the town, right opposite to the majestic, gothic cathedral. Other doctors were living there as well, and I got an offer of a nice, two-bedroom apartment on the eighth floor, where the large living room had wall-to-wall carpet that was almost new. I secured the apartment right away, leaving a down payment with the agent, and flew back to Boston. My wife was somehow bewildered by all the commotion — as she came from a small town in our native country — but she realized that a political refugee had not too much choice to choose. She tried to disguise her "pondering" about our wandering, taking it stoically, and she accepted the new reality. If it was good to her husband and professionally advantageous, then everything was in order.

Dr. A.S. Nadas was, of course, already informed about the outcome of my trip from his friend, and he congratulated me on my success in finding an academic position.

The last semester at the Department was rapidly approaching its end, and my departure filled me with an immense sadness and kind of separation anxiety.

After four happy years of my tenure and its security, leaving my boss was especially difficult. Our precious friendship somehow seeped under my skin, as an invisible Middle European kinship or perhaps even bond that cracked to the surface at some of his remarks, gestures, or oblique gist. Of course, our boss was for everybody residing on his "Olymp," but he was a human "captain," who especially in times of difficulty, was always willing to offer his helping hand to anybody. Dr. A.S. Nadas was also physically unique. He would not easily win a beauty contest, but his human personality radiated his genuine interest and friendship vís-a-vís "his" fellows. He was a uniquely particular or peculiar man, an emigrant from the thirties from Europe who never forgot his hardship and predicament, because it was impossible to forget your country and your poignant past. As I was weaning myself from the safe "womb" of the Department and the Hospital, in my minuscule study and privacy of my home, my eyes not just once welled up in tears. But in front of my wife and small children, I kept my positive disposition and kept smiling — the American way — even though my heart was aching. A faithful "lift up your heart" boosted my determination to march to my own drummer.

In our group, there were five seniors who were leaving Boston, and we were in a close, friendly relationship with each other. At that time, everybody was paying attention to his next step, to be on his own in the American professional structure. I was very close to Dr. Grace Wolf, a very intelligent cardiologist, who was leaving for Albany, New York. We stayed in touch at Christmas time and during her vacation at Lake George, where we met at their summer house.

I was very friendly with a handsome fellow from California, Dr. Bob Freedom. He was probably the most brainy member of our group. He was leaving for the prestigious John Hopkins Hospital in Baltimore and advanced to the Professorship

CONFESSION OF A REFUGEE

of pediatric cardiology at the Toronto Children's Hospital. In 1989 Bob curried a great favor for me when he accepted an assistant professor from Slovakia for a six-month training in pediatric cardiology, funded by the Heart to Heart program of the American Slovaks in New York.

Dr. David Maltz had a brilliant scientific mind, especially in mathematical interpretations, and he surprised everybody when he went to private practice.

The farewell party of that group in early June 1973 was ostentatious, cheerful on the surface, and bittersweet. We were quite a progressive group, where everybody published his successful research in peer-review journals.

Our relationships with our attendings remained strong for years to come. I stayed in touch with jovial Bill Plauth in Santa Fe, New Mexico, and the handsome Grant LaFarge, who anchored his roots and settled there as well.

For many years, I stayed in touch with Ami Rosenthal in Ann Arbor, Michigan, where I came with my wife to celebrate his professorship at his gala.

To my reverent boss, I sent every Christmas my heartfelt wishes and warmth of my feelings till 2000, when he unfortunately passed away.

Gratitude, the virtue many times forgotten in these rushing days, is a glue which binds together the human relationship, expressing our humanity, and was the embodiment of our kinship with our teachers and our boss, the ultimate "Mensch."

My personal "currency" as part of our team was my unconditional engagement in our common interest and professional mission — in the ultimate interest of our patients — supplemented by my personal integrity, an inheritance and message of my dear parents. During those four years, I intertwined the badge of my personal character with the solid advancement in my professional training into the well-rounded structure of a scientist, thanks to my exceptional teachers.

The personal goodbye with my teacher Dr. A.S. Nadas was very difficult for me. He managed it much better with his encouraging smile. My eyes welled up with tears as we shook hands. I expressed my deep and sincere gratitude, that at a time of personal tragedy in 1969, he indeed saved my skin and my family as well, as he offered me the last straw and opportunity to emigrate to the U.S. and be a fellow in his program. With a taut smile, he patted me on my shoulder and, through his clenched teeth, he muttered, "Keep your commitment high and work like in Boston."

In 1980 I welcomed him at our conference at the Saint Francis Hospital Heart Center, where I already worked as an Associate Professor of SUNY. I presented to him at the conference the result of our clinical research, as a pupil would to his teacher. It was my last and memorable meeting with my boss (Figure 42).

In the last days of June, I had to forget my personal and agitated emotions and face my immediate reality and professional change, moving to Buffalo and taking care of transporting my whole family there.

First of all, I went to rent a truck from the Ryder Company, and I was taken by surprise seeing the generous size of the "smallest " available truck (Figure 43). I, of course, never in my life had driven a truck! As a refugee, I couldn't be very choosy and had to face the harsh reality, even though I was not prepared for such an "exotic" situation.

At home we packed up our modest furniture and other "things," like clothing, shoes, and utensils for the kitchen. We crammed them into different cartons, which were more numerous than I expected. It looked like we were getting rich!

On the last Friday of June, I went for the truck with my wife. I came back with the truck while my wife drove our car. Our children were anxiously on alert. We all rolled up our sleeves and filled up that humongous truck, which looked huge to me. Behind my back, my wife muttered something like, "My God, how is he going to drive such a monster?"

I climbed up, high up, to the driver's seat, with its huge steering wheel, the largest I had ever seen. The seats were high but well-padded; the pedals were large, like for an elephant. The agent filled up the two gas tanks, both of them hanging under the truck's frame like two bombs.

On the other side of the high seat, my son, Robert, was sitting, ten years old. He was my navigator (no GPS at that time), and on his knees he spread our auto map.

Behind us my wife was following in our Bordeaux Renault 16 with our daughter, Patricia, seven years old. She had faith in her dad that he will lead us and manage as he always had. For my wife, who followed us at a safe distance behind the truck, it was her first trip on a highway and the longest one as well. The stress was palpable, but she had to face the facts and manage as well.

Our truck started with a mighty jolt as I pressed the gas pedal with the force of a beginner. My son glanced at me with some insecurity or fright, but my reassuring smile calmed him down. I had to get used to the heavy hand brake as well, which gave me a jerk at every start or stop.

But we buckled up, and in God's name, let's go! Fortunately in the early hours of the morning, the traffic was light, and I drove through that beloved town with ease, since I was familiar with most of the roads after four years as a resident of the town.

We drove along the lazy Charles River with its fluffed-up white waves, which were glittering in the morning sun, ending up in the huge Atlantic. After half an hour, we entered the Massachusetts Turnpike in the direction of Spring-field. After a while, we crossed into New York and bypassed its capital, Albany. Unfortunately I made a mistake and turned southward in the direction of Bing-hamton. Robert made me aware of my mistake; fortunately it was only a small detour. We were driving farther, and in my back mirror, I was glancing at the progress of my wife, but she just waved at me with her hand: go, go! Then out of the blue sky, an old dictum came into my mind from "a wise man" from my native country: "To go back is impossible. You have to always advance and go only forward."

As we were driving on the highway, somewhere from an obscure corner of my brain, an old song of WW II of a Russian, frontline chauffeur popped up in my mind. It had been sung toward the end of the war when the Russian Red Army had "liberated" Czechoslovakia. Suddenly I started to sing it:

"Ech dorožka frontovaja, nestrašna nám bomboška ljubaja.
Pomírat' nám radovado, jest u nás ješčo doma dela!"

Paraphrasing it in English:
"Hey, while trudging this frontline road, no bombardier will scare me. To die, it would be rather premature, as at home we have many tasks to do!"

Then I somehow felt like the frontline chauffeur, and I was singing, or rather yelling, that song as my son looked at me in bewilderment. What was his rather somber father doing? Had he lost his marbles? But I was just yelling and decom-pressing my stress as a Russian frontline chauffeur!

With the truck, I could not drive faster than 50 miles/hour, and eventually I got bored with the monotonous endeavor. Around Albany the red light from my gas tank started to flicker, indicating that the first gas tank was almost empty. I switched to the other tank, but after two hundred miles and before Binghamton, just as I was climbing up a hill, the red light from the second tank started to signal my empty tank as I reached to its top. My God, what am I going to do with my empty tank in this no-man's-land? The peak of the hill stopped my truck, and for a moment, I applied the brake. As I released the brake, the truck started to roll down the hill with the stalled engine, but suddenly my son started to point to his side of the truck and exclaimed, " Look, Dad, look!" On his side of the truck, on a little oasis, there was a Chevron gas station, which from my vantage point I could not see. I was immensely relieved, and so by its own gravity, the truck rolled down the hill and reached the small gas pump. We were very lucky because there was not any settlement or town around where we could find a gas station.

Right away we filled up both our fuel tanks and parked the truck in a small, surrounding garden under the trees, where we could have our lunch and some rest as well.

After a sumptuous lunch of tasty, homemade sandwiches and a strong coffee, as well as Cokes for the children, we rolled up our sleeves and faced the last trek of our frontline journey as a frontline chauffeur.

After four hours of driving, we noticed the skyline of the city of Buffalo in a green valley (Figure 44), and in about an hour, we hit the main artery of the town, which took us straight to the main avenue of the town, where we soon reached our building, the Delaware Towers. It was an elegant, ten-story building, where the facade of its front up to the first floor was decorated by turquoise-colored tiles, projecting a pleasant and cultured impression of the architecture of downtown, where the building was located.

We parked our truck before the large, glass entrance of the building, where the concierge knew about our arrival. He directed us to the back of the building into a large courtyard where we could park our truck.

On the elevator, we reached the eighth floor, and I could introduce my wife and the two children to our new apartment, with a large balcony on the back from where we could admire the outline of the neighboring hills. They were all elated by the apartment and the outlook. My wife was thrilled with the minuscule but modern kitchen with its microwave — her first — and the shiny steel kitchen range, equipped with an oven for baking. Well if my wife was happy, that was a promising start. She liked the large living room as well, with the wall-to-wall carpet in good condition. It was green, not to my liking, but we settled to that new reality. The bedroom was spacious as well, with a lot of sunshine with the bonus of inherited nice curtains. For the children there was a smaller room quite satisfactory, and they were jubilant to have their own quarters.

Then we all rolled up our sleeves, and with the help of a service elevator, we started to unload and move the furniture, the racks of cabinets, beds, our Grundig music box, and the TV from the truck and all the rest of the bric-a-brac. In about three hours, all four of us finished the grind at the dusk of the day.

The concierge let us park our truck in the back of the building till the morning, while my wife, with some pride of her accomplishment, rolled our car into the parking lot in the basement of or building. "Isn't this a luxury?" she quipped.

We were all dead tired but happy. The summer was warm and pleasant. We took a quick shower to get rid of the dust and sweat and went to a nearby charming restaurant on the main avenue and had a sumptuous dinner, which boosted the mood of everybody, as it was indeed what we needed. We went back to our apartment and made things ready for the night, that is, arrange the beds for everybody, fill in the mattresses, and cover them with clean sheets, which were already ready and cared for in foresight by my wife. The soft cushions were ready as well and the covers and blankets. The family was well-organized and well taken care of, as in the case of experienced refugees.

It was past 10 P.M. when, dead tired, we could retire, and we prayed with our thanks for some soothing, fairytale dreams. I dreamt that I had passed my exam as a frontline chauffeur.

We all had a well-deserved good night in that pleasant and peaceful condo. I was exhausted, and no soothing dreams lulled my weary mind. But in the morning while my wife and children were still lolling in their beds, I snuck out into a nearby supermarket and came back with milk, coffee, rolls, butter, eggs, jam, and some cheese. My wife, who heard my loitering, quickly prepared for us a wonderful breakfast of scrambled eggs with coffee and cocoa for the children. Still in pajamas, everybody was happy and smiling that we were lovingly all together, just in another town.

After the breakfast, I went to return the truck to the depot with my son, an associate "chauffeur." We had to ask and look where the Ryder depot was; eventually we found it on the periphery of the town. We returned the truck; it was checked out for possible damage. As everything was in order, we paid our bill and returned to our house in a cab.

At home, as we returned, my "two girls" were busy putting together the cabinets and neatly arranging the rest of the furniture after our third move in the U.S. They knew our routine well, and they realized that a refugee had to move with light gear and baggage.

After a while of rest, we went with our car to the First National supermarket to fill up our icebox and the cabinets in the kitchen under the "baton" of my wife. The children were running back and forth along the aisles, bringing back with joy all the required items. We returned home with a bunch of bulging, brown bags and were happy for the invention of the elevator. I left the unpacking to my dexterous bunch, popped a can of Budweiser, and enjoyed it in our beautiful Danish easy chair — the masterpiece of my wife — looking to the green hills around Buffalo. Well actually, life is not so bad, is it?

My skillful wife prepared for us our first lunch in Buffalo. On her shiny steel kitchen range, she fried a scrumptious crispy chicken with roasted potatoes and a fresh cucumber salad, sprinkled with black pepper and Hungarian red paprika. It was a well-deserved, enjoyable homemade "banquet!" A cool beer and soft drinks for children were an appropriate complement to the main meal. The children had, of course, their chocolate ice cream with a dollop of whipped cream. My wife and I were sipping a relaxing beer. After that tasty and sumptuous lunch, a well-deserved nap was desirable as a complement to the last leg of our adventurous trip.

BUFFALO

The city of Buffalo was founded in the eighteenth century on the sway of an ancient land with luscious pastures of the Iroquois Indian tribe and in 1789 was named Buffalo Creek. The settlement was established on the eastern cusp of Lake Erie, connected to the Atlantic by a channel. Not so far away on the Niagara River, huge and majestic waterfalls were discovered which later on we frequently visited and admired (Fig 45). The name of the river has its origin from the Native American tribes as well, most probably the Iroquois. The waterfalls were discovered for the "world" by the Frenchman Samuel de Champlain and researched in detail by the Belgian monk Louis Hennepin, which made them known and famous in Europe.

The town rather quickly developed into a large metropolis of four million inhabitants, coming mostly from the East, but a significant numbers of black Americans came from the South as well. At the end of the nineteenth century, the town was flooded by Polish and Hungarians from the "Old World." Rapidly in the city, different industries developed and flourished with mills and mechanical technology in different factories, but also centers for high learning, including the State University of New York with its huge campus and the Buffalo-Niagara Medical Corporation with its Center for cancer research, known as Roosevelt Park. The city, for the culture lovers, built a large cultural center, the Shea's Performing Arts Center, for concerts and performances.

The Children's Hospital was an integral part of the university of high learning and the Department of Pediatric Cardiology as well, where I had accepted the privilege to serve. On Monday morning, I was poised and ready for action to enter another unknown territory, the prestigious Children's Hospital, where its heart surgery was the jewel of the institution. As I was departing for another new "bat-tlefield," my wife gave me a tender kiss and quipped, "Have courage!"

The Hospital was only about a fifteen-minute walk through a manicured garden park of the town. I presented myself at the reception desk, where the officer directed me to the elevator and the fifth floor. There I was welcomed by the lovely secretary, Mary, with whom I had gotten acquainted during my previous interview, and she offered me a seat before the office of Dr E. Lam-bert. He soon showed up from his "wigwam" (office) and welcomed me very friendly. "Welcome, Zoltan. I am happy you made it and hope you and your family are settled comfortably." In a short exchange, I portrayed him briefly our adventurous trip as a "frontline chauffeur" and reassured him that myself and my family were settled comfortably and I was ready to roll up my sleeves and start to work. From the neighboring office, the haggard Dr. P. Vlad showed up, and his colleague, Dr. Henry Wagner, native of Switzerland, also a trainee from Boston. The highlight of the meeting was the arrival of the heart surgeon, Dr. S. Subramanian, who as a famous surgeon almost levitated into the meet-ing, except without fanfare. He was a tall, stocky man from India with a Creole complexion, with black, almost menacing eyes and a pitch black tress of curly hair and a small, black beard on the tip of his chin, made legendary by V.I. Lenin, the Communist leader. When I introduced myself to Subra, as every-body addressed him in that abbreviated way, he was very friendly and jovial to me. But when he heard my first name Zoltan, his reaction was abrupt, quite a "surgical" one, and he blurted out, "I am going to call you Boris. And with him, that nickname stuck with me while in Buffalo.

There were two fellows in training there and some pediatric Residents for teaching the art of pediatric cardiology in general pediatrics. It was a small but professionally excellent team.

The "uncrowned" king was obviously Subra, who had his training in cardiac surgery in London at the renown Children's Hospital at Great Ormond Street by Dr. Eoin Aberdeen, of Australian origin, and at Johns Hopkins Hospital in Balti-more. Dr. Subramanian introduced for the surgical procedures for babies the tech-nique of "hypothermia," lowering the body temperature of the patient during surgery from the normal temperature of 98.6° F, about eight to ten degrees lower, by surrounding the baby in ice while his core temperature was measured rectally. At that point, the circulation and metabolism of the body slowed down, as its ox-ygen consumption as well, to protect mainly the brain. To learn this technique, some other heart surgeons came from the U.S. and Europe as well and were visiting the division of cardiac surgery.

In the clinical field of cardiac diagnosis, a new, advanced technique was breaking into pediatric cardiology, the method of echocardiography and Doppler ultrasound. Almost unknown in our group was that Christian Doppler was an Austrian physicist who, from 1842-46, was a professor at Charles University in Prague — then Austro-Hungary, who in the academic year of 1947-48 spent a year as a Professor of the Royal Academy of Science, established in the year of 1763 by Queen Maria Theresa in the town that is today geographically in Slovakia: Banská Šiavnica.

The technique of echocardiography and Doppler ultrasound registered the reflected ultrasound or "echo" waves from the structures of the heart, developed soon into an integral part of diagnostic methods in conjunction of cardiac catheterization of the heart.

In the Center, the teaching and the diagnostic workup was at clinical level for preparation for open heart surgery and related clinical research. The anatomical diagnosis of the underlying anatomical congenital problem of the patient was — as in Boston — presented in weekly diagnostic conferences, where their main surgical input was provided by Subra. There as well, the discussions were animated and spirited about the optimal surgical solutions or its nuances for the individual patient.

As cardiologists we were providing our expertise and support in the postoperative care in the ICU as well, together with our surgical colleagues. One of the surgical fellows was from Italy, Dr. Ottavio Alfiery from Bergamo, who came to learn his surgical craft from Dr. Subra. Today Otto is a leading surgeon in Rome, a specialist of the repair of the mitral valve, with his invention of the "mitral clip" technique. We developed a warm friendship with this blue-eyed, blond Northern Italian friend during our work in postoperative ICU.

Not only surgeons, but many patients came to the center from the U.S. or Europe because of the excellent skills and surgical results of Dr. Subra. Teaching the younger doctors was always my favorite hobby and forte. I took the teaching to the residents in Pediatrics and younger fellows with great passion on the clinical floor, the ICU, and even the cardiac catheterization lab, where they could be observers. I was very busy the whole day and was coming home quite late, sometimes at 7 P.M. The tasty dinner within the family circle was a happy and uplifting event with our growing children.

Opposite to our Delaware Towers, just across the street on the main street, stood the beautiful cathedral in neo-Gothic style. It was a welcomed opportunity for our children to attend the parochial school there. At the crossing of the avenue, every morning since September they were welcomed by a smiling lady officer, who was watching closely as they crossed the street. Robert joined the group of altar boys, and every Sunday he served at the holy mass, to our joy and happiness.

In September, through a friend I was able to place my wife to work at the hospital for four hours a day in the Department of Medical Supply. The main goal was to get her in touch with people, enrich her English vocabulary, and polish her pronunciation, as well as for advancement of her qualification since her nursing diploma from Czechoslovakia was not valid in the U.S.

At the same time, by chance and by word of mouth, we learned that at the end of September, there would be a convention of Slovak expatriates, or diaspora, in the Canadian town of Galt in the state of Ontario at the mission of the Slovak Jesuits. In the garden of the mission, the statue of a prominent Slovak writer, Martin Kukučín (alias Dr. Martin Bencúr), was to be unveiled at that occasion. The statue was sculpted by the world-famous Croatian sculptor Ivan Meštrovič, who now sculpted and lived in the U.S. The statue had been originally procured by Slovaks in South America, where Martin Kukučín worked amid the Slovaks in Puntas Arenas in Chile. Originally the bronze statue of the writer was supposed to be unveiled at the Slovak Cultural Association in Buenos Aires.

Through some administrative glitch, the unveiling of the statue there did not happen. Consequently the Slovak Jesuits of Galt purchased the statue for five thousand U.S. dollars. Unexpectedly some other compatriots showed interest in the statue from the famous sculptor. A Slovak philanthropist and entomologist, Professor Július Rudinský, and his wife, Norma, asked maestro Meštrovič to sculpt two more bronze copies of the writer.

One of the copies was dedicated to the University of Oregon in Corvallis. The second copy was supposed to be sent from the Rudinskies as a gift to the main Slovak Cultural Organization, "Matica Slovenská" (Mather of the Slovaks), in the town of Martin in Central Slovakia. During the Communist period of Czechoslovakia, the unveiling of the statue was procrastinated until 1984 and was finally placed into the garden of the medical school (M. Kukučin or Dr Matej Bencúr was a doctor) in the capital of Bratislava. The unveiling of the statue was done by the Communist Secretary for Culture, Miloslav Válek, who did not utter a word about the origin of the statue, a gift from the American Slovaks (Figure 46).

We were quite excited and looking forward to meeting some of our compatriots. At the beginning of that crispy fall, when the Canadian maple leaves were getting their first "rust" on their petals, we departed in the morning on a sunny Saturday for our first Canadian trip. The mission had a sizable sway of the land with manicured gardens and trees. The gardens had beautiful, geometrically arranged patches of flower beds with rusty dahlias, autumn crocuses or "naked ladies" (belladonna lily), with their deep purple colors and bunches of pinkish heather flowers. The panoply of beautiful, bright colors, together with classical ocher autumn mums, gave us a joyful impression of the view in that serene habitat. The compound was full of visitors from the Slovak diaspora from all of Canada and the Northeast U.S., up to five thousand members. I did not know anybody, or did I know them all? Since we were of the same roots. Eventually I met a doctor who was originally an assistant professor from Bratislava, now residing in Toronto. We also met a couple, as he was a Resident at Buffalo General Hospital and a trainee in internal medicine. Since we were both clinicians and about the same age, we joined in a friendly conversation. His wife, originally from Poland and a doctor as well, was then working on her naturalization exam for foreign medical graduates. The couple had a nice, little, blond youngster, Bart, and our children were eager to have a new friend. Later we visited each other while in Buffalo and remain friends up to this day. They have since moved to Florida.

At noon a small lunch was served to the guests, during which the people cheerfully intermingled, chatted, and made new friendships. A festive celebration followed with the unveiling of the beautiful statue of the "thinking writer," who had his roots in the small village of Jasenová, from the quintessential Slovak province in the north of Slovakia, the beautiful Orava.

I had read in high school with great admiration one of his novels, *The House on the Hillside*. The ostentatious celebration continued with laudatory appraisals of the writer's literary work by speakers, as well his work as a physician amidst his Slovak émigrés in faraway Chile in South America. The celebration ended by singing an old elegiac Slovak national ballad:

O' Lord, who generously blessed our Slovak kin,
After the years of so many trials and sufferings…
The ballad ended: We are eternally thankful for all your blessings forever!

At the last stanza, eyes were welling up with copious tears, jugulars were swelling, and people were sobbing, as all the émigrés, who had shared their sordid fate of emigration were invoking the Almighty, as without His blessing, we would be unable to cope with all struggles and tribulations while finding our new homes.

Eventually a frenetic applause surged forth, and the tears changed to joy, and everybody was jubilant and happy that we were in a unique kinship, here and together. It was a memorable event and a joyous celebration for the Slovak diaspora in Canada and the Northern USA.

Buffalo was well-known for its early, cold winters and abundant snowfall. In October we got a foretaste and the first bout of thirty inches. And the forecast was foreboding much more compared to Boston. But we liked the snow, as in our native land we had always gotten plenty of snow in winter even though Buffalo surpassed our expectations. Nevertheless, well-dressed and warm, we strived rather well in that white paradise.

A white Thanksgiving sneaked on us coyly amidst our work, unforeseen in that country of Iroquois Indians, which gave to it a special flavor. Unexpectedly the lovely Mary, secretary of Dr. Ed Lambert, approached me and expressed her invitation and her family's, that they would be delighted if we could spend that quintessential American family celebration with them. I was surprised in a way, even though my wife wanted to try and master the art of roasting our first turkey in our new oven. Mary's invitation was so cordial with her enticing smile that we accepted the invitation and privilege. Anyway, I thought, my wife can wrestle with the turkey next year.

As the festive day of Thanksgiving arrived, we dressed up accordingly in our best attire for that family and at about 10 A.M., we departed to a small village in the hilly countryside. The countryside was all white in its festive overcoat; the country was slowly waking up, and the white, rural land was peaceful, almost pious. The silence of the land was spiritual indeed as our car — an intruder with its noise — was trying to "trespass" the snowy kingdom and dare disturb its serenity as it labored to climb up a small hill. Slowly but surely, we waded through first seen and unknown countryside with the help of a map from Mary.

It was just about noon when we arrived at the house of our hosts. The whole family was dressed up in a festive mood, ready for the celebration and in expectation of their guests, and their welcome was exceptionally warm and cordial. Mary and her husband were the first to welcome us, shaking hands with hugs and kisses between the women and for the children as well. Then the parents and the whole family joined in to welcome these battered people who had to flee their own home.

The welcome in that rural village, hidden in the white countryside, was perhaps more personal or genuine and had a more intimate, almost earthy chime in the white kingdom. The mood was more family-centered in the sense of neighborly love. The parents invited us to a spacious living room, and at the entrance, we were startled by the beauty of the bucolic decor of the room. The whole room was decorated in red- and green-colored decor with a large, red tablecloth, hemmed with colorful green leaves and red berries of holly on the margins around the cloth. Indeed only an impressionist painter was missing to save that colorful, bucolic beauty.

In the neighboring parlor on a small club table, all kind of bottles were standing in striking attention with whisky of Glenfiddich, bourbon and gin, but cognac and cherry as well, and on the side shelf, cool Coca-Cola was presented as well. We all filled our glasses with chosen drink and clicked them with a happy cheers and took our seats around a decorated coffee table. All of them wanted to know the story of our flight. I touched upon only the main points of it and rather switched the conversation in our admiration of their picturesque village in that fairytale countryside in the white winter and expressed our heartfelt thanks and appreciation for their invitation to be part of the celebration of Thanksgiving amidst their family. In a while, the lady of the house was calling on all of us to congregate around the festive table, where everybody had his name tag before his or her plate, flanked by an ornamental red and green napkin. We were all about a dozen of us around the festive table, and the mood now calmed down to an almost pious tone. The grandfather again offered his hand to his wife, and we all followed in a wreath of the whole family around the dining table. We all bowed our heads during the prayer of the grandfather, where he expressed his thanks to the Lord for all his blessings and gifts we were going to receive, in the name of the Father, Son, and the Holy Spirit. It was indeed very intimate and moving, and we were thankful that we could be part of that beautiful nuclear family. After the prayer, we wished to each other a very happy Thanksgiving and clicked our glasses again.

After a short time, the lady of the house came and brought a large, ornamental soup bowl, and the aroma of the steaming pumpkin soup spread around, arousing a happy smile of expectation. With a large, porcelain ladle, everybody received on his or her plate an ample portion of the soup, complemented by croutons or a dollop of sour cream. Everybody's mood was rising seeing the culinary gourmet potage, in expectation of the first warm gulp of the tasty and delicious soup.

At the same time, Mary's husband poured into our crystals a chilled California chardonnay, perhaps to please his European wine-drinking friends. After a short pause of conversation or chitchat, a domestic presented the golden, roasted turkey on a silver plate, amidst joyous cheers, and put it before the grandfather. It almost looked like a pagan sacrifice as the elder of the house took a long, somewhat-curved knife, resembling a Turkish scimitar sword, and plunged it into the protruding breast of the venerated beast. The first portion was offered to his spouse and then all around. It was indeed an esteemed ritual of the patriarch of that family, and we and the children enjoyed the festive presentation.

Everybody then received a piece of white or dark cut of turkey with a splash of creamy sauce from a gravy boat and added mashed potatoes or yams with a large spoonful of stuffing from giblets mixed with croutons and chestnuts, which surrounded the meat like an encircling mound. On the side were green peas, pearl onions, and also tarty sweet cranberry preserve. It was a "mega-feast," and everybody enjoyed the delicious and tasty harmony of the multitude of the produce of that blessed land.

The mood was cheerful and elated with vivid and amusing conversations, including our children as well, who were well-groomed in cultural table manners, mastering the simultaneous technique of the knife and fork, and our Robert excelled with his witty and sparkling remarks. The golden chardonnay was generously flowing, rising the mood and the tone of the merry ambiance amidst lovely hosts at a magnificent celebration of Thanksgiving day.

After a pleasant pause, the dishes and the cutlery were taken aside, and after a short intermission, the anticipated "sweet course" of desserts followed, to the great joy of the children. The luscious pumpkin pie with a dollop of whipped cream looked indeed delicious. I liked the homemade bread pudding with raisins, soaked in vanilla sauce with bourbon. A classic American apple pie or cherry pie was also available with different kinds of ice cream. Simultaneously coffee was served, which was most welcome after such an opulent and rich feast. The cheerful conversations were cordial, vivid, and happily flowing; hence we did not even notice that dusk was sneaking into the white horizons of the village. It was time — reluctantly though — but we had to say goodbye to this lovely family in the middle of that white, fairytale village. The parting with all those good and neighborly people was very emotional and teary, with many hugs and handshakes, but we had to go before the winter evening started.

It was really a memorable day, one of our highlights along our six years of pilgrimage during our flight, and it remains a precious, little jewel in our memory, that evening in a little, white village of the countryside amidst the welcoming and neighborly love of beautiful family and friends. It was rather late in that pitch black night as we were plowing through the countryside with our car in the heavy snow, the only car on that empty path, but we arrived home safe with a sense of joy and gratitude.

At the beginning of December, the snow was pouring heavily on the city, and it was really a struggle to get into the hospital by foot through the mounds of snow.

Christmas came silently, almost stealthily, into our family, and we spent it at home, rather alone. Christmas was always a difficult time for us. We bought a small Christmas tree and decorated it with colorful crystal balls and ornaments of snow with glittering electric lights.

Just before Christmas, I went for an afternoon walk with our children in the white and festive Buffalo. As we were walking on the main commercial street, we came in front of a store with antiques and other bric-a-brac. As I looked into the shopwindow, I was stunned to see a Bethlehem creche of fine ceramic that looked familiar to me. We entered the store, and I was almost flabbergasted; it was a piece of ceramic art originally from a small but acclaimed town for its ceramic art, from western Slovakia: Modra. I thought it was rather unbelievable. How had such a piece of art from Slovakia shown up there in Buffalo in 1973 or before? The owner had no idea how the piece had come into his store. And he had not the faintest idea where on earth the town of Modra, the "birthplace" of this ceramic, was!

I got into an emotional spell and nostalgia, especially at Christmas time, finding such a Christmas emblem, a creche from my native country, that I immediately purchased that little scene of Bethlehem (Fig. 47). I brought home the creche as a trophy in a jubilant mood, and this little Bethlehem has been for over forty years a dominant centerpiece on our Christmas table with its unbelievable story, found in snow-covered Buffalo in a small, shabby antique store.

In the last days before Christmas — as it is with some men — it occurred to me that I didn't have any present for my lovely wife. Rather foolishly in that harsh winter, I decided to go to some fancy department store in Toronto. Well it's only a stone's throw, I thought — or only some one hundred miles! I dressed up the children warmly, and they were joyous to go for an adventure with their sometimes silly Dad. I placed them on the back seats, where the heating was better in that dreadful winter cold, which was even harsher in Canada. It was really not a very good idea! Still I wanted to bite the bullet, and during the ride, I suggested to the children, "Why don't we sing some Christmas carols?" It was like an invitation for them to join in the act.

Robert took the lead, but Patricia quickly followed as they started to sing one of the most beautiful Christmas carols, originally from France in 1780, that crossed the channel La Manche into England and then sailed through the Atlantic over to the Colonies, or the U.S., and turned into a quintessential classic of the Christmas season celebration.

Its first stanza sings, "On the first day of Christmas, my true love sent to me, a partridge in a pear tree."

In the following stanzas, two turtledoves, three French hens, four calling birds, and five golden rings were sent to his true love. On the twelfth day, when the drummers were drumming, she was simply overwhelmed by his love, and so were our two children even though they were indeed in a Christmas mood.

Eventually we arrived in the center of frosty Toronto, and the only smart thing to do was, in the biting cold, quickly park our car in the basement of a large department store, get to a coffee shop, and have a hot tea or cocoa with some donuts to boost our energy. We darted then straight to the women's section of cosmetics, where we looked for some fancy French fragrance. On the recommendation of a salesgirl, I purchased an expensive fragrance, Lucien Le Long, in a fancy, crystal bottle in a Christmas package with a large, blue ribbon. As I paid my bill and picked up the fancy present, we looked at each other like three conspirators and started to giggle and smile, as with a successfully accomplished plot.

We turned around and hurried back home to Buffalo, where my wife was already worrying where we were loafing in the bitter cold. But we kept our mouths tightly shut; only our eyes were sparkling bright, like three rascals.

Just before Christmas, there was an ostentatious Christmas party at our Department for all the physicians and the nursing staff and the surgical team led by Dr. Subra, and his associates, like "Otto the Italian" were invited as well. Dr. Subra was a man of generous spirit, and he did not forget to wish Merry Christmas to "Boris" even though he was not a Christian. The doctors from the other departments dropped in with their well-wishes and to try our powerful "punch" and all the goodies, which were available for everybody who showed up. The cheerfulness and the celebration was festive and happy, and we did not forget to sing some of the familiar Christmas carols in the small group of doctors, which was perhaps more intimate.

The cultural highlight of the season in Buffalo was the concert given by the master flutist Jean-Pierre Rampal from Paris in the Shea Conference Center. There the world-famous musician, with his flute, introduced us to the elegiac folk songs of the season in the pastoral Auvergne of France. It evoked in all the listeners the bucolic countryside, with all its shepherds in that hilly province, coming to the biblical wooden creche, padded by golden straw in a simple stable, where the little

Jesus was resting and warmed up by the exhaled breaths of a small donkey and a young heifer, while Mary and Joseph were guarding their baby. It was a beautiful and spiritual concert and a proper prelude and induction to our own Christmas.

In that pastoral and pious spirit, we sat around our humble, but decorated table on Christmas Eve, decorated by mistletoe with its pearls and twigs from the pine tree and were happy that we were all together and well. After the prayer, we started our dinner with our quintessential and traditional tarty cabbage soup with bitterish mushrooms and their biblical overtones. The edge of the spicy soup was softened by the mildly blended boiled Idaho potatoes, an old custom in our family and our native land. The soup was followed by a tasty fried sea bass without bones, appreciated by our children, complemented by a piquant potato salad, or in keeping to the tradition, I stuck to the biblical challah with sprinkled raisins. Since my childhood in my family, I was used to the challah with raisins and liked when the sweet raisin "hit" the salty fish in my mouth, which evoked in my taste buds a sweet-salty sensation of my parents' home.

A chilled Chardonnay from the winery of St. Michel in Washington State, with its nice aroma and bouquet, was a complement to the main meal while the children enjoyed their bubbly Sprite.

As for the dessert, my wife inherited from my dear mom a recipe of chestnut-chocolate log with whipped cream on top, which was the epicurean finale of our dinner.

The gifts were modest but full of love: for Robert some interesting books and coloring books for our baby. For both of them, some warm items for frosty Buffalo. My wife was moved by the exquisite but expensive perfume that I had spent too much for her. I was surprised by a colorful necktie. Our joy of the birth of the newborn king was tempered since we were alone and rather lonesome, and in our thoughts, we were still "home" for Christmas in our native land with our dearest, even if only in our dreams. At 11 P.M. our son Robert hurried to the Cathedral as an altar boy to celebrate the midnight mass, and we soon followed. The Cathedral was just across the street. The midnight mass was celebrated by the diocesan bishop himself, with a long line of priests and deacons. The altar boys followed, amidst them our beloved son in a carmine cassock, a snow white shirt and laced collar, holding a ringing bell and smiling. We were really proud of him that he had followed in the footsteps of his ancestors.

The midnight mass was solemn but festive and indeed joyous. The main altar was decorated by surrounding tall Christmas trees with a lot of silver tinsel, emulating a snow-covered pine. The middle of the altar was lined up with beautiful, white chrysanthemums and hydrangeas, which under the strobe lights were gleaming their heavenly white purity. During the mass, the organ was sublimely intoning the refrains of the most cherished Christmas carols, when at the singing of the faithful, it increased its crescendo in its rich chromatic chords, eventually switch to a jubilant forte in celebration of the birth of the little Jesus. It was a ostentatious finale of this majestic but pious mass.

At the exit door of the cathedral, throngs of the faithful were full of smiles and happiness, wishing each other "Merry Christmas" with lot of hugs and hand-shakes in a festive atmosphere, and we were very happy that were part of that ju-bilant crowd during that Christmas celebration.

The bitter cold in that white winter with an abundant snowfall filled our terrace as well and the outside whole parking lot. Till the end of March, the town was cov-ered with about fifty inches of snow, and the snow was still pouring down from the skies. We were mostly stranded in our apartment, except my struggle through the abundant snow mounds in the morning and in the evening when I was coming home. For our weekly shopping, we drove from garage of our house to the garage of the supermarket and back. Occasionally I took the kids for a short walk when the wind calmed down, and a snowball battle evolved between the "two sides." Otherwise we just watched TV programs or read books. The winter was quite con-fining, and my wife started to be restless from the seclusion and started to work on me: "Perhaps we will not be in Buffalo forever?" We were also missing the richness of the culture of Boston, and we were starting to look for some different pastures or a more exciting or interesting milieu.

My contract with the Department was just for one year; hence at the end of the winter, I started to look for some information in pediatric or cardiology journals and was looking for personal contacts to get to a bigger university hospital where they would be interested in a pediatric cardiologist who specialized and had his forte in invasive diagnostic technique in children with congenital heart disease.

After some research, I received two offers to visit in the New York area. One was from a Children's Hospital in the Bronx, the other from the Downstate Medical Center in Brooklyn. I had to learn — eventually — how to take care of my liveli-hood and hunt for my job in a free society, where qualifications and market forces were determining the job market and competition was always just behind the cor-ner. Advice from a friend would open the door to a "paradise" and would be an important bonus.

I went to see the two institutions, and for that I flew to New York. I met the chairmen of the Departments and presented my curriculum vitae, where the years of my training in Boston were the main professional points, or the forte, of my qualification. I reviewed with the Head of the Division of Pediatric Cardiology, the division's clinical part and then mainly the technological strength of the laboratory for the diagnostic workup and the number of their procedures for a year. I was also interested in their number of surgical procedures and their eventual results. In other words, I wanted to have all the relevant information so I would know what I was going into.

Eventually I decided on University Centrum at the Downstate Medical Center in Brooklyn, which had a strong academic reputation and some Nobel Price laureates.

The Department of Pediatrics was chaired by Professor Charles Cook, a scholar from the Children's Hospital in Boston, with his alma mater Harvard Medical School. It played a significant role in my accepting the position. The Division of Pediatric Cardiology was led by Dr. Sydney Garber, who graduated from the Harvard School for Dentistry but then switched to pediatrics. The team was supplemented by two other Attendings in Pediatric Cardiology, and I would be their third member.

My wife was very happy that we would leave the fairy tale of snowy Buffalo, and my boss, the friendly Dr. Ed Lambert, understood that I didn't want to stay for good in that cultural backwater and gave me a letter of outstanding recommendation for my engaged work under his leadership. At Easter time, our daughter, Patricia, had her first communion at the Cathedral, where about forty little "white angels," Patsy included, gathered for a celebration. We brought her up in our faith and the faith of our ancestors, and the nuns prepared our daughter spiritually for the holy celebration (Fig. 48). At the festive and ostentatious mass, celebrated by the diocesan bishop, all the parents, in their festive attire, followed with great pride their offspring on that great day, perhaps reminiscing of their first communions many years ago. The mass ended with the solemn hymn, "Te Deum Laudamus," "We Prize the Lord". At the end of the mass, the Cathedral buzzed like a beehive of happy children and proud and happy parents. It was a joyous and memorable day for all of us.

My wife prepared just before the feast a sumptuous lunch for our daughter with her favorite food and dessert and surprised her with a small gift of white pearls, as it happened to be her birthday as well. We gave thanks that our daughter, in her faith, would remain in the footsteps of her parents.

In the following month, to everybody's surprise, an announcement spread in the city of Buffalo that Cardinal Joseph Mindszenty of Hungary, the jailed and proscribed warrior for freedom and against Communism — now in exile in Austria — will be the guest of honor of the city of Buffalo. He came to support and lift up the hearts of the exiled Hungarian émigrés of the Hungarian diaspora. The whole city was in great excitement and expectation, which extended to the large Polish population of émigrés as well. The whole city wanted to see the legendary warrior and fighter against Communism, and the preparations were huge to welcome and celebrate the great man. Of course, we wanted to be part of the celebration and rally of the faithful when our son was an altar boy at the cathedral. We never had seen the Cardinal before, but we were well-aware the history of his political "calvary," when first in 1919 he was incarcerated during the Communist putsch of Bela Kuhn in Hungary after the First World War. Next in 1944, the fascist government of the Arrow Cross jailed him as a protector of persecuted Jewish citizens, and in 1948 again the Stalinist Hungarian Communists jailed him, but in 1956, during the Hungarian Revolution, he escaped and found asylum in the U.S. Embassy in Budapest, where he spent fourteen years till he was allowed to emigrate to Vienna, Austria.

We did not want to miss this exceptional event. (He passed away a year later.) Cardinal J. Mindszenty was an older, haggard, gray-haired man, still standing ramrod tall. His stern, steely blue eyes revealed the ordeal of his trials in those exceptional times, revealing his notable personality. As he was approaching the main altar at the end of a long and festive procession in his ornamental mitre with his gilded shepherd's cane, he blessed the long line of his faithful. He gave the impression of a determined man willing to sacrifice his life for his faith.

The celebrated mass was festive with all the auxiliary bishops around the aging Cardinal with a flock of altar boys. The richly ornamental altar with white flowers was shrouded in a heavy cloud of incense from the fragrant myrrh, which permeated and filled the whole cathedral. We stayed through the long and celebrated mass, like a festive "marathon," and waited till the cardinal left the Cathedral with his whole entourage.

It was a memorable and imposing event in the history of Buffalo, not only for the Catholics, but for all the faithful who believed in the freedom to express their faith or their own consciences.

Unexpectedly in May, our beloved professor, Dr. Ed Lambert, fell ill. What started as a garden variety of the flu developed into a full-blown sepsis (blood infection), caused by the yellow staphylococcus bacteria. Despite five days of vigorous treatment, he had to be transferred to the Intensive Care Unit since his condition had turned gravely worse.

On the last day of his life, when nobody anticipated such a malignant turn of the events, I went to see and visit the Professor, the gentleman's gentlemen.

He was in an oxygen tent, and we could communicate only by gestures. As I was leaving, the professor tried to send me his lame smile as to a friend, since we had a very nice personal relationship. As I was leaving, I waved to him my blessing with my sad goodbye, as I was looking into a very pale face and forced grin. His clear blue eyes were giving testimony of his fading life.

The same evening, at 10 P.M., Dr. Edward Lambert passed away. The whole institution was in shock at the unexpected tragedy. He was a very kind, humane person, liked by everybody, a real gentleman and an excellent physician.

Since Prof. Dr. E. Lambert was a very good friend of my previous boss, Dr. A.S. Nadas, I raised my courage, and in the late evening after the death of Dr. E. Lambert, I called up Dr. A.S. Nadas and shared with him the unexpected news. On the telephone, Dr. A.S. Nadas was for a moment silent, as the unexpected news touched him personally. After a short pause, he thanked me that I had informed him about the loss of his close friend, saying, "Thank you very much, Zoltán."

The whole Children's Hospital participated in droves at the burial of that exceptional man who unexpectedly had passed away, showing that even modern medicine has its limitations. Dr. Peter Vlad delivered a solemn eulogy of the outstanding physician and declared properly that Dr. Ed. Lambert was one of the founders of pediatric cardiology in the USA.

The unexpected loss of that decent man and expert gave me some kind of absolution and quasi-endorsement that my decision to leave Buffalo was correct. His successor, Dr. P. Vlad, was a very different kind of human being. He was a hardcore, tough Romanian who would be less generous to accommodate somebody with a Hungarian tint in his first name. He was rather unpredictable, brooding in his decisions, even though he was a good specialist.

Just before the tragedy, I had made a short trip to New York, and with the help of a real estate agent — as I was then well-trained — I rented a two-bedroom apartment in the green side of Brooklyn called Bay Ridge. It was in a house along the coastline, close to the pillars of the longt and sleek Verrazano Bridge. The bridge was named after the famous Florentine seafarer Giuseppe Verrazano, who in service of the French king in 1524 discovered this ideal bay of the Atlantic Ocean, where the settlement of New Amsterdam was established, later called New York (Fig. 49). The slender bridge, which has an elegant design, connects Staten Island with the main periphery of New York. All the ships and cruisers coming to New York Harbor had to sail under the majestic arch of that most beautiful bridge.

Not far from its pillars on the Brooklyn side, we rented our apartment on the second floor of a three-story, red-brick building with a parking lot in the basement. The house was surrounded by a nice, green garden, and it was in the quaint part of Bay Ridge.

Our agent informed us that just at the corner of the street, there was a Catholic parish with a school, where our children could continue their studies. At the end of June, our story of moving westward to Buffalo had its repetition, just in the opposite, eastward direction to New York. Again I rented a yellow rent-a-car, and we all filled it up with all our stuff, perhaps with some more items than before. Again I climbed up to the high seats and the gargantuan steering wheel, and our son, Robert, was now my "experienced" navigator as we now drove in the west-east direction. My wife again followed me in her car, and I again boosted my energy by singing the now-famous song of the Russian frontline chauffeur, this time to the amusement of my son.

We started rather early in the morning, rushing through the town, and then turned westward and south. In a while, we passed Rochester and Syracuse and, for us, the "historical" Binghamton hill and turned more southward. Now I watched carefully that our gas tank would not go empty as before. After about four hours of driving, we took a short rest to stretch out our backs and have a lunch of tasty sandwiches prepared by my wife. Then I turned the truck more southward, passing the town of Scranton with its rich history of Slovaks who settled there in their diaspora. Those economic emigrants were coming into that area from the end of the nineteenth century to work in the neighboring coal mines and settle there with their families.

In another three hours of driving, we were approaching the west of Staten Island and its suburbs, and in a short while, we were driving across the beautiful Verrazano Bridge with its shiny, extended steel cables.

The street where we rented our apartment was not far from the pillars of the bridge in Bay Ridge. I quickly found the street of our house. Since we were in the middle of summertime, the sunset was just slowly, stealthily sneaking in, as the corona of the sun started to submerge to the bottom of the horizon. At that advantage, we rolled up our sleeves and quickly transferred our belongings to the second floor in our house. We all were now experts on packing, unpacking, and moving in or out. In a good hour, we arranged all our furniture in our new dwelling, my Castro iron bed included, which relentlessly was beating and scratching our knees and ankles. We were quite tired, but under the command of my wife and with her skills, the apartment with the bedroom was ready for our first night in Bay Ridge. Naturally we were then not only exhausted but hungry as well. We were lucky to find a nearby fish restaurant on the banks of the Atlantic Ocean. The restaurant had a wide assortment of different fish, with the obligatory golden, crispy French fries. As we were quite hungry, we ate without a word in silence, just the crunching of the French fries rattled the silence in our ambiance. We splashed down the tasty fried sea bass with an ice-cold Budweiser, or Sprite for our children, and our hungry mood started to soften. A happy smile soon appeared on the faces of our children first, and we happily joined in. The dinner was crowned by a glass of chocolate ice cream and a dollop of whipped cream.

We were then quickly hurrying back to our new home, as we were all dead tired. We fell quickly asleep, but I had to turn on my alarm clock. On the first of July 1974, I had to report at the Children's Hospital, which was part of the large building complex of Downstate Medical Centrum, SUNY, in Brooklyn. I looked for the Division of Pediatric Cardiology, where I was expected by the physician in charge, Dr. Sydney Garber.

BROOKLYN — ROSLYN, NEW YORK

I started to work at the Department Of Pediatrics of the Downstate Medical Center of SUNY, in charge by Chairman Dr. Charles Cook, a graduate of the Boston Children's Hospital. Based on my training in Boston, publications, and research, he appointed me as an Assistant Professor Of Pediatrics. My main assignment was in teaching the art of pediatric cardiology in theory and clinical practice, with diagnostic workup for fellows, residents, and medical students as well.

In the late morning, I had an appointment with Dr. Charles Cook, a handsome, tall, and lean Anglo-Saxon with a curly, salt-and-pepper coiffure of his hair and clear, blue, penetrating eyes, which had an inquisitive expression. At our meeting, he welcomed me on his faculty and was professionally courteous but rather impersonal. He regarded me and my qualifications as an important contribution to his staff. Following our brief exchange, he introduced me to the members of his faculty, about fifteen of them, who were about my age or older, specialists in different fields of pediatrics. What surprised me was that well over half of them were foreign medical graduates born outside of the USA.

In my teaching and training of the younger generation of doctors, I was mostly responsible for the two Fellows in training and the rotating Residents. I introduced the Fellows, besides the art of physical examination, to the forte of mine, that is, to the workup of patients and defining their anatomic problems before their surgery by an invasive technique. For that it was necessary to show and teach them how to advance a small, plastic tube into a vein in the groin and pass it into the heart to measure pressures, take samples of blood for oxygen content in all chambers of the heart, and making pictures (film) after a contrasting dye was injected into the heart and filmed by high-speed camera. I demonstrated to these fellows the "how to" of the technique with simple advice: "Pass the tube gently, very gently with an instinctive feeling" (Fig. 50).

In our Division, three of us attendings had the same academic rank. Unfortunately I soon noticed that Stanley, "the chief," viscerally disliked his associate Bob, who was mainly responsible for the postoperative care of our patients. It was a disheartening and disturbing revelation for our team, as well as our interdependence and teamwork. I tried to concentrate on my work and my responsibilities and find the best "modus operandi" between the two of them.

But Bob was a tough fellow, an introvert, and friendliness was not his strong trait. It did not portend anything positive for the future.

The Department had its weekly "grand rounds" where the members of the Faculty or the Fellows presented the results of their research or any novelty in their field of specialty. As I joined the faculty, in the coming month, I presented my research lecture, "New techniques and achievements in the diagnosis of congenital heart defects in children." The lecture was richly documented by slides of the different pathologies of the heart. Following the lecture, I experienced a very vivid discussion and exchange with the members of the faculty, and I was peppered with many questions, as I kept my answers right to the point. My "boss" congratulated me for my enlightening and innovative approach and presentation, and colleagues also chimed in. I was happy that my presentation went well and was appreciated by the plenum.

Socially as we settled down in that suburb of New York, we learned by word of mouth that New York had in its boroughs a large Slovak diaspora, which was quite active and meeting weekly in the Church of Saint John of Nepomucene on First Avenue and 66th Street. There after the holy mass celebrated in our native language, the faithful were congregating for a social hour and coffee in the basement hall of the church.

There I met the President of the Slovak League, John Holly, and his wife, Nina, who was active in presentations of Slovak folklore, such as beautifully embroidered costumes from our native land and folk songs by the ensemble of the choir. I also met Dr. Joseph Stasko, a member of the Parliament who had been persecuted by the Communists, and a whole group of other members and countrymen as well.

We were quickly accepted as newcomers into the group, and from then on, anytime we could we participated in those friendly Sunday meetings with our children, where we enjoyed common cultural roots with people from our native country.

The church, established by the Slovaks in diaspora, was inaugurated on October 25, 1895, originally on Fourth Street and First Avenue. It was a small church still in the time of Austria-Hungary before the First World War and part of the larger parish of Saint Elisabeth, led by Father Frank Pribyl. The beginnings of the small parish were very difficult. Everything was built only from donations of the faithful, and the frequent changes of the chaplains were less than beneficial.

A decisive and pivotal change occurred in 1916 during the First World War when a young Slovak priest (1887), Stephan Krasula, came to study theology in the U.S. as a twenty-year-old ambitious priest. He was a young and intelligent priest with solid organizational talent, and from then on, the parish started to flourish quite rapidly.

In 1925 he was successful to fund and build today's church of Saint John of Nepomucene on 66th Street, with its parish and school, for $300,000 U.S. Reverend St. Krasula led the community of Slovaks in diaspora for fifty-two years. In 1956 a beautiful altar of marble was installed with a blue baldachin over the main altar, and we remember it well (Fig. 51). From the beginning of the seventies, the parish was led by Father Robert Tomlian, and the Slovaks in diaspora got formally organized in a new body of the Slovak-American Cultural Center (SACC) established in 1967 in New York. The primary mission and task of the Center was to retain and cherish the cultural inheritance of our forefathers, with their language, art, customs, and literature further maintained and advanced for the young generation. The SACC was also presenting and teaching the youth the turbulent history of the Slovaks and their culture and art, as well as informing the younger generation of the achievements of Slovak-Americans in their new country.

We joined that cultural body with my family, and as a U.S.-trained physician and avid student of Slovak history, I had soon some informative lectures for the membership.

In the fall, our first in New York, we attended the traditional Slovak Heritage Festival organized by the Slovak League of America in New Jersey. We were surprised by the huge gathering of Slovak-Americans, probably from the whole East Coast. It started usually with a celebratory holy mass, followed by a rich cultural program of songs and dances by different dancing group in classical Slovak, colorful and richly embroidered costumes from different regions of Slovakia. The

Slovak folk songs were very popular since they brought back sweet memories and reminded us of our happy youth. For years to come, we were regular participants of this beautiful autumnal celebration, where we also nurtured our friendship with many of our countrymen from different regions of our native land, Slovakia.

The next year in 1975, we received a letter from the Department of State that we were chosen to be awarded citizenship in the United States of America. In some mysterious paradox, it shook us up and gave us some unexpected unease. On one side, we were elated that we, who as refugees were running for our lives and security, got a new home and belonging. On the other side, we were struck by inexplicable unease, as our roots were still elsewhere in our old country. Who can understand the human breed?

Eventually, as our real dream came through, my wife and I dressed up for the felicitous occasion and drove to the district court in Brooklyn, New York. We were welcomed and introduced into a festive hall by a military guard in full regalia, where about fifty future citizens were expecting to receive the great honor. As we looked around, people of all colors and races were gathered there for the festive celebration. We were seated in comfortable chairs while the somewhat strained and anxious atmosphere was tried to be somehow eased by the classic march of "Yankee Doodle Dandy" from 1775 in its soft presentation. (The march was "reincarnated" during the WW II in 1942.)

In front of us on the elevated podium, there was a large, ornamental desk with two empty chairs, flanked by the banner of New York State on one side, while on the other side the Star-Spangled Banner was floating. In a short while, an officer in a dark uniform came to the podium and asked for our identification. We presented our green cards, which he took in his professional possession.

Next the Senator of New York came to the rostrum, who in his professional presentation — lasting five to seven minutes — welcomed us as new citizens of the United States of America and called upon all of us to pledge our allegiance to the Constitution of the USA, during which pledge the Star-Spangled Banner was unfolded by an officer. We had to denounce our allegiance to any other foreign state or nation, and we pledged to defend the USA even with a gun if needed. After we finished our pledge, the Senator congratulated all of us that we had fulfilled all the requirements and were now citizens of the United States of America. With the American anthem, "The Star-Spangled Banner," our ceremony came to its end. During the celebration, many eyes welled up with tears of joy and jubilant smiles, and all of us realized our solemn responsibility and our commitment. Then all of us, the new citizens, congratulated each other and happily shook hands.

Slowly we left the auditorium in some solemn perplexity but eventually in a happy mood, and with our positive resolve, we stepped out into sunny Brooklyn. At the exit of the auditorium, we received our Certificate of Naturalization as written evidence of our new status: a citizen of the USA. In an upbeat mood, we had a small celebration in a nearby restaurant with a quintessential American brisket steak and a glass of chardonnay. We were, nevertheless, hastily driving home, as our children were coming home from school, and their mom used to always be at home at the time of their arrival.

While I was working hard to upgrade and secure my position in academic medicine, my wife took exemplary care of our two small children as they started to attend their new school. At that time, we were considering the possibility of having an additional economic line to improve our humble economic standing. To achieve that goal, it was necessary to upgrade the qualification of my wife in nursing, since her credentials from our native land were not acceptable in the USA. Hence in kind of a parallel to our children's schooling, my wife signed up to be a "student" again when she enrolled in the private Richmond College for nursing on Staten Island. Consequently every morning, all four of us departed for our assignments, and my wife travelled by bus across the Verrazano Bridge to her new school. I was, nevertheless, insistent, and we made an agreement, that my wife would attend all of her courses till 3 P.M., but she would be at home when our children came home from school to the loving care of their mom. All of us had, hence, a rather tight daily program, while I was usually returning home by car at 6 P.M. for dinner with the whole family.

On our floor as our neighbors, we had a lovely childless couple, a startling blond, Peggy, and kind, balding Walter. Peggy was eager and frequently available to help my wife, Judy, with the children. Peggy liked to supervise them during their piano lessons by banging on the wall at any misplaced note. We had a very warm relationship with the ever-smiling Peggy and the gentle Walter.

Now in our sixth year in the U.S., we could afford from our savings to buy a color RCA TV, and especially the children were elated. In those years of the mid-seventies, excellent educational programs were available for children with their didactic and social core and entertainment, which were interesting for the adults as well. These were very useful for my wife as well to upgrade her vocabulary and polish her English. We all liked *Mr. Rogers' Neighborhood*, and who could forget the warm and genteel smile of the unforgettable Fred Rogers and the baritone of Elmo in *Sesame Street*. We all liked them a lot!

Unfortunately from the second year of my appointment, some heavy clouds and unexpected problems started to lurk on the horizon of the Department of Pediatrics.

Our heart surgeon, Dr. A.G. was not able in his surgical technique to achieve acceptable surgical results in some more complex lesions of the heart; hence our mortality rate showed up to be unacceptable. It was a great concern of mine, since no cardiologist wants to lose the life of his patient in the hands of an incompetent surgeon. The second serious problem developed between the members of the Senior Faculty and the Chairman himself. It went so far that a group of Senior Faculty initiated legal proceedings against the Chairman, who disagreed that members of the Faculty in academic medicine should have a private practice at all.

For me that kind of litigation was totally new and unheard of, especially in my native land with socialized medicine, where the authority of the Chairman could not be undermined and challenged. The whole atmosphere in the Department was poisonous and unbearable. In principle and philosophically, I agreed with the Chairman, who put emphasis on research, teaching, and therapy for the patients as the backbone of the academia. As a younger member of the Faculty, I kept my mouth shut, like during socialism. But I had realized that in such a situation, my progress in my specialty had not much chance to go forward, nor my advancement in the academic field.

In that ugly and explosive situation, I committed myself to my work and research and prepared myself for the Board of General Pediatrics as a prerequisite so that I could next face the exam for the Board of Pediatric Cardiology to be on equal footing with any other American specialist. I wanted to be firmly anchored, along with my academic qualifications, in my specialty — or, in colloquial parlance, to be "second to none."

The task, to study for the exam of the board of general pediatrics, was perhaps the most difficult engagement of any of my previous examinations, since I had to go back about twenty years and reactivate my knowledge and training in pediatrics in my old country. I had to go back to all the forgotten textbooks of General Pediatrics and restudy the whole spectrum of the particulars in that field. In addition I had to face a new "monster" on the scene, "the computer," for the written part of the exam, with which I was rather poorly acquainted. Lo and behold, I passed the written exam without a hitch.

Next I had to face the oral exam of General Pediatrics before the Board of Professors in Chicago. I flew to Chicago under significant stress, well-prepared from my night studies of a few months. The exam was organized in a large hotel downtown. Each candidate had to face a Commission of five experts, who, in about an hour, showered the candidates with some specific or pointed questions and its minutiae in the field of general pediatrics. The examiners registered their answers with the faces of poker players, and it was impossible to fathom if the answer was right.

Incidentally there was one examiner who I trained with in pediatric cardiology in Boston, and he recognized me. Yet by the rules, every examiner had to excuse himself from the commission of examiners if they had trained the candidate. I was thus assigned to be examined by other commissions, and it was a grueling duel, but I stood rather firm with my theoretical knowledge.

I returned home after three days half dead, but within a month, to my great satisfaction and joy, I learned that I had passed the exam with honor and was named a Diplomate of the Academy of Pediatrics.

The irony in the situation was that in 1955, I passed the board of pediatrics in Czechoslovakia, an exam consisting only of three oral questions before a commission of three professors, well-known to me and vice versa. There was an immense difference in quantitative and qualitative content and methods of the examination regarding the objective assessment and the depth of knowledge between the two exams. It was a difficult hill to climb, but it was worthwhile.

In the third year of my appointment at Downstate, I attended a conference in Manhattan, where I met Prof. Dr. Welton Gersony, the Chief of Pediatric Cardiology at the Baby Hospital in New York. He was also trained in Boston by Dr A.S. Nadas at the Children's Hospital. There was some kind of "special kinship" between the trainees from Boston, like in some kind of tribe, where the trainees from the same clan could trust each other, like the knights of a special order.

As I talked to Welton, a very amicable guy, I confided in him that at our department of pediatrics at Downstate, there were significant problems and infighting between the Chairman and the senior faculty. I then confidentially asked him, as the leading pediatric cardiologist in the area, if he perhaps knew about an institution that was looking for a specialist in the diagnostics of cardiac catheterization in children. Welton promised me that he would ask around and let me know.

The next day, after the afternoon session, Welton contacted me with the information that at the Heart Center of Saint Francis Hospital on Long Island, N.Y., they were looking just for such a pediatric cardiologist. He added, "Wait, I will

introduce you to the Chief of Pediatric Cardiology there." After his kind introduction and recommendation, I had a meeting with Dr. Filippo Balboni, a graduate of
the University of Rome, Italy. He was a handsome, tall man in his late fifties, with
short, brown hair with some graying on his whiskers, and warm, brown eyes. He
was a pleasant and jovial Italian indeed. On that afternoon, I had a long interchange
with Filippo, which was quite positive and friendly. At the end of our talk, we
agreed that I would present to him my personal curriculum vitae and documents
about my training and Boards. He simultaneously invited me to visit his Institution,
the Heart Center, in the following days in Roslyn, a small but lovely town on the
north shore of Long Island, east of Manhattan.

The Hospital of Saint Francis was founded by the Sisters of the Order of Saint
Francis in 1922, when for their charitable work in that community, they received
from a local philanthropist and benefactor a gift of twenty acres of potato fields,
carved off from his huge land surrounding the town. It was in the area called
Flower Hill on the side of the sprouting town of Roslyn on the banks of the Atlantic
on the northern shore of Long Island.

At that time, the sisters decided to build a sanatorium for children inflicted
with tuberculosis, which was then rampant in the area. There was no other treatment available but isolation and rest since streptomycin was discovered a quarter
century later. They built on those potato fields the first units of wooden barracks
and an administrative building. The sisters were exceptionally skillful and experienced with a lot of organizational know-how and great enthusiasm for their project.
From the financial contribution and help of the local citizens, they hired a pediatrician, a general practitioner, and built a building for X-rays and a medical laboratory for children. All the patients were hospitalized free of charge, following the
commandment of Jesus: "love thy neighbor." That philosophy of charity was a
fundamental building block of their love for the suffering and sick as part of their
love for their neighbors. It was still well and alive when I started to work in that
institution many years later.

The sanatorium had changed by that time into a solid, red-brick building, but
the progress in medicine and the arrival of streptomycin after WW II had ended
the function and usefulness of the hospital.

The sisters, nevertheless, did not want to abandon the crowning achievement
of their success, and after some consultation and review with experts, the sanatorium was transformed into a Center for rheumatic heart disease in children, which
was then raging in the community and around that wet region.

The incidence of rheumatic fever was high in that coastal area of the Atlantic. Yet penicillin, which was able to subdue the streptococcal infection, the cause of rheumatic fever, was available from 1942-44 only for the military in war. Only after the end of WW II was it accessible to the general public.

Then the new Center was expanded in its size to a large, two-floor, brick building that could hospitalize up to one hundred children. In addition on the side of the center, a lovely chapel was built for the faithful and the public as well (Fig. 52).

What was most important and eminently professional was that the board of those bright and intelligent sisters invited the best-qualified physicians in the field from the House of Good Samaritan of Boston, which was affiliated and physically adjacent to the Children's Hospital in Boston. Coincidentally, in the House of Good Samaritans, I spent three months in the early seventies during my fellowship in Boston under the guidance of Prof. Dr. Benedict Massell, who was the physician in chief there. What a coincidence!

The Center started its work under the leadership of Dr. Leo Taran and Dr. Nelly Silágyi from Boston. These scientists advanced their pioneering research in etiology, clinical course, and treatment of rheumatic fever, facilitated now by the available penicillin, aspirin, and also cortisone. These two researchers laid down the foundation of the Heart Center by publishing more than twenty research papers in peer-review journals in the early sixties.

In the passing time again, the progress in medicine victoriously defeated the debilitating disease of rheumatic fever, and the Center concomitantly and physiologically changed its care for children with congenital or inborn heart defects.

Consequently the Center had to change and broaden its diagnostic armamentarium to diagnose the anatomic defects with new technology and, subsequently, also for their treatment or correction by surgical means. The new Cardio-Surgical Center was extended by a separate surgical pavilion, led by a new and prominent surgeon, who in time with his team advanced the Center into an outstanding Heart Center in the USA.

At the end of the seventies, a charitable Gift of Life Foundation was established in that Catholic institution to help children with congenital heart defects from developmental countries in the whole world. The children came for treatment from countries where the surgical know-how or surgical treatment of congenital problems was not available, such as Africa, Asia, or Eastern Europe. It was a God-sent institution for me, in which after my extensive training, I was well-equipped with all the modern diagnostic know-how to satisfy the professional requirements — intertwined with the philosophy of charity — to help those less fortunate children.

Eventually I left the Downstate Medical Center in the summer of 1978, with all its political and personal shenanigans that poisoned the whole working environment. Ultimately the Chairman, Dr. Charles Cook, left the institution a year later as well.

Incidentally at that time, my wife graduated with success from the Richmond College of Nursing and rolled up her sleeves for a struggle in facing the licensure examination in nursing of New York State. It was her turn to cram and study for the exam at night. But my industrious "bumblebee," my gracious wife, passed the exam with flying colors and received her Certificate of a Licensed Nurse for New York State. It was an insurance for our family. Just in case she had to go to work, she was ready to go. We celebrated the big event with our children in a Japanese restaurant, Benihana, and with a small gift for my accomplished wife.

In 1978, I was accepted as an Attending in Pediatric Cardiology in the Heart Center of Saint Francis Hospital and approved by the board of directors after my credentials of qualification were reviewed. The Chairwoman of the board was Sister Joan Kister. She was in her fifties, experienced in management and nursing with a Master's Degree, and lead the Centrum very professionally for many years. Joan was a women of medium height, clad in a more modern version of the habit for nuns, with a white skirt and a white jacket, with a white head scarf in the shape of corona. She looked quite spritely but professional. Her grayish blue eyes with a steely tint were measuring me up or assessing me during my interview in a subtle, but professional manner amid the presence of Dr. F. Balboni, my future boss. She was a self-confident professional, talking to the point and facts. The interview was only about my professional qualifications and experience and no small talk.

I was coming at the right time to the Center, as simultaneously an accomplished heart surgeon, Dr. Fred Thomson, was appointed as the head of the department of surgery. The Center needed a specialist-cardiologist who had the skill and command of modern diagnostic methods in the workup of a patient before corrective surgery, especially if the program Gift of Life would be initiated.

During the interview, through an oblique but nimble question, it transpired that I was of Catholic faith, and she was happy or relieved by that. It looked that I had come right in time into a right place and was fitting like a key into a proper lock.

As I quickly learned, the Department of Pediatrics had a huge backlog of local children with heart disease, and they needed a modern diagnostic workup before the surgical repair. The extension of the Gift of Life program of charity, as an addition, was especially appealing to me. As one saying says, "Who received a lot should return a lot." The program was, for me, kind of a personal down payment to my new country and society, which welcomed me and gave me all the opportunities — not free of charge — yet offered me a lot in my professional career.

The Gift of Life Program, besides its professional core at the department, had to have a parallel facility for lodging for the patients before all of the diagnostic procedures and to care for the chaperoning parent. That division served also as a preoperative and postoperative recovery department. It was in a nice wing of the hospital, which, for the patients from far and remote lands, looked like a luxury hotel. The kind and gray-haired Sister Mary Gobel, a French Canadian, was in charge. Her French accent and my Slovak mixed very well, and we had a wonderful professional and personal relationship. She was a lady with a big heart and was a solace and support for the patients and their mothers in their hard times, as most of them did not speak English.

As an Attending, I was assigned a nice office on the side of my boss, Dr. F. Balboni. Right away he took me to the Department of Pediatrics with its twenty-five beds and an adjacent Intensive Care Unit of four beds, equipped with up-to-date technology for monitoring the patient after an open heart surgery. He introduced me to the head nurse, Elaine, and to the rest of the nursing staff as the new Attending. Then he took me to the Cardiac Catheterization Laboratory, the pride of the Center with its modern and advanced technology and equipment. The Center had at that time two labs, but in a short time, it was increased to five laboratories. The lab was managed and serviced by an outstanding staff of nurses and technicians.

My first catheterization was indeed a memorable one in the annals of the center, which was quoted in years to come. As I changed into green-scrub attire and washed my hands, the little patient was already prepped and covered with sterile sheets. I looked around, and it was visible from the quivering glances between the nursing staff that they were tense and nervous. They did not know what to expect from this new fellow with his strange accent. The nurses, of course, prepped the patient the old way, that is, the area above the relevant vessel was covered. As I approached the examining table and the patient, I looked around, and in a rather accentuated voice, I asked the relevant question: "And what is this?" I pointed to the prepped groin, where I could not approach the vessel of my interrogation. The whole lab froze with all the nurses. But I changed to a soothing smile and resolved the tension and showed the team the preparation of the patient "a la Boston," when through a slit in the cover, one could feel the pulse of the artery with the vein was just on its side, and the area was then disinfected with iodine solution. The girls looked around, and they seemed to accept the targeted approach to the relevant vessels. And the girls watched me like hawks as I swiftly punctured the vein, inserted the plastic tube, the catheter, and under X-ray control, passed it into the heart of the small boy. With my catheter, I virtually "swiped out" all the chambers of the heart, taking blood samples and measuring pressures in every chamber. The nurses just watched and tightly muttered, "Hey! This guy, he knows what he is doing."

During the following two decades, that team of nurses were my most reliable, kind, and professional associates, with an exceptional rapport and respect of each other. Nurses such as Sheila, Claire, Joyce, Michelle, and all the rest of them, remain in my memory as shining jewels of our professional cooperation and human friendliness, as well as respect in our mutual relationship. In a short time, I was appointed the Director of the Pediatric Cardiac Laboratory.

With my full engagement and emergencies, the distance and driving from Bay Ridge to Roslyn showed up to be a significant burden. After some consultation with my boss and colleagues as well, we hired a middle-aged lady, Mrs. Brooks, and with her assistance and help, we filled our weekends with house hunting and looking for an acceptable house in the neighborhood. We reviewed about fifty houses, and the whole search or hunt for a house was getting on our nerves. But on one of the last weekends, Mrs. Brooks showed us a lovely house in the rather close neighborhood of East Hills, in the community of Roslyn. It was a medium-sized, split house with a half acre of garden and two birch trees in front of the house. In the back, two huge oak trees gave us nice shade with their enormous crowns of foliage. They offered a pleasant environment on the sizable patio, paved by travertine, fit for an afternoon coffee and cake. The garden was surrounded by a rural picket fence and surrounding junipers and golden yellow shrubs of laburnum and, on the side, some medium-size pine trees.

The house had the nice interior arrangement of a split house with three stories. The house had a well-preserved dry basement, and on the next level was a large living room with its adjacent dining compartment and social space. On the same level, there was a fully equipped kitchen and on the garden side a comfortable den. On the second level, there was a nice study, tailored for me, a large bedroom for the parents, and two sizable rooms for each of our growing children.

We looked at each other with joy, satisfaction, and smiles of delight. *Yes!* This sure will be a lovely home for our family! (Fig. 53). Mrs. Brook helped us with the mortgage — our first! — and in early fall 1978, we moved from Bay Ridge to the lovely and green East Hills.

The moving was accomplished by a professional moving company, and we enhanced and embellished our dining area with a Scandinavian rosewood dining set with an elegant sideboard and glass vitrine and a large rosewood dining table with a glass top. We had also a new Scandinavian leather sofa with two easy chairs and a large coffee table of rosewood for the social part of our living room. The sets in the living room were complemented by a sleek, upright, rosewood piano from Manhattan for our two children, yet neither turned out to be Franz Liszt after four years of piano lessons.

Our Heart Center was only five minutes by car from our home, a great advantage for me. But the children changed their schools as well, and we had to secure their transportation. While our daughter attended the School of Saint Mary in neighboring Manhasset, an adjacent village, still transportation by car was necessary. Our son, Robert, qualified to the distinguished Regis High School of Jesuits, and he had to be transported to the train station in Manhasset.

The only practical solution was to buy a second car, a small Volkswagen Golf, and every morning my wife drove the children to school in Manhasset and from there to the train station. From there she could drive to the neighboring supermarket in the neighboring Green-Wale Plaza for her groceries if needed. It looked so that eventually my wife had turned into a typical American suburban housewife with her morning duties, except that she did not drive our children to school in her nightgown or bathrobe. She was always fully dressed in her attire, spic and span, according to her upbringing in her native country.

Even though we lived a fair distance from Manhattan, about an hour's drive to the church through the Long Island Parkway, we tried to be present at the holy mass regularly as much we could and mix with friends of the Slovak diaspora afterwards amidst a good coffee and cookies. We also were participating in plans for social activities and social functions in that cohesive community.

In the early eighties, we started fundraising for a memorial for Colonel Jan Poloreczky, a graduate of the French Royal Military Academy and a Slovak hero of the American Revolution, who came to fight for American independence with his three hundred hussars, alongside Gen. George Washington. That elite unit was part of the seventeen thousand strong French Continental Army, which in 1781 at Yorktown forced the surrender of General Charles Cornwallis and his nine thousand strong Redcoats. Colonel Jan Poloreczky and his hussars made a significant contribution to the victory for Independence. A gray, granite memorial arching over his grave was dedicated to that hero in the cemetery in Yonkers, N.Y., in a solemn ceremony in the presence of over one hundred Slovak-Americans. We concluded the ceremony with an elegiac Slovak ballad, "Who Is Ablaze for Truth!" The whole crowd was very happy that we could pay tribute and honor that great man and hero of the American Revolution.

In our Center, with the collaboration of our team of nurses, we started a novel technique to open up and separate the leaflets of the pulmonary valve, which were stuck together since birth. With the help of that technique, a balloon catheter was inflated across the valve, which separated the leaflets and by that avoided surgical intervention. The patient could return home the next day and enjoy his or her life,

We also used a "coil technique" by which we could sneer of and abolish an inborn connection with a metallic coil, through the so-called "arterial duct," a connection between the aorta (the main artery of the body) and the pulmonary artery (the main vessel supplying the lungs). Again by this technique, surgical intervention was avoided.

The "girls" in the diagnostic lab were "elated and exited" that we were doing something new and interesting for the kids so they didn't have to have open heart surgery.

It was a great advantage and honor that our heart center was academically affiliated with the State University of New York and its campus at Stony Brook. I was very happy that I could continue as a teacher of my specialty in the academic program of the Department of Pediatrics of the University for the residents and medical students. Besides our clinical teaching at the bedside at our Center, we held regular lectures in pediatric cardiology at the Academic Center in Minneola Hospital or at the conference room of our heart center.

For one of our conferences, we invited Dr. A.S. Nadas, my teacher from Boston. We had a very friendly and heartfelt meeting during lunch. He let me know that he was very proud of his former trainee and fellow, Zoltán. We stayed in touch and continued to have professional cooperation and communication with the Children's Hospital in Boston and his Department through our mutual patients. It was my last encounter with "my boss" at the end of the eighties. He was an outstanding chief, leader, and teacher and a good friend (Fig. 42).

Our charitable program Gift of Life was successfully and steadily advancing, and in those early years, we were able to offer diagnostic workup and surgical repair for 120 children with congenital heart disease. Some children came from Africa, but the majority of children came from Gdansk, Poland. I had remained in touch with the Polish cardiologist, Dr. Kristina Dymnicka, since 1973 when we met each other during my presentation at the American College of Cardiology in Chicago. We also cared for thirty children from Italy, with their complete workup before surgery and their total surgical repair.

In 1987 President Ronald Reagan and his wife, Nancy, were on a state visit in South Korea. As their goodwill gesture and the goodwill of the people of the U.S. vis-a-vis South Korea, the President and his wife brought to the U.S. two Korean children with heart disease, visibly ill with their blue lips and shortness of breath. Those two children were transferred from Washington on a presidential limousine to the Saint Francis Heart Center in Roslyn for diagnostic examination and surgical repair. It was a great honor for our Center to be chosen for such a medically and politically delicate task. The media, TV, and newspapers were commenting on the charitable and humanitarian action of our Hospital, underlining that all the medical and surgical care would be free of charge for the patients.

The two children were immediately admitted to the preoperative department with Sister Mary Gobel in charge. After a few days, when the children had overcome their jet lag, the children were admitted to the clinical floor of the Department of Pediatrics, where first all the noninvasive tests like chest X-rays and echocardiograms were performed, followed by a cardiac catheterization, where the nature of the anatomic defects were identified. Those results were presented at the surgical conference, and following that our new heart surgeon, Dr. Paul Damus, performed the corrective operation. In about ten days, the children could return to South Korea. An unexpected happy ending turned out when the American public opened up their generous hearts and adopted those two children into two American families. The media, TV, and newspapers were elated and ecstatic with the happy end, like in a fairytale story of Hollywood.

In the last chapter of that American fairy tale, the President's wife, Nancy, came to visit the two "healthy" children and express her sincere gratitude to our Center for its charity, expertise, and care, giving those children a real "gift of life." In a more personal way, Mrs. Nancy Reagan thanked especially the surgeon, Dr.

Paul Damus, for his surgical prowess and me as the chief cardiologist for my expert preoperative diagnosis and postoperative care (Fig. 54).

In the evening, the first lady of the U.S. was honored by a gala dinner at the famous Waldorf Astoria Hotel in Manhattan. In a short speech, she warmly thanked and expressed her deep appreciation to all members of the Saint Francis Heart Center for the exemplary care and healing of those two children. She ended with, "Thank you very much to all!"

It was a memorable evening for all of us, where I was congratulated again with my wife personally by the first lady of the U.S., and many of the pictures were proudly posted on the bulletin board in the hospital.

As the result of this successful event, the Government of South Korea Republic cleverly yet generously invited our diagnostic team to examine and triage some children with congenital heart defects in South Korea, who could then be eligible for corrective heart surgery. We gladly obliged as a goodwill gesture of the American public and soon made preparations for the expedition. We also accepted the request of the South Korean Government to train one of its physicians, Dr. Kim, for six months in pediatric cardiology.

In a few weeks, two of us, the head of the division and myself, with one technician, flew to South Korea. We also took with us an echocardiograph machine — after it was checked out for explosives by the authorities.

Our flight from New York to Tokyo lasted over eleven grueling hours. Fortunately the next flight to Seoul lasted only one hour, yet at the end of the trip, we were quite exhausted. We were welcomed in the luxurious Hilton hotel for foreign guests, where we spent a refreshing night.

We spent in South Korea about a week — three days in Seoul, and then we were whisked by minibus to the University Hospital of Tegu and at the end of the week to the harbor city of Pusan on the shores of the Pacific.

In all hospitals, we were cordially welcomed by the Medical Staff and escorted to the clean examining rooms for the examination of the children and the following echocardiography, with assistance from the Korean nursing staff. In that whole week, from early morning till late evening, we examined about five hundred children with heart disease. The mothers came from the faraway countryside, as all the examinations were free of charge. Those mothers brought their sick children in different strollers, and some came on the backs of the mothers in a sack. It was very moving for us to see those struggling women from the rural areas, and many were expecting miracles, as the rumors had spread by word of mouth incorrectly that the children would be healed. It lasted a while, and the nursing staff explained to the concerned mothers that we were providing only a "triage," that is, assessing which children would be good candidates for surgical repair. Consequently for some, it was a huge disappointment, which we were unable to handle and had to rely on the local nursing staff. Most of the Korean mothers bowed deeply after the examination and repeated, "Ghamsa-mi dah" ("Thank you very much) or "Chak-ha-da" ("You are a good human being"). It was the highest honorarium and the most precious reward for all of us, from the bottom of the heart of a Korean mother.

Nevertheless, it was a huge clinical accomplishment to examine such a large number of sick children in such a short time. Every evening we were exhausted as we returned to our hotel.

Being in a different society and culture like South Korea, we struggled with indigestion from the Korean diet from the first days on. At lunchtime Korean girls offered their culinary menu with an inviting smile, the classic bul-gogi, a spicy, hot marinated baked beef, with a side dish, the so-called kimchi, a fermented, half-rotten, putrid cabbage, which stank like excrement. We were all sick, thanks to the quintessential Korean specialty of kimchi. It was fermented in large cans like amphoras with different spices and additives, and those amphoras were kept and were visible on balconies of many apartment buildings, and not only visible, but the whole area stank terribly from it, like from feces. It was obvious that for the locals, the smell of kimchi was equivalent to the smell of French perfume.

I carefully tried kimchi, which was spiced by a concoction of sharp black pepper and hot horseradish, and after the first lick, my tongue was burning, my face turned red, and I was ready to vomit. I lamely tried to apologize to my Korean neighbor and hide my embarrassment.

My real culinary "Waterloo" came at the festive lunch of the University of Tegu, where a local delicacy was presented to us on a large, porcelain plate. It was a "filled goat stomach" with some undisclosed stuffing. I hoped it would be something like turkey stuffing, but after I swallowed the first piece with closed eyes, not to offend our host, right away I developed severe stomach cramps, and I had to leave the hall immediately for my "Montezuma" finale. Fortunately some adjustments and simplifications were made in our diet to survive our trip.

Before my trip to South Korea, I recalled that while in Boston, I had befriended a fellow from Japan with whom I spent a month in the training of cardiac pathology with the whimsical but outstanding Dr. Richard van Praagh.

We had studied the specimens of abnormal hearts together and gotten along very well. Before my departure for South Korea, I wrote to Dr. Masahiko Ando a letter that I would be delighted if I could visit him in Tokyo since I would be close by in Seoul. His reply was encouragingly welcoming and positive, that he would be very happy to welcome me in Japan and rekindle our old friendship. I, of course, was interested not only to see his institution, but to see Tokyo as well and to get an impression of Japanese society and culture. After a tumultuous but successful week in South Korea, I said goodbye to the members of my group, as they flew back to New York while I was flying to nearby Tokyo. At the airport, Masahiko was waiting for me and was kind to welcome me in Japan as a generous gesture of Oriental hospitality.

Masahiko, a shorter, dark-eyed man with a thick, black hairdo and inviting smile, was now an Attending in cardiac pathology at the Japanese National Heart Center. He drove me to the center of that "megapolis" into an elegant hotel, New Otani, which was part of the center of the city, called Shin-djuku. While we were driving from the airport terminal to the city, I shared with Masahiko my intestinal problems, and he understood that I would need a day or two to recuperate and recover from my Korean experience. He gave me his business card to give him a call when I would be fit and back in shape to get together. The Hotel New Otani was indeed an architectural marvel, a beautiful, elegant structure with a central tower, giving an impression of a watchtower at the airport, while the main body of the hotel was built in a half circle around the central tower.

I wanted to settle quickly in my room, located high, almost in the clouds, on the highest floor, and I started to work and take care of my insidious problem. Before going to the buffet of the hotel to stock up with some mineral water, I noticed that on the side of the reception, there was small gift shop for guests. To my great surprise and relief, on the top shelf, I noticed in small boxes the classic German Zwieback, or rusk (double-toasted white bread). I immediately stacked up three boxes of that "medicine" of mine, and for two days I stayed on those double-toasted biscuits and lemon tea till my stomach and intestines finally calmed down. As I recovered, I wanted to stay a few days in Tokyo around the city center, which looked very interesting and very different from other American metropolises.

First Masahiko invited me to his home, a great honor for a foreigner in Oriental society. I ordered a taxi, which came right away with a chauffeur in braided livery and white gloves. As I was waiting at the back door of the cab, expecting that the chauffeur would open the back door, suddenly something hit me on my side. To my surprise, it was the back door, opened up by the chauffeur himself by pushing a button inside his cab. Well I never had seen that in New York, unless on a Hollywood movie screen.

As we arrived at Masahiko's house, I was warmly welcomed by his wife and his daughter of college age. Both of them were fluent in English, and the conversation was easy and cordial. We recalled our friendship and work in Boston, and his family cherished fond memories as well of the time spent in New England. A small but tasty lunch was offered of different sushi and other Japanese delicacies. As a dessert, Japanese "brownies" were presented, which were made not of chocolate but dark beans. It was quite tasty and interesting accompanied by green tea. Then Masahiko showed me the neighborhood around his house, which all had quintessential Japanese wooden architecture and gardens with a small lake and bridge. With a very pleasant social time and conversation with the family, the time passed quickly, and at dusk, Masahiko drove me back to my hotel.

The next day, we met again, and all of us went to see a huge bronze statue of Buddha, over twenty feet tall, in a classic Japanese garden full of vivid green, small bonsai trees and scattered little lakes and different wooden bridges over them. The ambiance in the garden was very serene and peaceful, almost pious. Surprisingly, by a back door of the statue, it was possible to enter the Buddha's body even though it was completely empty. We returned then to the center of the city Shin-djuku, where I departed from the Masahiko's, thanking them for their friendship and gracious hospitality, and went to try to explore the city on my own. After dusk the city was full of glittering lights from the bright, flickering neon of different colors. It was a dizzying sight on the main avenue of Shun-djuku. The shopwindows of the elegant stores were full of exquisite merchandise of any kind. It was surprising to see the businessmen in their three-piece suits and flashy attaché cases in their hand in great hurry; they were rather running as walking to their meetings.

On some prominent corners, before a building one could see college students, in the uniform of a particular school, standing ramrod straight, and it looked that they were practicing their rhetorical aptitude and proficiency. They were indeed shouting or yelling their message in full throttle of their vocal capacity, with eyes bulging in their effort and excitement, their jugulars swollen.

People were walking nonchalantly by, and nobody seemed to pay attention to their rhetorical mantra, no matter how loudly those boys were shouting. Of course, I did not understand a word, and somewhat perplexed, I joined the by-passing crowd.

Next I stopped by an exclusive pearl store, Michico, where an employee was performing the art of properly opening the shell of the scallop with the help of a special curved knife. It was an amusing ceremony with the potential reward of a pearl if the customer had chosen a scallop that disclosed a pearl during the opening. I chose a scallop as well, but luck was not on my side, as the scallop turned out to be empty.

Unfortunately I was not lucky to purchase a ticket for the world famous Kabuki theater; instead in a special store I would purchase a pink, silk kimono for my wife as a farewell gift from Japan. The rest of the evening I spent around the lobby of the hotel, where a festive wedding party went on. It was amazing that in that Oriental society, all the members were dressed in full dress-suit of a European background. All the men wore an elegant, dark gray tailcoat with a snow white shirt and a ruffled jabot and a black bow tie with a diamond pin. The ladies wore snow white frocks of layered silk with low necklines, glittering diamond necklaces and rings and other jewelry. The bride excelled with her diamond tiara and a long, white wedding gown, held by two little bridesmaids, all in white. I sure never had seen anything so opulent, elegant, and festively beautiful. That evening was my farewell event, with a visual bonanza and reward of a wedding ceremony of the upper crust of Japanese society. It was quite an overwhelming Oriental experience.

The next day, I said a good buy to Masahiko and his lovely family by telephone, and after an arduous two weeks in the Orient, I returned happily to New York, satisfied with our accomplishments in South Korea, as we had prepared some of the children to come to our Heart Center through the Gift of Life.

In the following years, we admitted to our Gift of Life Program about three hundred children from South Korea, our Chief Surgeon and I, as cardiologist, performed all the diagnostic tests and the open heart surgery for free, that is "gratis." Most importantly we did not lose one patient!

During my appointment at the Heart Center of Saint Francis Hospital for two decades, we took care of and treated about six hundred children from all over the world, which was probably the highest number of children in the U.S. cared for in the eighties and nineties (Fig. 55).

Our institution developed a parallel social program in support of the program of Gift of Life and a public-relations campaign to raise funds for the success of the International Program. While the physicians offered their services for "gratis," funds had to be raised to cover the expenses of hospitalizations, laboratories, surgical suites, medications and technical staff to be reimbursed to the heart center.

By that impetus, a department of public relations was established, led by an exceptionally gifted and astute administrator, Frank Regnante, who had a big heart for the program. He was able to mobilize the community of Polish-Americans and Korean-Americans, who joined in their responsible organizations to help the Gift of Life Program for the children from their native country. Their contribution supported and secured the success of the lifesaving program. Frank was also able to mobilize the business leaders in the North Shore area, whose important contributions were instrumental for the success of the program.

During those years of the successful public-relations program, I befriended Frank and got close to that magnanimous man. The experience working with him gave me an idea and impulse to try and help some physicians from my native country behind the already rickety Iron Curtain in those years.

In the middle of the eighties, 1985 to be precise, I was able to invite a younger lady, a doctor, for the World Congress of Pediatric Cardiology thanks to the generosity of Frank. Frank purchased the airline tickets for Dr. Sonja A. and secured for her a suite in the exclusive Waldorf Astoria Hotel. The suite had a small lobby with a divided living quarter and a bedroom. In the lobby, there was a bar with bottles of different drinks, hard and soft, with salted almonds and pretzels, that our guest from Czecho-Slovakia could, in the social customs of the U.S. during such meetings, welcome her colleagues or friends from other countries for a drink or a chat. Frank was very generous, and he wanted to boost the ego of my Eastern European friend. During the recess of the congress, friends from different corners of Europe and Eastern Europe as well welcomed her invitation indeed and were happy to come for a drink.

In the old country, Dr. Sonja A. was Resident doctor at the Heart Institute for Children, where I had been the Physician in Chief. From 1962 till my unexpected emigration to the West in 1968, we worked together at the Children's Hospital in Bratislava. She was my clandestine and pivotal informer since 1969 when I arrived in the USA. From her I received information about the gradual decay and professional deterioration of the conditions of pediatric cardiology at the hospital.

Through her I sent every Christmas a package of books for the cardiologists in Czechoslovakia or in the old country to stay in touch with the latest advancements of Western medicine.

My wife and I welcomed Sonja at JFK Airport. We hadn't seen each other for many years, and the welcome was very cordial and emotional as well.

We drove her to Manhattan, straight to the Waldorf Astoria Hotel. While standing before the elevator, two well-dressed young men pushed forward to the elevator. It was obvious that those two were there for the Congress. One of them, a tall, blond, blue-eyed fellow, was startled seeing Sonja from Slovakia at the Waldorf hotel. They were acquainted and new each other from medical meetings in Prague or Bratislava. Suddenly he quite loudly and brashly vented his unexpected surprise and quasi-indignation and addressed her impulsively, "How come that you are here?" We were quite surprised by that outburst of his reproach with its hidden meaning: "How come that you, from Slovakia, dare to be here for this congress." He was a Pediatric Radiologist from Prague, and he perhaps felt that only he from Prague or Bohemia had the right and privilege to be there. Sonja, in her surprise, blushed in her embarrassment, and I looked at him askance, rather miffed by his unacceptable invasion, and ushered Sonja and my wife into the elevator following the "brotherly" incident.

Sonja was very pleased with her marvelous suite. Every morning I picked up Sonja from the hotel and drove her to the congressional center. The World Congress of Pediatric Cardiology was particularly useful for all physicians from the countries behind the Iron Curtain, since during the week of that Congress, all the pertinent and newest information and achievements in the field were presented quasi "on a plate."

After a hectic week of deliberations during the Congress, we invited Sonja to our home in Roslyn, and I spent a week with her in our Heart Center. During that time, I acquainted her with our clinical floor and the adjacent postoperative ICU and the technologies in our labs of echocardiography and mainly the laboratories for diagnostic workup, which were all new for her. Sonja was ready to make a presentation to the members of our Department of Pediatrics about her collection of rare afflictions of the heart muscle in infancy, which was well-received in our group.

During the week, I also learned that after the invasion of the Red Army to Czechoslovakia in August 1968, altogether six senior professionals, myself included, had left or fled the country. It was an enormous loss for the institution and especially for pediatric cardiology, as four of the refugees were cardiologists. The Professor was now of advanced age, and she was being pressured to relinquish her post to a younger, most importantly a "politically correct," member of the Communist Party. That painful change led to further deterioration in quality of care, especially for children with heart disease. In our free time with Sonja, we racked our brains about what could be done and how we could help to redeem the division of pediatric cardiology, once the "jewel in the crown" of the Children's Hospital where I had spent six productive years.

I slowly acquainted and interjected to her the idea that in the USA, the care for children with heart problems — mostly congenital or born with — was realized and performed in Cardio-Centers, where cardiology, heart surgery, and postoperative care were intertwined in a physiological unit, embedded usually in a Children's Hospital. In Bratislava the clinical cardiology in the Children's Hospital was miles away from the Department of Surgery, which was also isolated from ancillary pediatric services, a great disadvantage for a patient.

We were trying to figure out how to be helpful in solving such a complicated "Gordian" problem.

Earlier I had passed my last hurdle in my specialization when I passed my Board in Pediatric Cardiology. About two decades before, I had passed a test for that specialization in my native country as well, but it was not accepted in the U.S. and rightly so. The test in Slovakia consisted of only three questions regarding a medical problem; it was not a comprehensive exam that would address the details and go into the depth of main pertinent question. Again I had to first pass the written part of the Board through a computer and answer all the multiple choice questions and riddles presented by the questions of the computer. Since I successfully had passed that part of the Board, I qualified for the oral examination. For that I had to fly to San Francisco, where the Board exam was given only on one day in the whole U.S. We gathered in a spacious hotel, about eighty of us would-be specialists. On the morning of the exam, the Chairman of the Board announced that each professor or examinee who trained any of the candidates had to excuse himself and couldn't examine his trainee.

Individually each of us were examined by members of three commissions consisting of two professors, who were personally unknown to us, and none of us had been in their training programs. Each commission individually examined and interrogated us for forty minutes, and then we were passed to the next two commissions. The questions of any particular topic was in great detail, tough but fair. At the end of the sessions, all of us gathered in the conference room of the hotel, where the Chairmen of the Board announced to us that the results of the test would be mailed to us.

The test was, of course, quite stressful, but I was well-prepared and trained, and in a month, I received a letter of congratulation from the Board that I had successfully passed the test.

At the next Annual Conference of American College of Cardiology, we were all inaugurated into the College of Cardiology as respected Diplomats (Fig. 56).

Subsequently on the recommendation of the Chairman of the Department of Pediatrics and the Medical Faculty of the SUNY Stony Brook, I was appointed an Associated Professor of Pediatrics (Cardiology). The Chairman of the Saint Francis Hospital Heart Center sent me his congratulations and his appreciation of my work on behalf of the Heart Center.

At the end of 1985, my dear mom passed away, but the Communist authorities of Czechoslovakia denied to issue for me an entrance visas; thus I could not be at her funeral. I was devastated by that political and inhumane decision of the authorities.

Two years later, as the political winds started to change in the USSR, thanks to Mikhail Gorbachev, a political thaw spread to the countries of the Soviet Bloc, and in 1987 I applied for an entrance visa again. That time I was somehow incomprehensibly lucky, and I was able to pay homage to my dear mom at last, at least at her grave.

At that time, with some trepidation, I was able to visit the Children's Hospital in Bratislava, where I had been a happy warrior and pursued and followed the goals and targets of Western standards in the medicine of my specialty. Almost twenty years had gone by — gone with the wind — in the grim times of the Cold War in Europe.

I took a cab from my hotel in Bratislava, and as I was getting closer to the hospital, I felt my innermost senses start to quiver, feeling some anxiety and trepidation as I noticed the rather humble building where I had spent six prolific, bittersweet years, where I was quite happy, despite all the adversities and hardship.

In the porters lodge, an unknown woman was present, not the pleasant and cheerful Mrs. Lukach, who had welcomed me every morning with her cheerful smile. The lobby at the entrance looked shabby, worn-out and tired gray. The once bright paintings of local village children of Slovakia in their national costumes by J. Hála were now withering.

I climbed up to the first floor of the hospital, as it would be "yesterday," and unexpectedly I faced the new politically correct Professor, who obviously had been notified by the receptionist. He welcomed me, so to speak, with a pretended surprise, with a poorly guised smile or rather a frozen frown. He was obviously not thrilled by my arrival. The approaching residents did not know who I was or what to make of my visit. My attire revealed that I was a foreigner from another country, and the Professor introduced me as a former associate of the hospital. Then he rose above his displeasure and invited me to the clinical floor where the older children were hospitalized. That was the floor where I had cared for the children with heart problems, virtually my headquarters. Everything was the same, but shabby and worn-out, displaying the signs of significant destitution and decay. I entered the diagnostic laboratory — once my pride — and I froze in pain in my consternation. All the old, worn-out machines and decaying technology were still there in a desolate condition. No rejuvenation or new technology was acquired to replace the aging and decaying old ones for two decades. On the X-ray machine, the visor and its rubber frame were in full decay and sticky and virtually falling apart. I stood in the lab like the biblical Lot in deep distress and disbelief. I couldn't imagine how the doctors could do their diagnostic workup with that obsolete equipment. It was a very disappointing and painful "homecoming" for me indeed. Eventually some younger physicians showed up after they learned that I was a pediatric cardiologist from the USA. They did not know what to do or what to show me, especially when they saw my bewilderment and poorly disguised disappointment at the entrance of the lab. Consequently no meaningful professional exchange followed in that awkward situation — not even a coffee of collegial courtesy was offered. My visit was, therefore, cut short, and the Professor was rather happy to see my back.

After I returned home to the U.S., that disheartening experience gave me paradoxically a positive impetus that something had to be done for that hospital and mainly for the suffering children. The whimsical question often quoted by V.I. Lenin was: What to do? That was the question for me as well. At that time during the Cold War — in the late eighties — it seemed that on the political horizon, signs of a new dawn were breaking through, and the tensions between the East and the West were softening. Still Czechoslovakia remained one of the last and faithful bastions of Communism in Europe, with the slogan, "Forever with the Soviet Union."

I was coming home to New York with very mixed feelings. Still I wanted to share with my fellow countrymen in the Slovak diaspora in New York my dismal experience of the bleak medical conditions in Slovakia, especially for children with heart disease.

At the first meeting of the American-Slovak Cultural Center (ASCC), where I presided over the section for science and medicine, I presented to the Chairman and the Board of Directors my appalling experience regarding the obsolete and dilapidated medical care for children with heart disease in Slovakia. The whole Board and its members were listening in great discomfort to my experience and its narrative about the lack of technology and the know-how of medical care in our native country.

In 1988, in the midst of the times, the Cold War was only slowly coming to its end. In the convergence of political events and the dramatic rupture and change of the political landscape of Czechoslovakia, whimsical fate was perhaps offering us an opportunity to intervene with our help. The turmoil of the political events redoubled and boosted our determination "to do something" for those less-fortunate babies and children afflicted with heart problems. In the Board session, we decided to go the "American way," that is, to establish a professional Foundation and raise the necessary funds for the ultimate goal to develop a children's heart center in Bratislava, Slovakia.

We began with the establishment of an incorporated foundation, according to the counsel of our legal experts, and entitled it with a logo, Heart to Heart Program, with an additional declaration: "Let's give hope and new life for every child with heart disease in Slovakia" (Fig. 57).

To begin with, we established a working group of leaders under my professional guidance. There my leadership was jacked up and boosted with my experience and close working relationship with Frank Regnante in the Gift of Life Program. Frank was a master in the art of PR (public relations) and carefully watched our audacious experiment. He pointed out for us some pivotal tasks in the endeavor, and most graciously he gave to our disposition an excellent printing company.

At the end of the same year, we dispatched 2,500 elegant pamphlets of semi-soft, glossy cardboard as our bulletin, with the same logo of two hearts, one with the star-spangled banner and the other with the Slovak tricolor. The central text summarized our message, to establish a Children's Heart Center on behalf of the Slovak children inflicted with heart disease. It was a proclamation and informative statement from SACC in New York to raise funds for the benefit of children behind the Iron Curtain and to appeal for donations and generous help for the lofty and important goal. We sent five hundred pamphlets to Europe as well, and the rest were to be distributed in the USA.

On a cold and rainy weekend, about twenty of us gathered in the conference room in the basement of our church. The room was full of boxes of our pamphlets, which should be posted and sent out. We rolled up our sleeves and methodically, by hand, addressed two thousand envelopes since we did not have a computer then.

Likewise two thousand stamps were moistened, or licked, where the accompanying children had a ball in competition —who could lick more stamps and seal more envelopes. Each envelope had a small return card for the donation to be returned. A special courier took a large box of five hundred pamphlets to West Germany, where members of the Slovak diaspora there took care of their distribution.

By the dawn of 1989, the first donations started to arrive at the headquarters of SACC in New York.

I tried to boost the economics of our Heart to Heart program with personal engagements and presentations of our Foundation to companies or known philanthropists in our area. I made a presentation to the general secretary of the swiss pharmaceutical company, Sandoz, who honored me with a check of ten thousand U.S. dollars. The Gift of Life program in our hospital doubled that gift, thanks to Frank Regnante. I made a presentation about our program to a local philanthropist, Mrs. Barbara Gagnon, in her mansion on North Shore, and she generously supported our program with a check of five thousand dollars. Some physicians of our heart center generously pitched in with a thousand-dollar donation. One of my patrons was Dr. George Stefanik, whom I met at a surgical conference in California. When I informed him about our program for Slovakia, he generously donated one thousand dollars as well. As it turned out, he was the cousin of General Milan R. Stefanik, one of the founders of Czechoslovakia in 1918. The donations and gifts slowly, but surely were pouring in in different denominations, but every denomination was appreciated, even a five-dollar bill from a retiree, since it came from the bottom of the heart.

Nevertheless, there were some negative reactions, not only from the members of SACC, but also from members of general public from the Slovak diaspora. Letters came with some angry replies: "We don't give the Communists anything!" I was not an exception either when I was personally verbally attacked at a meeting for my initiative to help the children with heart disease in our native country. We understood these disgruntled and angry voices from some of our citizens, who had been harshly persecuted by Communist authorities before they could escape to this country of freedom.

Despite those isolated attacks and outbursts, the donations were arriving, and reasonable people understood that it was not a political action, but an activity of pure human charity "from heart to heart." Toward the end of 1989, we had collected over $100,000 dollars, and the collection continued for more than a year.

Our first goal was to delegate some physicians into prominent hospitals in the West, to advance their theoretical knowledge and get some experience in applications of novel diagnostic methods like echocardiography. The second goal was to update the technological equipment for the Children's Hospital and achieve a convergence or merger of Pediatric Cardiology with pediatric heart surgery within the new Children's Hospital.

An unexpected chance of a Congress of European Pediatric Cardiology in Prague (Czechoslovakia) gave me an opportunity to extend my tentacles in search of training possibilities by meeting the professors and chairmen in prominent hospitals of Europe and the U.S. as well. In addition that Congress in May 1989 gave me the opportunity to meet a young doctor from Bratislava, Dr. Joseph M., whom I had met shortly during my visit in the Children's Hospital in Bratislava. As I learned then in 1987, he had started to follow in my footsteps, to learn the technique of cardiac catheterization for the diagnostic workup, but more opportunity to learn and experience was needed.

There I took advantage of my previous acquaintance with Professor Gladys Hayworth, the Chief of Pediatric Cardiology at the renowned Hospital on Great Ormond Street in London, a charming, rather young lady of ebony black hair chignon and dark eyes. After some greetings and courteous politesse, I raised right away the question of if she would accept a candidate for training in pediatric cardiology from the Soviet Bloc, provided funding was offered for the training. She asked me politely to consider the matter for a day. Eventually she came with an affirmative answer, provided our foundation could offer $20,000 U.S. I immediately agreed, as I realized that to get to the top-notch institutions was a great honor and the best opportunity for training Europe. Later, as a token of my appreciation, I presented her with a small platter of Carlsbad china with its quintessential blue, onion-shaped ornaments.

In November 1989, in a dramatic change, the Government of the Communist Party collapsed — in conjunction with the fall of Communism in the Soviet Union. It was the most welcomed convergence of events in regard to our Heart to Heart Program. Unfortunately the "old cadres" still remained in place, mainly in the administration of many institutions, such as the Children's Hospital.

At that time, the physician in charge at the Children's Hospital in Bratislava was Dr. E. Cz., a "politically correct" cadre. It was transferred to me through a back channel that unless Dr. E. Cz. was the first to go for training in a Western center by our foundation, that nobody would go. I decided to meet that nemesis of mine at a Conference in Vienna (Austria) in 1988. She was a middle-aged, quintessential "proletarian" with the sinister look of an ideological enemy, but my arguments were in vain. She was the "physician in chief," and she must go first.

I had a bad feeling from that meeting, and I realized that my principles would not break the political, ugly obstacle, and eventually I would have to swallow the bitter pill, in lieu of the other younger members planning to be placed in other training programs in Western centers.

In my pain, I called up my good friend from previous years in Boston, Dr. Bob Freedom, who was Professor of Pediatric Cardiology at the renown Children's Hospital in Toronto (Canada). He was very generous, and he agreed to accept this "politically correct" lady doctor for training for a period of six months, provided our foundation would foot the bill.

Through the diaspora of the Canadian Slovaks in Toronto, we rented a room for the doctor with a Slovak family. The relationship turned quickly sour with the arrogant doctor and her exaggerated expectations, and eventually she left the family. To my chagrin and embarrassment, the whole training of the doctor turned out to be an unmitigated disaster. She did not master her English, let alone the medical jargon, and the level of her professional erudition and knowledge was unacceptable. For five months, she was just a bystander and did not participate in any procedures or professional exchange. She had nothing intelligent to say! Eventually she left the Department a month early, but did not forget to take the thousand-dollar stipend from our Foundation. It was a total fiasco and tremendous embarrassment for me, and I had to apologize to Bob, who vented his frustration about the waste of his time for that political dilettante.

Later in the year, I met this doctor at the Children's Hospital in Bratislava, where between "four eyes" I gave her an unmitigated dress down.

I reported her unbecoming conduct to the Dean of the Medical School, and she was later demoted from her position.

Despite that letdown, I was able to arrange a training for a fellow in echocardiography at the prestigious Baby's Hospital in New York, where the head of Pediatric Cardiology was Dr. Welton Gersony, a friend from Boston. There Dr. Martin C. had an outstanding teacher, Dr. Fred Bierman, a leading professional in the field. Unfortunately the insufficient English of the candidate was again a great disadvantage to take full benefit in the teaching of the excellent teacher. The final results of the training were obviously less than satisfactory.

The lack of knowledge and competent English communication skills were the major obstacles for those cardiologists from Slovakia to gain the benefit from the integral programs in those outstanding Western institutions, where they had the privilege and opportunity to learn, train, and gain the maximum of the art of Pediatric

Cardiology. Most of them remained only as bystanders, without participating in particular procedures, that is, in hands-on training. A particular exception was a young and talented surgeon, Dr. Viktor H., for whom I secured a hands-on training in surgery at a course in Paris, France, funded by our program. It was a special course in repair of a specific and difficult heart condition given by Dr. Claude Planchet in Paris at the Hospital Mary Lelong. Next that talented man spent a year at the Children's Hospital in Boston in the Department of Cardiac Surgery. He left for Germany, establishing an excellent Heart Center at Asklepios Klinik in Sankt Augustin near Bonn. Today Viktor is a Professor and Physician in Chief at the Herma Center for Cardiovascular Surgery in Milwaukee, Wisconsin.

Throughout our Heart to Heart Program, we opened up the gates for the avant-garde Western medicine for physicians behind the Iron Curtain, to advance their knowledge in that particular specialty. Each of them received an exceptional opportunity "to grab the horse by the reins" and take advantage of an exceptional professional chance. Unfortunately few were ready and prepared linguistically and, likewise, professionally. The end results recalled the biblical parable of the sower. Some of the seeds fell wayside, and the fowl came and devoured them. The others fell on a stony ground, where the seeds had not enough soil and perished. The next one fell among the thorns, which choked the seedlings. But the one that fell into a fertile soil yielded the richest harvest. That story was poignantly the same of the doctors, where the science was politically choked and interfered by a defunct political ideology in Soviet Bloc countries behind the Iron Curtain, where few were ready for the advanced West.

In the spring of 1990, I was asked to join a delegation of the Slovak World Congress, an organization that tried to integrate the different groups of Slovak diaspora worldwide. I was asked to be part of the group as a physician who understands the problems of healthcare. The delegation was led by Mrs. Betty Roman, the wife of the Chairman, and by his brother and joined by members of different business groups, such as the Canadian CEO Andy Miklas, to bring the know-how in business and economic enterprise for post-Communist Slovakia. I had an advantage that through the Heart of Heart program of the SACC, I already was in contact with some authorities, such as the Chairman of the Slovak Parliament. Our delegation was welcomed by the Prime Minister of Slovakia, Mr. Milan Číč (Fig. 58) and next by the President of the republic, Mr. Michal Kováč. The President, who to my surprise, somehow knew and was interested in the Heart to Heart Program of SACC, and he was curious regarding our approach of training of the physicians from Slovakia in Western institutions. At the end of our audience, the President reached into his drawer and handed me an ornamental box with his personal silver medal. I was taken by surprise by the unexpected, "ad hoc" reward and expressed my deep thanks to the President for his appreciation of the work of SACC in New York. I still cherish this medal from the President as a small memento of his acknowledgement to this day.

At this opportunity, in the early days of the fall of Communism, I took the opportunity to visit the managing Director of the Children's Hospitals, where the management was still in the hands of the "old cadres." The lady Director welcomed (?) me with great unease and a great deal of suspicion; perhaps she still regarded me as an "imperialist agent." She was rather aloof and not interested in our Heart to Heart Program even though it was for the benefit of the children in the hospital. As I handed over for her our elegant bulletin of our Heart to Heart Program, her interest suddenly changed when she realized the available money donated by her compatriots in the U.S. listed in the document. I left with great disappointment after meeting with that "politically correct" administrator.

Next I visited the Department of Cardiac Surgery, where I knew the Surgeon in Chief and presented him the idea of a Children's Heart Center by joining the medical and surgical part of the cardiac care intertwined and in the bosom of the Children's Hospital. This kind of "symbiosis" and approach was totally foreign to him, and in his "surgical mind," he was dreaming of a surgical center from the newborn period up to advanced adult age, an idea totally unphysiological and disadvantageous for the children. The heart surgeon of the old school and his opinion had still significant weight in that ossified medical environment even though his surgical results did not support his overrated confidence and expectations.

It was obvious that a political action and public pressure would be necessary to sow the seeds and the idea of a Children's Heart Center, an idea totally unfamiliar and foreign to the present medical community.

Therefore, I personally visited and lobbied the Secretary for Health, Dr. J. Polák, and the Secretary for Social Affairs and the Chairman of the Slovak Parliament as well. I presented to all those political leaders the modern and physiological concept of a Children's Heart Center, separated from the adults, which would offer comprehensive medical and surgical care for newborns and children afflicted with congenital heart disease. It seemed that the ice was slowly breaking up.

After I returned from Slovakia in late March, I received a "godsent" telephone message from an unknown Dr. Viktor Kugajevsky from the U.S. Department of Health. Viktor was the son of a renown Physician in Chief and the Head of the Department of Urology in the Western town of Nitra, Slovakia. Viktor heard of our Heart to Heart Program, and he informed me that it would be possible to receive a

Federal Grant through the Agency for International Development (AID). He recommended me to get in touch with Dr, William Walsh, the chairman and executive
director of Project Hope.

Indeed I called up Dr. W. Walsh and presented him my proposition, that the
AID grant of $2.5 million be awarded to Bratislava, Slovakia in the "post-Com-
munist era" to establish a Children's Heart Center in my native country. I was
aware that there were some other candidates for the grant from the former Eastern
Bloc as well.

My suggestion was very appealing to Dr. W. Walsh, with a caveat that he had
to present the suggestion to his professional expert, Prof. Dr. Aldo Castaneda, the
Chief of Cardiac Surgery at the Children's Hospital in Boston. When I revealed to
him that I knew Aldo from the seventies as a former Fellow in cardiology at the
Children's Hospital in Boston, Dr. Walsh was quite surprised by the coincidence.
He suggested to me that I call up Dr. A. Castaneda and discuss my proposal with
him. He also asked me to submit my CV to him.

Consequently I had a long conversation with Dr. Castaneda by telephone. I
explained to him that in Bratislava, there were already some solid building blocks
present for such a Children's Heart Center, namely a group of pediatric cardiologists and heart surgeons as well, even though they were physically not in a joined
medical unit. In other words, there was already significant professional potential
present, which need an American reorganization and overhaul, as well as a hands-
on professional upgrading in that specific specialty.

Fortunately Aldo was familiar with those problems since he previously had
established a similar a program in Kraków, Poland, with Dr. John Murphy, a good
friend from Boston who had given me some insight into those proceedings.
Through those channels, I was quasi a professional guarantor for Dr. A. Castaneda
to guarantee that the investment in Bratislava was a worthwhile and justifiable endeavor. There in Bratislava, Slovakia, there was an excellent potential that the un-
dertaking would yield positive achievements and results in advancing the care for
children with heart disease. With the recommendation of Dr. A. Castaneda, the
grant from AID was indeed rewarded to Bratislava in 1991.

The main goal was to bring together the group of Pediatric Cardiology with
Cardiac Surgery in the new Children's Hospital. The incoming group of specialists
from the USA would offer for two-year, hands-on training in cardiology and cardiac surgery, with supplemental support of specialists in pediatric anesthesiology
and postoperative care in a comprehensive program.

In the following two years, a team of specialists came to Bratislava from the prestigious Boston Children's Hospital under the leadership of Professor Dr. John Mayer, the head of the surgical team.

My good friend and interlocutor, Dr. John Murphy, gave hands-on teaching in the art of cardiac catheterization, and Dr. Stephen Spivak taught the art of cardiac echocardiography. A team of anesthesiologists and doctors and nurses of postoperative care supplemented the first-class team. In four- to six-month lasting courses and teaching curriculum, a new team of experts was developed or "born" in Bratislava for a new Children's Heart Center. Some of the physicians and nurses were reciprocally invited for two-month training sessions in Boston to have a deeper overview and experience in the Hospital where cardiac surgery was born.

Thanks to the original and bold idea of the members in the group of SACC in New York, a Children's Heart Center in Bratislava was born. The institution was inaugurated at the end of 1992 thanks to the significant financial support of AID of the American Government. The grant made it possible to train a group of doctors with new technology to take over with new professional expertise the treatment of children of Slovakia born with heart disease, as the Heart to Heart Program had promulgated and declared in 1989.

Today this children's heart center is providing first-class diagnostic and surgical care for the whole country of Slovakia thanks to the generous and big heart of the United States of America.

During those years of exciting scientific fermentation in my native country, I continued to work in my heart center, but regularly, on a yearly basis, I visited Bratislava with the contribution of my lectures, teaching, and expertise to help and stimulate the cardiac group at the Children's Heart Center.

Yet my intensive work in the diagnostic lab, postoperative care, and night calls was giving me some definite signs of chronic exhaustion, portending that I was getting slowly but surely burned out. It dawned on me that after forty-five years of active practice and Academic Medicine, I would have to accept the unthinkable and unacceptable, that I would have to say goodbye and hang up my precious stethoscope (Figure 59) and end my beloved work, my other personal "alter ego."

It was the most difficult decision to make, as I was emphatically devoted to my profession and my work, especially to my patients, indeed "my children," my second family. I loved my hospital, which offered me a wide opportunity to work, grow, do research, and publish. The charitable work of the hospital was very close to my heart and personal philosophy "to help thy neighbor." My nursing staff in the catheterization lab, which I surreptitiously all loved, as well as our clinical floor of the Department, with all its patients, nurses, and even our scrub lady, Tina from Greece — these were all part of my professional life, my second home.

As they say in a Latin proverb, "Jacta alea est," "The die is cast." In summer of 1996, I had an appointment with the Chairman of the hospital, Professor Dr. Allan Guerci, with whom I had an excellent personal relationship, and handed over to him my letter of resignation. He was very sorry that "his friend and workhorse," a man devoted to the institution, was going to leave his post. We remained for a few minutes in cordial discussion, talking about my plans for the foreseeable future. Eventually I thanked him for his friendship, which he reciprocated cordially, shook my hands, and said the inevitable goodbye.

The nursing staff from the diagnostic lab gave me a surprise farewell party, where amidst a glass of Champagne, we recollected many of the funny and memorable events that their Zoltan had provided for them during the two decades of our wonderful and professional relationship. We said a bittersweet goodbye with teary eyes, hugs and kisses, but outbursts of laughter as well. At my departure, Sheila surprised me with a precious gift of a beautiful wristwatch, which I cherish to this day on my wrist.

Likewise the nursing staff of our Department was most generous during my farewell party and in our small classroom. I had to dip my palm into a pot of blue color and make my mark on the wall for years to come.

All my private patients I transferred to a younger colleague for further continuous care.

Nevertheless, they came like a caravan of pilgrims to my office. Most of the moms came with their small children directly into my office to say a warm thank you and goodbye to their "doc." In hard times, we struggled and fought together for the well-being of their offspring and had great joy during the recovery after successful surgery.

I had a very humane and close relationship with my patients, who were quasi my "parallel family."

Some of them were really special, like Rocco Brussezi, whose parents had emigrated from power-stricken Calabria in Italy. Now the five-year-old Rocco presented to me at Christmas time a small but beautiful artificial Christmas tree, which to this day is part of our Christmas celebration in our home.

And the "rascal" Joe Betz, in his teens, frequently tormented his parents while severely ill. His father was my confidant when Joe was in trouble, and we tried to alleviate or solve the problem. Now Joe, a lanky sixteen-year-old, came with his mischievous, kind-of-awkward smile and handed me over a hand-carved name tag from a fine, light wood and surprised me with his hug and thank you for my care and understanding. The name tag remained part of my office on my desk (Fig. 60, in front) and is now on my bookshelf in my study. The story of Joe had an unexpected and awkward ending when he died in an accident on a merry-go-round. The centrifugal force of the carousel compromised the blood flow in his sick heart, and Joe was found dead at the end of the ride.

Perhaps ten-year-old Tommy McGuire was specially unique, born with Down syndrome, who turned out to be my most devoted friend. He was a son of Irish parents, the last offspring in the family. His father was a captain at the local police force, and Mom was a teacher. When she was expectant with Tommy, the sonogram revealed his heart problem and the Down syndrome as well. The obstetrician was ready to perform the abortion. Mrs. McGuire, a deeply religious Irish Catholic, resolutely refused that solution with her remark, "Let it be done in the Lord's will." Indeed Tommy was born with Down syndrome and a severe heart problem; hence I knew Tommy since the day he was born. I performed on him several diagnostic catheterizations, and Tommy had two open heart surgeries. It turned me almost into a member of the family.

At the time of my departure from the hospital, Tommy showed up in his best attire with his beautiful mom. He was very well brought up, thanks to the excellent care, education, and love of his mom and his whole family. He was then successfully attending a remedial school. As Tommy entered my office, with which he was familiar, he came straight to my desk and handed me a huge bottle of Coca-Cola with an orange-colored balloon and a message on it: "I love you."

It was the most difficult farewell from this special little boy for whom I had cared for ten years. My wife, who helped me out as a licensed nurse, was present as well, and she knew Tommy and his mom very well. The parting from that boy and his wonderful mom was teary and emotional with their heartfelt thanks for our special care. At the end of the parting, we were both emotionally quite drained.

On June 30, 1996, with a heavy heart, I left the Saint Francis Heart Center. I left there a large part of my professional life, filled with lot of happiness and joy. In addition to my professional devotion to my work as a physician, my leading philosophical motto remained the eternal dictum, "Love thy neighbor."

EPILOGUE

I never had any intention, not even in my dreams, to leave my native country where I was born. The word refugee or emigration had, for me, somehow a foreign, awkward, or even sinister sound, as the word "migrare" in Latin means departure (1778), to which the French revolutionaries added an "affix" or the vowel "e" for the birth of the word "emigrare." It meant a forceful departure or exodus on political grounds, where the issue for any citizen was the question of freedom or his subjugation to an alien ideology or force. In the midst of bygone times and a given reality, being behind the Iron Curtain — where somebody else made the decision for you — in the "socialist" Czechoslovakia, I had a rather rocky start in my career. Still it turned to be ascendant, thanks to my passion for medicine, intelligence, and willingness to fight, even as a citizen. I turned inward in taciturn disagreement with the political climate. In the early sixties, I was quite content and happy but was like a donkey with its blinders on in that peculiar professional atmosphere. The Chairwoman and Professor of the Children's Hospital was politically able to establish and maintain an acceptable, even positive, "modus vivendi" — way of professional life — even though everything in the hospital was under the tutelage of the Communist Party. The staff of the physicians was "invisibly" divided between the group of physicians, the "doers" who were running the well-qualified clinical care and research, and the other group of "political mock-ups," cleverly pretending that they were working as well.

That political dichotomy was blatant and poignantly demonstrated once a month at the presentation of the physician on the night call. That once-a-month event had a political knell and was tagged as the "political ten minutes." After the nightly report, the Professor reviewed our daily program and planned tasks, addressing the main responsibility of the "working bumblebees." After the review and planned assignments, lasting about thirty to forty minutes, the professional meeting ended.

Then the Associate Professor and the Party Secretary raised their voices and announced that for the following "political part" of instructions of ten minutes, only the members of the Communist Party should stay, and the rest of the Faculty should leave.

Then the Professor rose from her seat, and with a visible sneer and disdain, left the hall with all the politically "incorrect" members of her team. It was, for all of us, a deeply degrading gesture and distinction, and we left the hall like some kind of lepers or beaten-up dogs. It was a blatant demonstration of a political discrimination, indicating that even in medical care, we were the "different ones" from those politically anointed. In truth we never asked or searched what that feeble-minded gang of political cadres had in their political program. We simply ignored them! That quasi-selective "mafia" was yet exercising their surreptitious political power and giving the seal of their endorsement in every major decision in our institution. The sword of Damocles was hanging over our heads all the time! In that politically perilous situation, we, as political unreliables or "enemies of the system," were well-aware that we are dispensable by a stroke of their pen.

Despite the politically poisonous atmosphere, I had a rather solid position in the Department, perhaps even prominent, thanks to my work, research, and publications and a breakthrough in summer 1967, and I took over the preoperative diagnostic workup from the surgeons for the first time in the history of the Department since 1952.

Unexpectedly the invasion of Czechoslovakia by the Warsaw Pact Armies under the leadership of the Red Army on August 21, 1968, was the greatest shock of my life, which surprised me and my family on our return home to Bratislava, Slovakia, from our vacation. We were totally unprepared to leave our native land to an unknown and insecure future into an unknown land.

We were not ready to flee our country mentally, psychologically, nor materially and leave behind our "home sweet home." On the last day of our vacation in Belgrade, Yugoslavia, we had money only for the gasoline to drive home. Our clothing was only for summer vacation, light, cheap, shabby, and "socialistic."

Yet as we watched on the Yugoslav TV the Soviet Tanks T34 run over the country from Prague to the eastern metropolis of Košice, our mood turned very somber and rather desperate. We could see the brutal, menacing soldiers of the Red Army in their army fatigues and helmets with their Kalashnikovs on their shoulders, roaming around in our land. The killing of many citizens who were demonstrating against the military aggression was especially menacing. The invasion, of course, changed the whole situation, not only for us, but also for fifty thousand Czechoslovak citizens strangled in Belgrade.

For our nuclear family, with two small children — two and five years old — the situation turned really upside down, and my responsibility for my family turned to a millstone around my neck. The fundamental question for us was, of course, what could or should we do now? That was the Rorschach question for me: to go home into the military quagmire and chaos or perhaps turn as a refugee and emigrate? I got a lot of goose bumps on my back every restless night pondering the idea: Should we flee and to turn refugees? It was something totally foreign and never considered by me.

Yet in that real reality and in the light of the brutal occupation and political strangulation of the country, the future of my position in my job and academic medicine — not being a member of the Communist Party — fundamentally had changed and portrayed a totally different angle and future for me and our children.

Even though at the time of my departure for my vacation I had submitted my postdoctoral thesis for approval by the professors at the university in Bratislava and Brno, the conclusions, as far as my research, were positively solid, and the end results of my research were endorsed. But my research did not have a political angle, an almost "condition sine qua non" for every work.

How could I continue in my further work at the University when I was not a member of the Communist Party and I had twice refused to join the Party and left the submitted application form blank?

It eventually turned out to be our decision that we would rather bet on the future of our children in a country of freedom and opportunity and not in a country of strangulating socialism. Especially my wife was petrified and scared to death seeing the rumbling tanks of the Red Army, with their red stars on their turrets and the Siberian or Asian look of many of those armored soldiers, who were not hesitating to kill every opposition.

We wanted to give our children a fair chance to study in schools in a free country, according to their choice and on the merit of their achievements. We did not wanted to expose those innocent kids to the political shenanigans of the so-called socialist system. I did not want that their views, opinions, or religious affiliation would be part of a political record in the "cadre files" for their political screening, victimizing, or punitive judgement, with subsequent forced assignment to their work, as had happened to their parents.

In that dreadful and seemingly hopeless situation, nevertheless, I had two "secret" trump cards that offered me the potential and professional scaffolding to have a chance to find work according my qualification and to get to a professional medical center in a free country.

In 1967 I had passed the entrance exam for physicians entering the U.S. for training, an opportunity that was thwarted by the political climate of my country. Later that year, my application for the Alexander van Humboldt stipend for West Germany was successful and gave me the opportunity to work at the University of Tübingen as a temporary bridge till I could advance for a Fellowship at Boston's Children's Hospital.

Thanks to the temporary "waiting" bridge, I got the opportunity in the summer of 1969 to receive an invitation for the Fellowship at the Children's Hospital in Boston. It was a dream come true and the ultimate and most fortunate outcome of the Russian Invasion. It was indeed like in a fairy tale, where my "blue fairy" stood again at my side in that totally unexpected moment in my life and offered me her helping hand.

It should be said, at the same time, that being a refugee meant a long and arduous journey to be successful to achieve the targets of my ambitions and to succeed in academic medicine. Nevertheless, "when the going gets tough, the tough get going," and I had to tough it out. Because as the saying goes, "In life, there are seldom failures, only people who give up too soon."

It was a providential advantage that for four years, I could, as a Fellow, work, learn, and do research with the best professionals in my field at the Children's Hospital of the University of Harvard. Those professors were my best and most generous teachers, as well as models and examples in academic and Hippocratic etiquette and human behavior, who gave me the best gift in my professional life: *knowledge*.

In that institution, I understood the full depth of the meaning of the biblical rabbi or teacher, who in his wisdom shared with me his experience with clarity and objectivity, and, as a matter-of-fact, remained still my colleague and friend in his humble demeanor. I learned there the beauty of analytical thinking based on the facts supported by their numerical scaffoldings, leading to objective assessment instead of subjective impression only. It was the best education in my professional life, which gave me that crucial "kick" and equipment in theory and practice to have a successful takeoff in the struggle in the following professional years as a physician and scientist teacher. But most of all, a human being and a former refugee, a badge many of us are carrying with fondness and pride.

The years of my academic position at the Downstate Medical Center were rather a "sojourn" and temporary landing to look and find an optimal opportunity in my medical career, which I incidentally found at the Saint Francis Hospital Heart Center in Roslyn, New York. Simultaneously our family could settle and take roots in our new home and country and fulfill our most important obligation given in August 1968 to our children, to offer them the best professional opportunities to study in Ivy League universities (Columbia and Tufts University), based on their intellectual prowess, talent, and hard work.

After almost two decades of clinical and academic work, as a specialist and teacher in Pediatric Cardiology, I was then in the last chapter of my professional career. At the very beginning of my American journey, I had grabbed the tress of my "mustang," and by my personal initiative and resilience, I was able to climb up on the professional ladder, intertwined by elements of Hippocratic humanity and charity. It was a prolonged struggle, not an easy one, but always personal, exciting, and precious. After forty-five years of my cherished struggle, I had to, with great humility, hang up my beloved stethoscope (Fig. 59) and with certain reverence, I could humbly whisper to myself an old proverb from the land of my fathers: "I did fight a good fight in valor." I safeguarded the stellar crest of my honor and my personality, and I remained truthful to the faith, moral code, and principles of my dear parents and my forefathers.

CPSIA information can be obtained
at www.ICGtesting.com
Printed in the USA
LVHW071124110420
653034LV00001B/1/J